SO YOU WANT TO BE A "REALITY" TV STAR

EVERYTHING I LEARNED ABOUT SEX, DRUGS, FRAUD, ROCK AND ROLL, AND VIPERS AS TEAM LEADER OF DISCOVERY CHANNEL'S TREASURE QUEST: SNAKE ISLAND…

CORK GRAHAM

D1572249

ISBN: 0-9703580-2-8
ISBN-13: 978-0-9703580-2-8

DEDICATION

For my ladybug

In memory of combat buddies, who died in Central America and other places, in what was incorrectly labelled a Cold War, and to their families, who, through the travesty of political "plausible deniability," may never know how, where, or why their loved ones perished, from North, South, and Central America—Anti-totalitarian Americans all!

CONTENTS

ACKNOWLEDGMENTS

Good books aren't written in a vacuum. Good books come about through good research, good resources, and not giving up on game trails so small, they initially seem imaginary and non-existent, until they turn out to be major highways to facts: Special thanks to the following people: my birthday brother Captain Mykel Hawke US Army (RET), who has been going through his own hell as a result of a major lack of integrity at Discovery Communications. Officer Ed Stading, of the Homer PD, who helped me get a handle on the aspects of criminal cases involving pedophilia, which sadly greatly effects our society more than most of us would imagine. With help from Lt. Larry Richard, retired from the Santa Cruz PD, I was able to fully understand the considerations and effects of cyberstalking and harassments on its victims. It was always a joy to talk with my friend US Army Special Forces Major John Donovan (RET) about those years in Central America that was so unknown to those who were most likely to have been effected by it had we lost, and it was a comfort to know I wasn't paranoid in thinking that Discovery Communications continues to hire supposed authorities and specialists not on their true experience and knowledge, but on their ability sell tales like snake oils salesmen of old, and some who fit a certain character profile. And finally, special appreciation to District Attorney Pat Knauth of Jefferson County, TX, for assistance in understanding how a past drug tax law deemed unconstitutional, along with a TREASURE QUEST: SNAKE ISLAND co-star's perjured statement, could have aided in the release of a reality TV cameraman and drug smuggler arrested with 48.8 pounds of marijuana laminated into the hull of his boat...

PREFACE

As I write this tell-all memoir of my experiences behind the veil at Discovery Communications, I'm in conversation with the office of the Inspector General for the FCC (Federal Communications Commission), and I'm in a lawsuit against Discovery Communications, and my former co-star Brett Tutor, for battery, and seeking retribution from the first tortfeasor who attacked me on set in Argentina, while drugged up on cocaine, Jeremy Whalen, presently hiding out in Salinas, Ecuador, while he and his younger brother Jaime, or James Kendall Whalen/Kendall D. Mckibben (take your pick of an alias) in Washington State, cyberstalk, harass, and libel me through the Internet. It's mind-blowing that I'm in this situation right now after simply having accepted an invitation to lead a team on what I initially was told was to be a historical fact-finding mission of exploration for Discovery Channel, instead of what turned out be a charade, fully scripted to make Discovery Communications many more millions on the cheap.

I'm here because I've reported Discovery to those who should have been covering this story from the moment I reported it to my old employers, the Associated Press and Reuters. I've only got guesses as to why I've not heard a word since the day I contacted Anthony McCartney at Associated Press, and Peter Henderson over at Reuters, and the ambassadors of Peru, Ecuador, Argentina, and Brazil, along with the FBI's Internet Crimes Division, ICE, and INTERPOL. Mind you, I was a combat photographer in Central America and Southeast Asia, who frequently worked on assignments for the news services. This press corps would be what I'd call my alma mater over any J-School in university.

When I contacted the news bureaus, again, almost a year after I initially brought the story to them, I asked why nothing was ever followed up. Stories about the media industry often got shuffled to the entertainment

1

desk, which is how I was referred to McCartney in Los Angeles, but Henderson in San Francisco should have recognized the international historical implications of this story. Alas, all I got from Henderson, was, "I remember the story, but"…I could tell he was overburdened as many.

But, this is the day and age of "fake news" and propaganda set to either sway the public to any agenda, or just make a quick buck. If only it were just attempts by such small factions trying to sway masses, or advertising broadcasts to sell a product.

Instead, what we have now is a media and education services company offering fake material as fact, and what were bastions of truth, the press corps, following fast in step, journalists turning into a speaking box, instead of reporting on fraud, and lying to the masses that goes far beyond what I saw in the Central Intelligence Agency.

At least in the CIA, for a moment, the secrets held, and the lies and facts initially delivered were with an intent to protect Americans and the "Free World," until these facts and lies were then bandied around to protect everyone's career asses and pensions—and those of us who did the up close and dirty work (the "expendables," those they used up and died, or they wished and hoped just faded away, depending on which presidential office was in power), were left out to dry.

It's pretty sad when even your friends in the military special operations community ask you to always tell them the truth, as though the assumption, that once you've worked for the CIA, is you will always lie. Frankly, I'm pretty disgusted with the new terminology that's taken wing in the community: "If you ain't lying, you ain't trying."

With Discovery Communications there's no patriotism involved, though they're quick to throw former SEALs, Green Berets (former and active), and Marines at the audience as if to say, hey, we're good and we're okay, we can be trusted by the major audience; we have credibility—we're one of you (those living in the "fly-over" states, which is predominantly patriotic). After all, doesn't Discovery Communications sell itself to its shareholders and the rest of the world as the last "true-life" documentary network out there, a bastion of education? Don't they invest all this money into education around the world, especially in third world countries and a variety of states within the United States, making millions in the process?

What if it was just like everything else in Hollywood: a total smoke screen? It's nothing new. Oil tycoon John D. Rockefeller, the man who was totally despised by his generation to the point he would surely have been imprisoned for years for his actions, but learned that if you tossed a dog a bone, they'll be happy. In one of the biggest whitewashing events to occur in history, Rockefeller hired an advertising agency and began a public opinion swaying campaign that would last for decades. Even my mother, an Ecuadorian by birth, felt the Rockefellers were the greatest Americans in the world for all the money they spent in Ecuador.

It didn't seem to hit her that the reason there was so much money being spent in Ecuador was there was so much fossil fuel to be drilled for in Ecuador. The rich become rich because they've learned to calculate whether the juice is worth the squeeze. If that financial potential of the squeeze can be abated with public relations measures that let things fly under the radar of scrutiny, so much the better.

In a third world country rich in oil or copper deposits, it's the bringing of clean water to a village that brings smiles and good thoughts about foreigners. Oil and mining companies doing so will look good to those on Main Street. When a media corporation, most especially one that needs to garner attention, especially having gotten its hands dirty in poor programming that goes counter to the company moto, with fakeumentaries on mermaids sold as fact, what better than bringing laptops to a village in Africa—and what better way than through a corporate division that specializes in cheap to produce educational materials?

When my father worked for the CIA (but everyone, even his family, knew only that he worked for USAID—until the week he died and I went through his old IDs and papers from Vietnam: all those years, and neither of us talking about what we'd gone through under our old employer and how much it could have been a place of connection, instead of a point of contention and lack of understanding), this worked in two ways. When he was doing his PR work for US Embassy in Saigon, he was a project manager putting up communications installations around the country. When CIA case officers came to him needing technical advice, he wired their Vietnamese agents and other assets to be able to record conversations and eavesdrop. When he needed medical attention, he had it done by the CIA doctors, who also did two jobs. One was patching up paramilitary officers, case officers, and other employees of the Agency; the other was providing humanitarian aid, otherwise known as good PR in village and provinces.

This is how the world works. The US learned this from the lessons of the British as they built their empires in India and Malaysia, and the Brits got it from the Romans and Macedonians, who brought "peace," the rule of government, and "bread and circuses" to their subjects, and the subjects of their allies. In the corporate world, which is becoming hard to discern from the government world in its giant, elephant-like bureaucratic movement and waste, it's the same with regards to covering ugly deeds with the distraction of supposed good deeds, that are to come off as if from the goodness of the institution's heart—it's because of this need to be believed that PR firms and PR departments of corporations actively hire "true believers," because good intentions are best sold by these people, who are far from the rubber-hits-the-pavement ideology and philosophy of the other departments and agencies. Of course, what fuels all this is money, and the pursuit of great wealth.

For a country, it's the leadership and the ruling body, for the corporation, it's to make the board happy. At a corporation like Discovery Communications, it's ALL about keeping the board happy, as that's the job of the CEO. It wasn't always like this, and you can see this in how programming has changed at places like Discovery Communications, A&E and sadly, even what I thought was the final bastion of getting the story right, and that's National Geographic.

Two things have happened since the days when these documentary and education networks got it right. First, there was the screenwriter's strike of 1988 that started things going downhill as networks searched for options to keep productions coming and not be held at the mercy of the screenwriters. Secondly, Michael Moore became the first TV/film documentarian to make major money with such fabricated offerings as BOWLING FOR COLUMBINE, offered to the public as true documentaries, when they're some of the most made up propaganda at the beginning of the 21st Century. But, they were moneymakers, and in the world of corporations, if it pays, it stays: no better way to do this than keep your overhead very, very low, and returns astronomically high.

Fine for sophomoric entertainment directed at teens and millennials. Not fine when produced for networks and channels that purport to be proponents of education and protectors of history. Big Brother has moved from the world of seeing how twenty-year old coeds act amongst each other with only a camera, like a fly on the wall, to what were previously real documentary networks that offered historical programming that often got it right, even when reporting ancient aliens. At least it was reportage of what had been recorded in history for centuries. What is happening now is much, much more insidious.

Normally, it's a conquering army that rewrites the history of a nation. Have you ever wondered how the Celts, Visigoths, Spartans and other long-dead cultures would have recorded their history, had they continued as the main culture of their nation, instead of having been forced to take that of their conquerors? Who's to say who are the conquerors of this present time and these contemporary events, but what they are doing in the media is writing and rewriting history. Can you imagine the dangers?

When I shared with a good buddy of mine, a well-experienced combat veteran and retired Marine colonel, the extent and ramifications of Discovery Communications' criminal actions that stretch across many borders from South America to Europe and many other parts of the world, and have blown through the ruins of history the way Panzers blew through the walls of the Warsaw Ghetto, and how much was at stake for this megalodon-sized corporation, he told me, "Geezus—watch your six. They might try to take you out!"

When I later told my lawyer, who has been my counsel in an assault and battery case against two of my TREASURE QUEST: SNAKE ISLAND co-stars, Jeremy Whalen and Brett Tutor, that I wanted to send the leadership at Discovery Channel and Discovery Communications a list of questions to hear how they explained their actions, or refuted them, he said, they could pull a TRO, they could use Discovery Communications' aircraft carrier-sized legal team to remove my First Amendment rights through a temporary restraining order. He said that that's exactly what he would do had he been representing them, instead of me.

What has happened in this country where a person's rights to free speech are infringed on by the very institutions that are supposed to protect them? Is this the country we want, where a large, mega-media corporation, that is itself the first to abuse the privilege of free speech, would so quickly muffle a whistleblower—informing on actions they've committed that they fully know are wrong?

Somehow, Discovery Communications has been running its programs like a bad CIA, thinking that a non-disclosure clause in their employee contract is as binding as the NDA shadow warrior agencies use to keep a lid on the actions of their clandestine operators in foreign countries. Ironically, unlike the CIA, Discovery Communications has a clause that states no employee or representative of Discovery can break the laws of the US and other nations—yet, Discovery still seeks plausible deniability for their actions of bringing fraudulent programming.

What is fraudulent programming? It's no different from a manufacturer of a product making false claims about their product in order to garner a sale. The horrific part of this sale is that world history and record is being rewritten by the media and bought by the audience as truth, when it is so far from it—and so destruct to the society that believes its veracity.

Now that you've been forewarned, I invite you to join me in reliving this surreal treasure hunt that Discovery Communications invited me on under false pretenses, and warn you that the little gems we'll find will be truly mind-blowing...

BRAZIL

1 JABBERWOCKY

Cappy was three sheets to the wind, stuck in a hole in the jungle, and screaming, "WHERE'S MY RIFLE? THERE'S GOOKS EVERYWHERE!"

A variety of stunned looks covered the faces of cast and crew in that moment of shock, that moment just before bystanders realize a real emergency is unfolding. This was no acting we'd been experiencing for the last two months and last year's first season of TREASURE QUEST on Discovery Channel...this was the real thing!

With eight years' experience as a drug and alcohol counselor, with a specificity in helping those confronting post-traumatic stress disorder (PTSD), I quickly ran to my fellow actor, Keith Plaskett, and did what I knew. Only problem was Jeremy Whalen, the actor who I'd always wondered why he was on the show. After all, Discovery Channel had hired us in order to bank on our personal histories, bringing credibility to a totally fabricated TV show.

What a group we were. Keith Plaskett was a bonafide treasure hunter, retired from the US Navy diver and EOD programs to a boat captain plying the waters of the Caribbean and the Latin America. Mehgan Heaney-Grier caught the public's eye when Manny Puig and her cameraman boyfriend Mark Rackley realized they had an opportunity to catch that eye by turning her into a freediving champion, which led to modelling contracts and TV appearances for the three on Animal Planet in 1996. International notoriety caught me in 1983 and 1984 when I was a fledgling combat photographer who had followed a treasure hunter to west Vietnam and paid the price of eleven months imprisonment on trumped up charges of spying for the CIA.

Now, there was Jeremy Whalen, and for that matter, Brett Tutor, our new "survival and security guy"—I never did get the reason he was here, other than Whalen had found a golden goose in Plaskett. I would find out later from Plaskett, that after Whalen had found out about the casting for TREASURE QUEST, he hounded the MAK Pictures office until they put him on the show. From day one he had come off as the weasel who had found a shirt-tail to ride in on. This fact didn't mean much back during casting, and even during first season in Brazil, but here in Argentina, especially with the lively playing out of the cast's dynamic, it meant everything.

"Get out of the way!" I said, "Your friend needs help."

"And what are you going to do about it?"

"You friend needs help, man," I said and just moved around him.

Kneeling next to Plaskett, I put my hand on his shoulder. "How are you doing Cappy?"

He clutched my hand and said, "I'm back there, Cork. It all came rushing back. You know what I'm talking about. You're the only one here who knows."

Just as I was about to respond, Whalen, who had positioned himself on the other side of Plaskett, guffawed, "Yeah, right!"

Ignoring Whalen's slight, I focused on Plaskett. He was in bad shape. All morning he had been hitting a bottle of rum to deal with the stress of being on the show. Just before we started this scene, he said he had been hitting it since the evening before. His anger, at how he felt what was a betrayal of his trust by Jeremy, had been gnawing on him for days.

Only a few weeks earlier, he said he had heard Jeremy and Mehgan having loud, drunken sex in the room above his—he thought it was Brett Tutor, but it was Jeremy Whalen's room. Cappy had said, Jeremy had entered into an illicit lover's contract with Mehgan to make TREASURE QUEST: SNAKE ISLAND all about them, and that they were trying to get rid of him and me.

Cappy lay curled up in the fetal position, releasing outbursts between sobbing, which would be broadcast in an episode of TQ:SI. What wasn't broadcast was the previous morning's drinking, and buildup of stress and rage waiting to be indiscriminately unleashed on the unsuspecting.

For now, he was just seeking help, pleadings I'd heard many times before as a veteran of counseling those dealing with PTSD (post-traumatic stress disorder), which I fell into after coming back to the US from five years in the Central America War and working on my own. I went to him as I did in the war with the wounded. Instead of applying tourniquets and bandages on the battlefield, I applied my words and empathy to help him calm down.

"You understand," he said.

"I do," I replied. "It's okay, man…"

Whalen chortled—I kept my focus on Cappy. I just didn't know yet how toxic Whalen really was, and what illegal activities he had been up to behind the scenes with his brother, in order to attack me, in an ongoing attempt at discrediting me toward his goal of becoming the show lead. It would all be clear, soon enough.

Plaskett took about twenty minutes to come down from his abreaction. It would take until the next day for him to come out of his drunk. What I had to do was go and take care of my own memories of five years in one of the most depraved fighting to hit the Americas since the Aztecs, Mayans, Incas and Spanish conquistadors were violently killing each other in the 1500s. Memories of humans killing humans have turned some to drugs, others to alcohol, and yet others to suicide. I refused to follow either of those roads back in 1990, when I said I'd had enough and the proxy war against the Soviets was well on its way to being won.

Like I did when I came back from that war, I sought solitude. For me in 1990, it was a cabin in the wilds of Alaska, near a town Discovery Channel would also produce another TV, one called ALASKA: THE LAST FRONTIER. Back then, Jewel Kilcher wasn't even out of Homer High School, and Homer was just a sleeping fishing town that had the reputation of having been named after a conman by the name of Homer Pennock from New York, who lured people with the promise of gold in 1856 and went bust in 1902. And in that moment on set, I wished that I could go home to that town that I had returned to only four years earlier, an event that drove me, after years of living and traveling the world, to go back to the only place in this world that I truly missed: that's the thing about Alaska—if it touches you, it will bring you back either physically, or at least in mind.

But, I was deep in a fucked-up jungle in Argentina, with a madhouse field production company and working for a TV network that had no respect for reality or true documentary—and it was killing all of us. What sanity was left, I was reaching for at every nook and cranny in that deep, thorny, venomous bug and snake-infested place. Done helping Plaskett, I left him to the rest of the crew and cast to deal with my own PTS as I had been trained and experienced enough to do on my own.

Breathing, meditation, healthy introspection, sober thought, physical exercise, these are all the tools God gave us to deal with the effects of traumatic events that haunt survivors. Plaskett preferred to confront his with a bottle of rum, after coming back from Vietnam the first time, a drug I was well acquainted with through my Central America years. The year after I came back and drank myself into a stupor on the deck of my cabin on a hillside near Homer, Alaska, I having drunk so much beer, and mixed it with brandy my fishing buddy's from San Francisco brought, that I just rolled over on that deck, puked onto the fireweed below the deck and curled back up in my sleeping back to fight the chills of alcohol poisoning.

Unlike Plaskett, who became a functional drunk, only drinking when off the job, I went cold turkey for five years, delving deep into the Native spiritual ways of the people who first came to Alaska, and their descendants who moved south, especially the Apache and the Oglala Lakota—who would give me the name, Cork.

My respite of introspection was short-lived, perhaps only about three minutes, before co-star Jeremy Whalen, the deck monkey who'd gotten on the show because he'd heard about the show from his drinking buddy Keith Plaskett, came up to me and repeated what he said when I told him to stop blocking me from aiding his friend. "Nobody tells me what to do!"

"I was trying to help your friend—"

A true friend of Plaskett's would never have needed something like this explained to him. But, it wasn't Whalen's words which would replay in my mind for months to come. First, to hit me was I had ignored the signals that told me Whalen was a threat, and that I had let him get too close—distance equals time, which equals safety in reaction—much less than the twenty feet it takes an assailant to close the distance and stab someone drawing a pistol from a holster to defend themselves. Had I referred to my training so many years ago, I would have told him to stand his ground and personally moved away to a range from which to verbally de-escalate the situation. Second to hit me, was that the shape and color of his irises reminded me of a great white shark's.

That's when his sucker punch came and ripped open my left eyelid. My hand came up to touch the eye I could only see red through as blood gushed. In shock, I dropped my hand to see it covered in blood. That's when I went into a form of rage I hadn't since so many years ago.

Whalen threw a few more punches at my chest and stomach and I plowed into him and grabbed his legs to put him on the ground to defend myself. On top of him to hold him down, I was suddenly yanked by my neck in a choke hold by our new cast member, who had been hired by Discovery Communications' field production company, MAK Pictures of Los Angeles, to play our "survival/security expert," Brett Tutor—qualifications be damned.

Insult to injury, as the sudden victim of an assault and battery, I had now just been jumped by our survival expert who had proven himself of being even incapable of starting a campfire a cub scout could easily prepare. Yanked by my neck from an almost prone position on Whalen, I was on my back on Tutor, him asking me if I was done. Yes, I was done—I was more than done.

All fun and games on the set of a Discovery "reality" TV production—more common than I had yet to learn…

2 GOING FOR THE GOLD

As I had said in my 2004 bestselling memoir, I would never, ever go on a treasure hunting expedition again. In 1983, while documenting a British comedy actor-turned treasure hunter's pursuit of Captain Kidd's treasure as a photographer freelancing for the Associated Press, and in the hopes of finding possible signs of American MIAs still being held in Indochina, I participated in a covert insertion into western Vietnam which ended that night in automatic fire over our heads. We were being bound and transferred to the communist re-education prison system of the Socialist Republic of Vietnam. From 1983 to 1984, I had spent 11 months in Vietnam, and as a result, I had no interest in such endeavors as treasure hunting. In 2014, I received a message from a Facebook fan of my memoir, THE BAMBOO CHEST, who mentioned that there was a casting call for an adventure show, and would I be interested?

I'd already been working on a variety of show proposals for TV and had interest from National Geographic on a project about low-impact gold mining in Alaska and internationally. But, then I had a talk with my birthday brother, retired Green Beret captain and survival TV personality, Mykel Hawke.

I was new to reality TV and thought it was just like any other type of documentary programming, and so whenever I made progress, or had a stalemate, and had to bounce things off someone who had been more experienced than me in this field, I talked to Mykel. After all, he'd been in the TV business for almost twenty years, in a variety of positions from fixer to producer to talent, his biggest hit being MAN, WOMAN, WILD, at Discovery Communications.

TV news was where many journalists in Central America ended up, either as reporters, or TV crews. Being behind the camera early in the game, I knew the ins and outs of cameras and sound gear. Being on the other side of the lens was something those of us who considered ourselves cameramen, was something so abhorrent, we didn't even joke about being on the other side. That was left for the prima donnas of the time, like Peter Jennings and Dan Rather.

Figure 1. The author on arrival at Don Muaung Airport, Bangkok, the day of release from Vietnam, May 17, 1984 at age 19, led by American Consul Frederick J. Vogel, and trailed by reporters from AP and UPI. ©AP/Wide World

My first hint of what was to come from Discovery Communications was the contract that included a non-disclosure clause. I would learn during the broadcast of first season that was how Discovery Communications keeps the crew and especially cast from saying anything about what was really happening on set. If only the others had fully read their contracts and understood the full implications of that contract, that when a corporation breaks the laws, both US and of a foreign country, they effectively cancel the contract, per the wording of that contract meant to protect the corporation's secrets.

What becomes even more amazing is when such a large media institution as Discovery Communications breaks the laws, not just once, not just twice, but almost frequently. It's a lesson in the manner of how a large elephant moves through the forest.

Large media corporations, like large elephants, just amble along, pretty much not paying attention to anything except their stomachs and making sure their stomachs are full. Corporations are like that in that it takes a lot for them to know anything is affecting them until it's too late. They move along often through momentum, their weight just seeming to carry the behemoth through inertia.

This momentum is their aid, but also their detriment. They can't adjust fast enough to immediate threats, most especially by those that are able to move fast enough, and in enough number, to create effect on their travel. For this reason, a department, or department employee, in corporations can just keep their head down and not only will survive, but actually rise through the ranks.

Unless there's some major shakeup as had happened in the past with corporations that found themselves not above the law, the elephant just keeps moving along. This is one of the reasons why Discovery Communications has never been talked about since the turning of it from a company that truly offered documentary content to what it is now, a corporation whose hollow slogan is that it's the "last true documentary network."

Had I known this before I accepted dialogue with Discovery about being on a show about hunting for treasure, I'm sure I would have stayed with my initial objective, which was to get a show produced on low-impact gold prospecting and mining. As it was, my co-producer and I had already received interest from National Geographic about a show in which I travelled into the wilds of Alaska searching for likely areas of placer gold for later mining. This was my antidote to the type of mining that had taken the airwaves with ridiculous multimillion dollar investments that looked more like gambling or tossing money in the ground, instead of gold mining. Real miners don't gamble…

Happy to go off into the wilds of Alaska and quietly exploit some solid gold deposits, with or without a TV crew along, I set about preparing myself for getting out into gold country, as there wasn't much more time left before the gold season was over: we were almost half-way between Spring Breakup and the end of summer, signified by Termination Dust covering the mountains of the Kenai Peninsula. I was working away on some new gold mining gear I had designed and was looking forward to putting it to use when a call came.

After an exchange of greetings and how's the weather, and saying how impressed he was on my background and writing, Aaron Burk of MAK Pictures asked me if I'd like to be on a TV show about treasure hunting. "Where's the treasure going to be searched for," I asked.

"We can't talk about that right now. What I'd like to do is get you on a casting call on Skype. Would you be up for that?"

"Sure."

A week later there were several questions on a Skype video call that Aaron Burk and his boss, Mark Kadin, owner of the company, for whose name was constructed from the initials of his first, middle and last name. A few weeks later another call came, and Aaron Burk asked me if I wanted to come down to LA for a chemistry test with all the rest of the potential cast.

"Sure," I said again, with that sure-what-the-hell, attitude I've gotten myself into adventures before, and trouble, too, namely Vietnam 1983.

Chemistry is important in TV. Chemistry means many things in TV. Most viewers think it's the chemistry between two actors playing lovers on a drama. Chemistry tests are given in the TV business on a much larger scale, that goes far beyond romance. On this production that would become titled TREASURE QUEST: SNAKE ISLAND, the question of chemistry came down to potential teams, how we interacted on camera, and how that "chemistry" translated through the lens to the viewers.

Cast introductions came about at dinner at a local Santa Monica Italian restaurant: that's when I met Keith Plaskett, Bryan Grieg-Fry, Jeremy Whalen, and Meghan Heaney-Grier. Like every first-time meeting, new employees are apt to check the others out to see how they stack up; and if they can razzle-dazzle, so much the better.

Bryan Grieg-Fry, or more accurately Dr. Bryan Grieg-Fry, a herpetologist who sounded like he was from Australia, but was born in Philadelphia and raised in Portland, Oregon, was first on the exhibitionist's stage. A true actor, seeking to get cameras on him always, he told us over servings of pasta and bread how he had been bitten twenty-six times, one nearly killing him with its hemotoxins, causing him to bleed from every orifice. As he talked, I couldn't help but be concerned with the relish and delight he conveyed at how he had come so close to being killed by the snake. It was very unsettling to learn he was to be the show's snake specialist who would venture forth on *Queimada Grande*, known famously since the piece by VICE TV, as "Snake Island." His job would be to move ahead of us, collecting the truly deadly *bothrops insularis*, the golden lancehead viper, and moving them out of the way.

Bryan and I soon struck up conversation about writing. He was working on a memoir about his reptilian adventures and knew that my Vietnam prison memoir had been a bestseller. Hunter S. Thompson was his idol, I quickly learned, but the ramifications and realizations were far from being understood, yet. Time in the field is always the final teacher. For now, he was just a jovial, well-educated doctor of snakes.

Talking across the long dining table to Mark Kadin, was Mehgan Heaney-Grier, famous for her freediving and appearing with sharks and alligators with her boyfriend at the time, cameraman Mark Rackley and her Animal Planet co-star, Manny Puig, the Cuban-American spearfisherman and naturalist, easily recognized by his beard, long hair, and alligator teeth around his neck. Most famously, he led the JACKASS movie cast on several animal adventures.

Seated next to me was Keith Plaskett, Senior Chief USN, (RET.). He had entered the military through the draft in 1967, which put him in Vietnam as a combat engineer with a US Army airborne unit. He was in Vietnam in time for the Tet Offensive, so of course, I gravitated toward talking with him. There are two kinds of responses I get from connecting with someone who was in Vietnam during war, whether civilian, expat, or military. One is surprise that someone who wasn't in the military was there. The other is a look of suspicion, one more critical as to why in the hell was my family there. My automatic response was that my father worked out of Tan Son Nhut with a US Army signal corps unit that placed large, remote communications stations throughout Vietnam for units to use when operating nearby.

Plaskett interacted with me from somewhere in between, one where I was too young to understand the combat I had seen in Saigon, and the perceived difference of being in the Central America War, even though those who were there on both sides called it Vietnam II. Seated next to him was his friend, Jeremy Whalen, who worked the table, clearly sizing up everyone and seeing how he stood up. When Whalen learned I wrote product trial and evaluation articles on a number of products in the outdoors field, and had been since I came on at THE TIMES of San Mateo County, in 1994, and became their last outdoors columnist as the result of the Alameda News Group buy out leading to the complete lay off of the editorial department in 1997, he was all excited to find out how to write to manufacturers to get what he thought was "free stuff."

By the end of the night, he was even asking me to give him a template, as if there was one. It was clear that to him it was a game, not to achieve anything, such as become a writer in his field of choice, freediving and spearfishing, but just to see if he could get people to do things for him. His first pleasure of course, would have been to manipulate me into giving him a copy of a letter, instead of him learning how to write his own. As it would soon turn out, he would do just that with Minelab, the metal detecting company that I would be asked by MAK Pictures to request items for product placement on the show. It would become one of the biggest placements of products for Minelab on a show that wasn't gold prospecting and mining related.

The problem with getting the truth out of people, is that most of the healthy of us, brought up in a society that prefers to work for something better is that we often ignore the darker parts of society and focus on the brighter. Whalen had that friendly quality he used to hide his much, much darker past and much darker inability to have dealt with that childhood experience. In the future, he would become a reminder to me to never, ever forget my training that kept me alive during those five years I spent in Central America. Reading people is one of those trainings and it evidently served me well, until I got lazy, as I did in the moment I subconsciously began just let things slide with Whalen.

Unbeknownst to me, this would a be lesson that would play out for two years, involving Whalen's deceit, and participation in such illegal activities as defamation, character assassination, cyberstalking and harassment...

It was an early morning wakeup to get to the harbor and out to Catalina Island from San Pedro, entertained between production sequences by Captain George Elliot, a former Marine who loved bringing out his bagpipes. The pipes were almost as entertaining as hearing our soundman, Ryan Canestro, puking between catching soundbites. It was beyond professional; it was impressive how he was able to notify us, cut, and then run to the rail.

Aboard Captain Elliot's boat, the white, blue-trimmed Bottom Scratcher, that normally took divers out for weekends of underwater exploring, spearfishing and diving for lobster, we anchored off the island I had last been to on a romantic trip to Avalon in the mid-1980s, Mark Kadin, Ty Clancey, the one who would become our director during the first season of TQ:SI in Brazil, and Andy Ruggles, head of production at MAK Pictures, talked amongst themselves.

Out on deck, the potential cast sat around and moved around talking and chatting. We were still getting to know each other, and we still wouldn't know if would have a show. What we did have a hint of as Will Ehbrecht,

Kadin's partner and executive producer, had shown us the sizzle sent to Discovery Channel, was that they were interested, and this chem-test was about getting the final okay to go south and shoot the documentary, or what I thought was going to be a documentary, otherwise known as a "reality TV" show.

We had shot a bunch of video already on the way out. It was interesting to see how we moved together on camera. Keith Plaskett, who preferred to be called Cappy, because he'd been a boat captain specializing in tourism and deep-sea research for decades. He had piloted a research vessel from the US to Peru more than ten years ago, and was residing there, even getting a small moringa tree farm going. Of all of us, I truly considered him the true "treasure hunter."

Plaskett and Whalen had brought with them examples of the finds they'd found off Ecuador and Peru. The two had met at a bar in Peru, and sharing a love of diving and caught by the romance of treasure hunting, had been on a number of dives together: finding silver coins, musket and cannon balls, and other artifacts before the collecting of national treasures was made illegal by Peru and Ecuador.

Clancey had me talking with Plaskett about the "find," which would be either a coin or a musket ball and acting as if our dive team had just pulled it up from the depths. Other times on the voyage to Catalina, they would just have the camera crew video us while we had casual conversations about our lives, interests and aspirations.

They would also have us do specific scenes that they thought would best represent what they thought would happen on the expedition. Mind, you as I participated, I thought this was just an idea of what would happen. After all, this was just to give the production board back at Discovery Channel an idea of how we would appeal to an audience. One of the scenes was interesting because it was now becoming clear that though Plaskett would be cast as the boat captain, I would be set as the team leader.

Jeremy Whalen, clearly did not like this, as he went around to the other cast and said, almost out of earshot, in a hushed and agitated voice, "They're making him the team leader!"

MAK had one camera crew covering Plaskett as he captained the boat. Another was tasked with shooting other scenes while we traveled to Catalina.

It was clear, though that they had to do a test, and this was where they had everyone except Plaskett sitting around the galley table, with a map of Snake Island. What Clancey and Ruggles were trying to produce was an operation planning meeting where they had me telling everyone gathered around the table the background of Snake Island and our initial plan.

As I would later learn, this was a shakedown cruise on so many more levels than just a chemistry test. It wasn't only an understanding of how the director, or as it's now called in the reality TV industry, the showrunner, would direct a scene by referring to a script he'd been given early that day, but also how he would tell us not only what to do, but also what to say.

Sometimes it would be, "in your own words, say something like..." Other times, it would be them telling us to repeat with our own fabricated emotions the exact words as they read to us from the script.

Figure 2. Boat Captain George Elliot, a former Marine playing his bagpipes on enroute to Catalina.

When we arrived at the island I hadn't visited since the 1980s, I was taken by how beautiful it had remained, and how blue and clear the water was. My last time in the water was at 100 feet, laying with my back on the bottom, on SCUBA, my bubbles floating up toward a school of tuna swimming just under the surface, their silhouettes like a flock of geese in the sky. Some beautiful things in the world, happily, never change.

"Get suited up, Mehgan," Ruggles said, as the crew dropped anchor. Both crews would be needed to properly cover the action that MAK had written for this scene. The plan was to have Mehgan over the side and have her swim down along the anchor.

A drone was launched to shoot gorgeous aerials of the boat and blue sea, points of view that would be a highpoint of footage in Brazil and Argentina. Early September is truly one of the best times to visit Southern California. The skies were clear and the weather wasn't too warm. Most of all, the seas were calm, except for the patch that almost took out our trooper soundman Canestro.

"Go down to the anchor again, Mehgan." Clancey, yelled off the bow, and then moved off camera, and said, "Cork and Jeremy, call back to Keith, worried that you can't see Mehgan."

"Where's Mehgan?" Plaskett said immediately after Clancey called, action.

"We can't see her!"

"Now look at each other, Cork and Jeremy, with a look of concern."

Jeremy and I traded looks and it looked like he was about to crack a smile. Thankfully, Clancey called, cut, and we retreated from the bow, while filming continued underwater with Bryan slipping into a farmer john and jumping over the side with a pair of fins. It was amazing how much a scientist who preferred to work among lifeforms that were pretty much silent, and reserved, was so happy and elated to jump in front of the camera.

Before our first day at sea, it had been Bryan's day, a reptile shop in Fountain Valley, called The Reptile Zoo. I'd never seen so many reptiles and arachnids collected under one roof, except for a national zoo. Case after glass case lined the tiny halls with a jungle theme captured by all the plants that looked more at home in the wilds along the equator than the Los Angeles. Frogs, snakes, lizards, venomous and non-venomous, they were everywhere.

Production led us in and had us walk amongst the reptiles in their cases, trying to capture on camera the way they thought we'd react when we came across venomous and very deadly snakes for real, having us comment on what it would be like to come across them in the field. As Bryan talked, it was clear how he could connect to these snakes, especially the venomous ones. When I was in combat, we used to call these guys lead magnets. The key was to put them on the next plane out of the combat zone, before they not only got themselves killed, but also those around.

After the first broadcast of TQ:SI, my combat buddies that I still keep in contact with from the Central America War, and others who worked with me in other parts of the world, flat out said, "You didn't put this team together, did you?" I'd only grin and you say, "What do you think?"

I was just along for the ride, and so curious as to how this would all play out—and I had hoped that the appearance would do something for my books sales. But, as I looked at Bryan as he lit up for the camera without much prodding from Clancey, other than perhaps to keep the rest of the cast actively in the scene, I wondered how in the world casting could have thought someone who had been bit more than twenty-five times would be good for a team trying to stay away from snakes.

If this were a team I'd put together, my questions would have been, so how many snakes have you found that had never been recorded, and how many life-threatening events did you come home from unscathed, instead of nearly killed? In combat this would have been comparable to how many high-quality prisoners were collected, how many high-value targets destroyed, and how few KIA did it cost? It was disconcerting to realize that the reason Kadin, Ehbrecht and Discovery were excited to have him on the show was that he was careless and dangerous, and he was famous for it: oh, the drama, oh, the excitement...

The only time that I thought I was truly going to die, aside from being put up against a wall in Vietnam in 1983, was when I was at a Salvadoran Army base in San Miguel that was being overrun by the FMLN, and one of the tactics they used in their operation was to infiltrate some of their guerrillas as Army recruits, who then went about killing soldiers and taking the weapons, creating the worst case of friendly-fire I'd ever witnessed.

All those life-threatening events reminded me of a quote my father had used on me from Roy Chapman Andrews, an adventurer, explorer and paleontologist, about how adventure is just the result of accidents and errors—when everything goes smoothly, there are no risks and threats to life and limb. There's just getting a job done, and getting that job done right. It's one of the reasons I emotionally and psychologically didn't feel the full effect of what I'd survived in Southeast Asia and Central and South America during the 1980s, where I was first just a journalist doing his job, and then an anti-communist frustrated with how many successes they were having with a nod and wink from the media that was supposed to be reporting the injustices and atrocities communism was committing in the Western Hemisphere.

What I found interesting and lodged in my mind was that Bryan and Jeremy hit it off immediately. Jeremy was good at that. I'd seen it in these kinds of people who live by their wits and skill conning others. They're the kind of people who need to remember who they've told what. It takes a lot to run to another country and try to make a new life, as Jeremy had done in Peru, and not so scrupulously I would learn the hard way.

Bryan did it by leaving the Pacific Northwest and gaining a name for himself in Australia. He even took on the accent of his adoptive nation, to distance himself from his nation of birth. Jeremy tried to do it by moving to Peru, marrying several Peruvian women and even getting a Peruvian passport. This is that form of greener grasses on the other side of the fence, that many don't realize can lead to not being allowed to come back over that fence, if you decide to change your mind. Many realize it too late, having destroyed all their chances of returning to the home they miss in the later years, and wish they'd never left.

Me, I was raised in Southeast Asia by an American who only dreamed of hot, warm climates in the tropics, so different from the cold of Spokane and Chicago in which he was raised. Is it any wonder that my preferred climate has snow, conifers, birch, and the aurora borealis? I had also learned at a very young age that you can try to run away from yourself, the idea that you're your father's son, but where you end up, you've got yourself with you—so make peace with yourself, first.

Plaskett was also in this group, but he was a totally different kind of conflicted. He liked to think it was Vietnam that set him on his way to being out of bounds. Personally, I think it started with the paternal abuse he would regal us with over drinks or a meal. Like Whalen, who said he doesn't do well in the US, Plaskett would mention later, he would be in jail if he stayed in the US. That always got me: does being an expat in another country mean that it's fine to do things there you wouldn't do in a country from which you emigrated—and people wonder why travelers from the US, UK and Canada get such a bad rap in other places?

We shot for the full day in that reptile shop. Each of the producers asking us to do something that they thought would stick out. With me it was the tiny bottle of Prell that I would use regularly. I'd learned from a friend who licked a turtle that you just don't do that. Me, I carried the Prell because getting sick on planes is just not something I can afford the down time to recover from. In this situation, though, it was to keep from getting salmonella that many reptiles carry.

At lunch everyone was asking for that Prell when I told them how great those little guys were at carrying a disease that can make you deathly ill, shooting fluids out of both ends. We were back to the reptile shop for more intimate moments with monitor lizards, corn snakes and even rattlers. The rattlesnakes were all Grieg-Fry's. I was happy to stand back and watch the PhD. showman, but perhaps not as much Plaskett. He'd been hit by a rattlesnake. This fact was disturbing to say the least—What if he needed anti-venom again?

"I hate snakes," he said. He would say this often. I don't know if his hatred was really to the level that he needed to say it that often, or that the reason he did say it so much was that it played to the producer's idea that there was something they could work off in their search for drama.

What I was reminded of as we continued in our chem-testing was that the more I was exposed to something, the less it was that I was affected by it—dating, combat, travels to new countries; exposure and experiences create confidence. On a small level this was occurring with the spiders that have always given me the heebie-jeebies. The more time you spend in war, the less jumpy and reactive you become. The dates you go on, the less intimidated you are by them. Just makes sense. If you continued to jump at everything that initially shocked you, you'd fall to the ground fatigued, or you'd lose your mind, much worse than getting a case of post-traumatic stress.

Overcoming fear was why I lived the life I lived during my late-teens and throughout my twenties. War, risking life and limb for various causes and other reasons put me in a place where calm would overtake me instead of crippling fear that often takes most with a moment's hesitation, or a full-on moment of being unable to move at all as the result of shock. In combat, the best thing to do is something, anything, but most often something moving you forward: most ambushes are designed with the idea of keeping you in a kill box or directing you out of fear into one. Sometimes, doing the illogical can save your life.

On camera, it's a different matter. Emotional connection is what the director and producer want from a personality in front of the lens. Expressive faces, interesting dialogue, these are the bread and butter of TV and film, and that's what Kadin, Ehbrecht, Clancey and Ruggles were always trying to get from us. Personally, I found it weird. After all, wasn't this supposed to be a "reality" show? Wasn't it just supposed to happen, and the job of the director and camera and audio crew to catch the moments, like I did when I was working on real "true-life" documentaries, and photographing news?

What I saw and experienced in those two days showed me everything I needed to know. But, I'd only worked on bonafide documentaries. I'd only covered the real news. I'd never, ever dealt with a reality TV show, other than being friends and acquaintances with a variety of cast from other Discovery Channel shows, like ALASKA: THE LAST FRONTIER, and BERING SEA GOLD. I'd never seen anything other than what others also saw as an audience.

What I saw as we did the chem-test was what I saw when I was an actor on the hottest English language TV show in South Korea, MBC's SURPRISE, and my first time on a movie that would become an Oscar-winning film called THE KILLING FIELDS—all scripted, dramatic theater. When I was an extra running around in Marine fatigues with a rifle, to and fro in the scene where the US ambassador leaves Phnom Pen in

THE KILLING FIELDS, the director was telling us all exactly what he wanted us to do.

In those dramatic scenes they wanted us do things that were totally scripted. But, that was dramatic media filmed off the script in Thailand. Well, I thought, this is just a sizzle to sell the idea to Discovery, so of course it's going to be scripted and I thought that was that.

When the day was over, we headed back our separate ways. Mehgan headed to her room to talk with her husband and manager. Keith and Jeremy went off for a drink at a local bar. I headed for my room, the professor in tow. He was coming out with a book and wanted to pump me for ideas, as he knew the reason I was on this new production was the result of my success with THE BAMBOO CHEST.

He asked me if I wanted to go smoke a joint. I chuckled because I knew that things were a lot more lax in Australia with regards to marijuana (one of the reasons I think Aussies are so surprised when countries, much less relaxed than the US, execute their citizens for smuggling drugs, such as Malaysia, Indonesia and Thailand), but recreational drugs aren't my thing— I love driving and flying and getting an infraction of that kind would be a real downer. How much they were Dr. Grieg-Fry's thing wouldn't come clear until we were underway in Brazil. A hint would be his memoir on chasing snakes, titled VENOM DOC, that he offered to send me in pdf format for me to read and make any suggestions.

Tired, I was curious about what he put in his book. As I read about his adventures, I couldn't help but think that the best suggestion I could give him was the same that First Lady Nancy Reagan was hammering everyone with during the 1980s: "Just say no."

October 9, 2014, an email came in from Mark Kadin:

"Hello All!!!

"We've got some spectacular news!! We just got word that Discovery has picked up "Journey to Snake Island" for at least six episodes and possibly eight, depending on how filming goes in Brazil!

"This is no small feat! We are the first show the network has greenlit in many months, and everyone is very excited for it. You guys really brought your A game, and it showed. This is going to be amazing, and I have no doubts that while it may be challenging at times, you will have a fantastic adventure together.

"Over the next several weeks, we'll begin to figure out many of the logistics behind the

series, and we'll fill you in on how the process will work. It's going to take a fair amount of pre-production to get this going, and as of now, we're looking at beginning principal photography the beginning of January. I am hoping that this won't conflict with any schedules, as we need each and every one of you to make this series a success.

"Again, congratulations and I hope you guys are excited by the news! Feel free to reach out with any questions, and otherwise, we will be in contact very soon."

Figure 3. (l-r) Will Ehbrecht, MAK Pictures Partner and Executive Producer; Laura Crowson, Sr. Director of Development at Discovery Channel; Ty Clancey, director; Tarina Van Den Driessche (Reed), videographer/former US Army combat photographer; Mehgan Heaney-Grier; Jeremy T. Whalen; the author; Bryan Grieg-Fry; Keith Plaskett; and Aaron Burk, MAK Pictures Sr. Director of Development, returned to LA after our successful chemistry test at Catalina Island. Photos tell a lot: Who knew how prophetic this photo was in showing how much Jeremy Whalen had his eye on making the production centered on him, the narcissistic predator. When I now look at this photo of a smiling Jeremy Whalen, a photo of a smiling, charismatic Ted Bundy comes to mind.

3 CHEAP EATS

For the last week, I'd been in conversation with my birthday brother (November 29), Mykel Hawke, combat veteran, retired US Army Special Forces Captain (retired), and long time TV producer and personality. The topic was my negotiation with Discovery Channel.

"Can you believe that they opened with $1,800?!"

"That's normal," he reminded me.

"Normal is $25,000 an episode and something like 5 points on the back end," I responded. All my friends on TV in Hollywood were making at least this. "I don't know, man, this is pretty fucked up!"

"Get on TV and then use the publicity."

"I've been on TV," said, referring to my international fifteen minutes fame that put me on every major news network and on the front page every city's main paper. International print, TV and radio coverage received me when on my release from Vietnam. I was unimpressed, especially when 20th Century Fox carpetbaggers came knocking with an offer to buy my story for less than the amount that was paid for the ransom to get me out.

"You need new publicity. Get this under your belt, and then you can do the other shows you really want to do." I'd been so fed up with Andrew Zimmern and Anthony Bourdain butchering every foreign language they've tried to speak, while in the same breath saying how much they loved traveling and experiencing foreign places—no one is a master of any language at the beginning, we just need interest and we need time to learn. Some people, like those that say they have an ear for languages, just started younger. I had to start picking up languages quickly, having been raised as an expat. I wanted my own food shows traveling around the world showing people, new, interesting and delicious foods, while, in contrast to these two former drug addicts, acting like either a know-it-all, manic depressive sour-mouthed wannabe Parisian or a utopian idealist using the media rewrite world and US history to fit their socialist ideals.

"Ok," I said, "I'll see what I can negotiate."

While my frustration was at its peak, it was nothing like Bryan's in this email:

"On Fri, Oct 24, 2014 at 1:55 PM, Bryan Grieg Fry <bryan@xxxxxxx.com > wrote:

Hi Krystyna,

I hope all is well.

Just a quick email follow-up to our phone conversation on the financial side of things.

My services are being contracted out for the show on a time-served basis, not on a per-episode basis. However you wish to cut together the footage is your side of things and thus that side of the financial shell-game does not concern us. If I am on location for a set period of time, I set my rate by that period of time. Not by how many episodes it is cut together into or how many of those I actually appear in.

My standard rates for dangerous shoots such as this one is
- $1,500 a day for up to 7 days
- $1,000 a day for shoots up to 14 days
- longer shoots are negotiated based upon total time.

For month long shoots, I charge a discounted rate of $25,000. For periods longer than this there is no additional discount due to the significant time spent away from family and also professional responsibilities. So for a two month shoot such as this, my professional rate would be $50,000.

Similarly other cast members (all CC'd in this email) charge their time out at professional rates on a time-contracted basis. They also have similar levels of professional committments that need to be put on hold for this shoot. We are all in fundamental agreement that time spent on location is time paid for and that the rates are set to reflect the professional services we are providing. We are all experts in our respective fields, not Jersey Shore wannabes. Thus the rates are reflective of our professional services provided.

Not having seen the contract yet, I cannot comment on other areas at this time. But upon receiving the contract, naturally we will doing due-diligence and seeking legal advice both in regards to the terms of the shoot, any ability for us to do other shoots afterwards, medical insurance etc. I shall quickly note that in the screen-test, there was a section regarding non-compete clauses. I am fine to sign something saying that I will not film anything else in the 'treasure adventure' genre for a set period of time. I will not however accept any contract that affects my ability to do filming within my area of professional expertise: venomous animals. I regularly appear in documentaries as well as being an expert commenter in the news for venomous bites or stings. This is a integral part of my professional responsibility in addition to how I obtain a significant part of my income. Thus, I will not accept any restriction upon this in any form of the contract.

All the best
Bryan"

The banter of emails went back and forth, until a send from Mark Kadin to all the potential crew, except Bryan:

"From: Mark Kadin [mailto:mkadin@xxxx.xx]
Sent: Monday, October 27, 2014 12:42 PM
To: Cork Graham
Cc: Mehgan Heaney-Grier; Jeremy; keith; Eric Christensen; Will Ehbrecht
Subject: Re: Snake Island shoot

Hey all,

Thank you so much for your responses. It sounds like you are all dedicated to making this work which is extremely exciting news.

I know that many of you have brought up something that the Discovery talent folks mentioned, which was that you would only be paid for the episodes in which you were featured. I want to let you know that you will ALL be in every episode, so that will not be an issue.

As you continue this process with Discovery, please let us know if we can help in any way. We will give you the best advice we can to ensure you get everything you can from this process.

Thanks all and we'll be in touch soon.

Mark

On Fri, Oct 24, 2014 at 4:47 PM, Mark Kadin <mkadin@xxxxx.xx> wrote:
Hello talented folks,

I just wanted to touch base with you as a follow-up to Bryan's earlier email. He has not been CC'd on this email, only for the purposes of making an effort to understand the feelings of this group aside from Bryan's sentiments.

We have been down this road numerous times before in talent negotiation, and it's always a little shocking when our talent receives the first contracts. Unfortunately, there's often quite a misconception about non-fiction shows having large budgets and people getting rich off them. Perhaps that's true for Seasons 3 and 4 and beyond for talent on Duck Dynasty and Pawn Stars, but truthfully (and I know this to be fact), on both those shows, the talent made no more than $2,500/episode in the first season. This is not because the networks are making massive amounts of money and not sharing with the talent. It's because there is little upside to any show in the first season. The networks invest in many series, and only a small number of them hit and actually make money for them. Therefore, they really won't negotiate much on a first season. If we are fortunate to make it to a second season (which means the show has had success), the leverage and power shifts to the talent, and a little secret in that even though you technically are signing a document for "several cycles", the truth is, if the network wants a show and you guys want to re-negotiate...there will be room to do that.

Please know that I will fight tooth and nail to get you guys everything you can get from Discovery at this point, but I basically know where the limits are. I think I can get them up to about $3k per ep for you, but I know it's not going to be much more than that for these first episodes. We absolutely think you guys are an amazing team and are going to have a great adventure together with us by your side. We are beyond ecstatic about the future for this series and we believe this is going to be a major hit for the network. Obviously, if the sole purpose of doing this show is simply about the financial gain right now, then clearly doing a reality series is not the right way to go about that. However, in success, talent on our previous shows have gone on to do endorsements, book deals, speaking engagements, along with a myriad of other financial opportunities based on the success of a show.

Just to be clear. MAK Pictures is hired by Discovery Channel to produce this show and we are in no way benefitting one way or another depending on your negotiation about talent rates. I believe that you guys are the stars and the heart and soul of this series, and I hope you make every bit of money that you deserve. However, I've been here before and Discovery will quickly make this show go away if talent is unrealistic in these early stages. And frankly, we would be terribly disappointed if that happened because we truly believe we have something special here.

Feel free to email me back privately or as a group and let me know your thoughts. I will be happy to discuss the contracts with you, and will do my best to make sure you get the best possible deal on all points. And definitely email any questions you may have. We will be open and honest with you every step of the way.

Thanks guys and I hope we can move forward soon!
Best,
Mark"

I told them I wasn't interested with how poorly they were going to pay us, especially with the amount of danger involved by going to the Snake Island. Discovery was up to $3,000 per episode for the cast, and I was still uninterested. Why would I go off, spending months in a jungle doing an adventure? I don't do that anymore.

When I was in Nicaragua, helping the Contras, a coworker, a contractor for the CIA, a Vietnam veteran who had done tours under Johnson and Nixon, told me as the result of his disgust of what had happened, "Don't ever fight for your country, unless you're fighting for money."

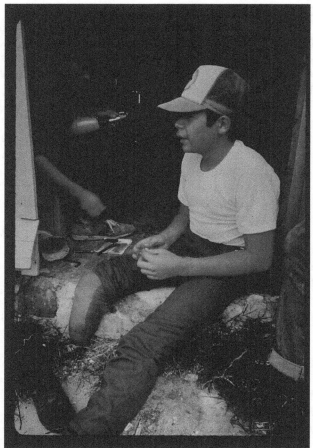

Figure 4. An FDN/Contra hospital outside of Tegucigalpa in 1989, where the author provided medical attention to Nicaraguan refugees wounded by the Sandinista mines.

I was young, dumb, and so patriotic, that my indigenous counterparts in Central America would call me Captain America because of it—not a good thing, when you're trying to stay alive and make your team feel you have their best interests at heart. Later introspection told me that it was likely resulting from being American yet not being born or raised in the US, that that drove me with such a patriotic idealism and a need to prove my loyalties, along of course, with a prior solid, up close and personal experience and understanding of a country in which the communists ruled. Unlike the rest of the cast, it seemed, I'd had my fill of adventuring for the sake of adventuring.

When Discovery came back with $6,000, I still wasn't interested. I had other projects I was marketing, books and another project that National Geographic had shown interest in, and just the manner in which Discovery was trying to nickel and dime me. But, I thought about Mykel's words about publicity—what he and I didn't know was that this wasn't the Discovery Communications he worked for. This was the now the post-Hollywood opening of offices at Discovery, that replaced him with Joseph Teti, as if thinking that one former Green Beret could replace another.

Kadin called and said he wasn't going to get into it, because the negotiations were between Discovery Communications and us. But here he was telling me that no one else was going to get $6,000 an episode.

That's nice, I told him, but I couldn't see myself pulling myself away from a home that I'd made for myself in Alaska and I was bringing with me a whole lot more than the others on the show. As far as I was concerned, they were all being brought along to fill out a specific character-type and I was the one who was bringing credibility to the show. It may have been a while ago, but God damn it, I was fed up being taken for a ride by those who sought to benefit from some major pain and duress I had gone through in a communist re-education prison system. The first of these insults happened within a week of my release, with that 20th Century Fox carpetbagger saying that they would like to buy my life story for $10,000. That was the exact amount of my ransom paid to free me from what was basically a Vietnamese debtors jail: it didn't matter whether I stayed ten years or one in their prisons, $10,000 had to be paid out.

That's when Kadin finally said, "Without you, we have no show."

Not totally sold, I went back to Mykel Hawke, and told him the latest offer. He didn't miss a beat, saying, "Take it."

A bit more soul searching, and I let Krystyna Lab at Discovery Communication legal department know that I would accept the offer.

What could happen, perhaps a dud of a show? Perhaps it might even be a hit, and I'd be travelling around the world hunting a variety of treasures and historical mysteries—I started recording history as a photojournalist, but real history and the accurate telling of historic record is what really excites me.

In my Vietnam prison/treasure hunting memoir, I stated that I wouldn't ever go on a treasure hunt again. Now that I was standing back and really looking at what TV was to offer, I was in conflict that I might actually break that promise—what I didn't know was that I had nothing to worry about that promise, as Discovery Channel would help me keep it, to never, ever go on a treasure hunt since the day I made that promise in a Vietnamese re-education prison. I thought was going to break that promise, especially as I felt swayed by what Hawke said, that it was going to sell books and I'd get to do the types of TV that I now wanted to do. This would be my first step on going down a road that I thought would lead somewhere. It worked for Hawke, after all: books, speaking, product manufacturer sponsorships, spokesman gigs, and travels engagements.

What Hawke was also dealing with now, that I should have paid much more attention to, was that if you hold to honor, Discovery will throw you under the bus. Discovery Channel's Dual Survival personality Joseph Teti had modified his records when he walked them to the National Guard and joined their Special Forces Group. What all this had led to at Discovery Communications was that it put my good friend through the emotional grinder, a precursor to the hell I would learn was common at Discovery Communications, because they thrive on getting drama on camera for their female audience, and nothing delivers drama in front of the cameras than a predator, otherwise known in the law enforcement world as a psychopath. The problem with predators is that you can think you can control them, like putting a leopard in a zoo, but it's still a predatory animal pacing in the cage and eyeing a piece of meat; it will never change its spots.

There was the war on Facebook orchestrated by Teti, using innuendo, hiring a cyberhacker by the name of Mark Ryan of the Mahalo Agency, to create a variety of internet campaigns to attack Mykel, and to get the psychologically imbalanced of his fanbase to do bodily harm to Hawke and his family. There was Discovery Communications still making money and holding Teti's reputation in esteem, when it was clear someone like him should be sitting in a prison cell, or at least in the holding tank of a sanitarium. All this started because Discovery Communications doesn't do its due diligence in vetting a person's background and psychology— regarding the psychology part, I think it's much deeper than that. And if it gets controversial, so much the better, more people watch the show to see what all the huff was about: CEO David Zaslav has truly taken to heart that no publicity is bad publicity.

In the wake of "reality TV" are strewn the lives of many who thought it was just a straight gig where you're the personality, and your experiences and your responses to the events were what make the show. This was before we started reading about Richard Wyatt of AMERICAN GUNS who got fifteen years for conducting firearms sales without a federal firearms license, and of course, William Hayden of SONS OF GUNS, who is presently serving two life sentences, plus another forty years to be served concurrently, for aggravated rape in Louisiana. Wyatt got $500,000 from Discovery for his show…$6,000, much less $3,000 doesn't look like much does it, when you're in danger of being bitten by a golden lancehead viper?

But it's Joseph Teti's attempts to defame, libel, slander, harass and cyberstalk that I should have paid most attention to in the coming years…a person who Mykel Hawke thought was a friend, someone he had brought into his private world, his confidence, as a bodyguard (even living at Hawke's home) and used that proximity to get himself into TV, someone Hawke thought he could trust because Teti had been member of his special forces group.

What Mykel missed was that Teti was in his group until 9/11—and then, just before "stop loss" was implemented (and "it got real" with Mykel Hawke already on his way to Fort Bragg), Teti jumped ship. Three years after stop loss, three years of unsuccessfully trying to get training contracts with the Las Vegas PD, quitting on a DYNCORP contract in Israel, and a failed carwash business (where he burned down a competitor's business— true psychopath/predator behavior), Teti was saved by a contract working for the CIA through the Viper program at controversial MVM, Inc. Teti was pulling in much better pay as a contractor, than he ever would if he was in the military—mind you, this wasn't even with the CIA's Ground Branch, as he likes to infer: this was a contracting deal in support of Ground Branch. Even that gig, he couldn't keep from screwing up, and was fired by the CIA after only one year.

If he hadn't threatened to compromise operations, he would have been gone immediately. As it was, the CIA/MVM, Inc. kept him on as a "coffee boy" until the end of the two year contract. It was during this time that he was able to get all his fake, set up crispy critter photos, that he would then intimidate the hell out of poor hippie wild child, wouldn't hurt a fly, Cody Lundin—remember, predators never go after lions and bears; that would cost them. They go after easy prey.

I should have paid much more attention when I was in my negotiations with Discovery. There was the money, but it was the psychology of those who wanted, almost needed to get onto a reality TV show. There's a certain type of psyche that feels a need to be and stay on TV. So many aspects of fame draw the personality, that the networks rely on that psychological need to wrench what they pull: fame, celebrity, the possibility of wealth, and for some the opportunity to lose themselves in a TV identity that far removed from their own personal realities.

When I was doing the chem-test back in September it struck me that out of the all the potential cast, there was only one who made me ask, why— Why him? Jeremy Whalen brought nothing to the table, other than he was Keith Plaskett's friend.

Everyone has a sixth sense about people, places and situations. Those of us who are good at paying attention to this innate ability we all have, do well in business and keeping undesirable, and frankly dangerous, people out of our circle and even be forewarned about upcoming dangerous events.

In war, I learned that those senses are heightened by the subconscious need to survive. But, in our complacency in average modern life, where the government and media try to make money by making us feel good, disconnected from our personal realities, we lose those skills—more, we just ignore them. What I shouldn't have done was ignore the unsettling feelings I felt every time I was around Jeremy Whalen...Within the coming two years it would become clear that not only had I taken Mykel Hawke's mentorship to heart by succeeding and getting on TV again, but that I was about to have my own, personal Joseph Teti.

4 VIPERS TO THE LEFT OF ME, JOKERS TO THE RIGHT...

Rain had hammered the island of Ilhabela for almost the entire week since we arrived on January 29, 2015, making it seem as if the production team was hiding in their office on the second floor of the Ilha Flat Hotel. All of us were pretty much going nuts. If not for a number of books so easy to carry on Kindle, I'm sure a bunch more crew and cast would have been hitting the walls.

Only some of the crew were in the production office working. Camera crews were out shooting B-roll, and production in Ilhabela was sending information back and forth to help the office back at MAK work on the script with Joseph Boyle, Discovery Channel's lead on this production. It was as though the production was still on location scouting, though the cast had arrived to begin shooting.

Part of the reason were the dealings with local culture that many Americans who want things done yesterday have problems with, especially since most of the time when the Brazilians respond with *amanha*, the Spanish equivalent of *mañana*, it could be tomorrow, or it could next week...or it could be done the next time you ask, whenever that is. People who come to the resort of island of Ilhabela, a place that seems like it was a designed by someone who watched a slew of US TV shows about Hawaii would imagine our 50th state to be—they even have the triathlon competitions and outrigger rowing teams, and not bad surfing on the Atlantic-facing side of the island.

If we had sun I would have been out and about having some beach time while we waited for MAK and Discovery to get the shooting schedule in line. I knew that when the sun did come out, it was going to be gangbusters to get as much shooting in as possible. What I was curious about was that I had yet to get anything from MAK Pictures, except requesting me to make sure Minelab, and HotfootRUG, which both make highly sensitive types of metal detectors, were sending product for placement on the show: I had yet to understand why I wasn't being asked anything about treasure hunting, or being told where we were going to be going and why all the ideas about where we were planning to go was coming from LA and not from a researcher down here in Brazil.

I was told that they had contacted a number of authors about the *Tesouro de Sombrio*, the mysterious treasure in Brazilian Portuguese, also known in Brazil as the *Tesouro da Trindade*, or the Treasure of the Trinity, that was made famous by the efforts of Belgian engineer Paul Thiry (not to be confused with Paul Thiry, the father of architectural modernism in the Pacific Northwest), had a small cottage on Ilhabela. This would be the same small house on the other side of the island, in the *Saco do Sombrio*, that Jeremy and Mehgan would go off to investigate, on the show. They came back with the knowledge that a later owner, after Thiry's death, blew up several stones with a number of markings. It must be said that Thiry moved to Ilhabela in order search for Treasure of the Trinity (TT), because he felt that the treasure was located on THAT island.

It would perplex me as to why Discovery had fixated on Snake Island. When I would later learn the reasons and how Discovery Channel came up with the idea for going after Aleixo Garcia's Treasure of the Trinity (TT), the Brazilian Portuguese name, *Queimada Grande*, the name would make me laugh: Snake Island's real name means "The Big Burn."

Many people north of the equator don't know the story of TT. In Latin America, and especially Brazil, it's folklore that keeps treasure hunters looking all over that country for quick wealth. Treasure is interesting in the US, Canada and Europe, but in Latin America, Easter, Europe and Asia, some look at treasure hunting like geologists might look at mining, as another form of potential income. Areas of dire poverty and few opportunities really draw the local enthusiast, somehow hoping that if they follow one more lead, one more hint, they'll somehow find El Dorado. After all, didn't Mel Fisher achieve just that with finding the Our Lady of Atocha that sank in 1622?

Fisher did find old Spanish treasure, and at what cost: decades of hardship, even losing his eldest son Dirk, when their vessel sank due to a bilge pump failure—everyday he rousted his crew with "Today's the day!" So many treasure hunters come into the endeavor thinking that they know something that no one else knows, and they'll be the ones to find that treasure. What many miss is that many treasure leads are actually red herrings and misdirections that are intended to keep treasure hunters from finding the treasure.

Hints and indicators are not often left for later generations to find, as many think and hope. Most treasure hunters search for treasure on the assumption that it'll be quick money, if they're lucky. Often, they don't have enough money to keep going on a long run. If they're unlucky, they're lying in bed and dying from the effects of years of alcoholism, as happened to the British comedy actor-turned treasure hunter, Richard Knight, who I covered in Vietnam as a young photojournalist.

On this Discovery Channel adventure, I was told that we were being used as field specialists (that's how Discovery told me that they were hiding the fact they were paying me twice as much as the rest of the cast—half my pay came through as the same payment as everyone else on cast, and then Discovery added my higher pay than the rest of the cast as a "consulting fee") Yet, they never really asked me for ideas, nor even the rest of the cast. It was beginning to look more and more like they had hired us to just be the personalities on the show, not because of the knowledge and experience we had, but solely, and I mean, only, because of the credibility our backgrounds brought to the story—it just wasn't clear yet that the credibility was in order to make the story, instead of just augment what should have been solid already.

This, of course, brought me back to my question of why Jeremy Whalen was on this cast: Keith Plaskett would confirm this when he let it slip that all the photos Jeremy had were the result of his hunting treasure with others, never really organizing and running a treasure hunt—he was our proverbial hanger-on, hoping to get something out of those with whom he had had his pictures taken. We normally call these kinds of people users.

Keith and Bryan were wanting to check out the night scene in town, so when there was a break in the rain one evening, we headed out over to the Estaleiro Bar, one of the dance clubs on the resort island. There was dancing and chatting: Brazilians are very friendly, and especially near the beach, where everyone either comes to get away from their workaday lives, or those who live by the beach because they've found a way to avoid a nine-to-five.

The owner of the Estaleiro must have been making a mint. The bar was packed, and it wasn't even a Friday night. Though predominantly a twenty-year-old demographic because of the music, all ages up to sixty were covered that night. A Russian-Brazilian who worked at the local bank struck up a conversation in English, which kept me from pulling my hair out trying to learn Brazilian Portuguese. If you speak Spanish (though a hodge-podge because of the places I've worked in Latin America, it's actually my first language, because my Ecuadorian-born mother didn't speak English by my birth), heaven help you when you try to pick up Brazilian Portuguese. Like so much Spanish in Latin America, Brazilian Portuguese is influenced by the local indigenous peoples, and words and inflections brought by African slaves and European immigrants, namely Italians.

Ironically, Italian is not as destructive to your Spanish, as Portuguese, because Italian is phonetically like Spanish, and often has the same meaning. Portuguese might have written words similar to those in Spanish, but it can often be totally different in not only pronunciation, but also meaning. I finally stopped rolling my "R"s and began pronouncing Spanish words as if I was British or French, and Brazilians started understanding me. What I was ending up with is what's called *Portuñol* in Latin America, a mix of Spanish and Portuguese.

A few hours at the bar and I was ready to get back to the hotel as we were supposed to head out to an island off the coast of Ilhabela. Both Keith and Bryan had gone off to their own diversions. One of the patrons had come up and said that Keith was being rude with one of the patrons. So, when I went over to them and asked them if they wanted to go, I was happy when they said, "Sure." Both were three sheets to the wind as I guided them out of the bar. Keith let fly with an insult to one of the women he was talking to, and I realized that he had been trying to hook up and ended up rebuked.

It wasn't just the booze he'd had that caused him to lash out. I think it was fact that he had crippled himself in learning languages by convincing himself that he wasn't good at it. Keith had told me about how he had a horrible French teacher in elementary school, and how she made him feel dumb for not doing well in her class. It had always been interesting to me that someone who could attain a high rank, or title, either in the military, or corporate, or whatever, which a senior chief is for a non-commissioned officer, could still be held back by event from all the way back in their childhood.

Thankfully it was one of the things that I had an opportunity to philosophize about in my seven months of solitary in a Vietnam political prison. My issue was with mathematics, and I realized that my anger at my dad for riding my ass every weekend about getting better grades in math, actually had the opposite effect. Nowadays, I love using a variety of mathematical calculations from geometry, algebra and calculus for navigation, surveying, flying planes, long-range shooting, ammunition reloading, and building log homes and homestead outbuildings. It all comes about through forgetting the messenger, and focusing on the message, especially if it's a good one—knowledge is good; and knowledge applied is even better!

We made it out of the bar and started making our way back to the hotel which should have been a quick walk. It soon became clear that not only was Keith totally plastered, but so too Bryan. To say they had gone on a major bender was an understatement. At every few blocks, Bryan was either trying to lay down on the sidewalk or even the street, traffic blaring by, as if he expected in his drunken stupor, and who knows what high, that he would get a wake-up call right there and be ready to head onto production tomorrow…which was already today, considering the hour.

Keith was trying to pick a fight with me at every block, too, as if trying to goad me into a mine's bigger than yours contest. "Common," he'd say, "let's fight!"

His fists would come up, as he also fought to keep from wobbling over, and I would quickly deflect with, "Oh, common, man, you'd kick my ass— where's the victory in such as easy one as that?"

We'd go another few blocks, and we'd repeat the charade. Then, about twenty blocks down, I came to a realization. "Where the fuck is Bryan?!"

"Oh, shit!" Keith responded. Was Bryan stupid enough to become "that guy," the one on our production who gets knifed for trying to score some recreational drugs in a dark alley?

No Bryan, no production. For the first time, I saw Keith afraid. He wasn't the only one. For some twisted reason, I was now actually falling into the role of team leader, or it was overtaking me. After the first episode would come out, many of my old combat buddies from Central America would ask me, did you really put that team together? I'd grin, and every one of them answered themselves, and laughed, knowing immediately the truth.

Yet, in that moment, I was beside myself that Bryan was gone, and I somehow felt responsible for not getting him home safe. It was the beginning of what I called taking on the role, and the role taking us on, as if in a demonic possession. How this would make itself apparent would make for interesting introspection throughout the coming seasons of TQ:SI. It had more to do with what we had experienced in our lives before the show, as compared to what we were in fact doing during filming. A strong sense of being was not that much affected, and brought about what I, and evidently the audience, felt, was good TV presence. Not having this solid sense of self could lead to some very interesting developments as I was about to see.

"Stop walking," Keith said, sitting down to catch a breath and stop the spinning in his world that had been filled to the gills with rum. "I'm telling you, I'm going to kick your ass!"

"Where's the victory in kicking my ass, Keith? You'll do it so quickly it won't even register—it won't be any fun for ya."

"Yeah, you say that, but you'd probably be able to kick my ass."

I smiled, relieved we'd never have find out that night: no matter who ended up the victor in such a trivial and stupid fight club of drunk, everyone always loses.

"Come on, amigo. Let's get back to the hotel." I pulled him up from his seat on the bus stop bench he'd plopped onto. "Hopefully Bryan doesn't get himself killed tonight."

Bryan had a that innocent wild child look on his face the next morning, as he chatted about the toxicity of various types of snakes with MAK's local crew, Bruno Prado and Heron Alencar. Local cameraman Prado shared a love of surfing with Bryan and me. Alencar, a fellow expat, except instead of an American raised in Saigon, he was a Brazilian raised in Paris—I took our conversations as an opportunity to regain what little was left of my fourth language I was introduced to after Spanish, English, and Vietnamese. Like any language, or even the skills shooting and fighting, if you don't do the drills, you rapidly lose the skills. It had been many years without practice for me, but Heron went back to France as often as possible. Prado was the more serious. Alencar was laid back, and yet you could see that he was feeling slightly uncomfortable about Bryan's description of how the golden lancehead viper's hemotoxin attacked the system. Every once in a while, he'd release the tension with a chuckle.

There's a reason Cleopatra chose the asp for her historically romantic suicide after Anthony's death. Cobras use neurotoxins to incapacitate. Vipers get you with hemotoxin. One puts you to sleep and you feel nothing, the other leaves you screaming in unbearable pain to your last breath as you bleed out of every hole.

Me, I was just floored that the amount of alcohol, and who knows what, that must have been coursing through his veins from the previous night, seemingly hadn't left him with a hangover. He had shown up in the lobby with his panache that would constantly make me smile at how much he was the comical contrast between a flamboyant character played by Peter O'Toole in MY FAVORITE YEAR, carried with the swinging shoulders of John Wayne in THE LONGEST DAY. I would soon find out why Bryan had that walk so full of bravado, and it would terrify me, along with the rest of the crew when we got into the jungle.

"Where in the world did you end up last night?"

He plopped down on the sofa next to me, and said, "Oh! I found a bus and then I was in a part of the island I'd never been."

It was just like that with him. No real explanation, just here I am, so who cares where I was...

Plaskett looked at me and just rolled his eyes and shook his head.

"The gist of this scene is that you're not happy with how long it's taking for the Jeremy and Cappy to finish building the dredge," Ruggles said as he reviewed the script received the night before. We had been sitting in the car, in the rain, for a few minutes, while Clancey went about giving Keith and Jeremy instructions as to what to say. This was beyond just putting people in situations and recording what they do. This was full-on Hollywood film drama scripting—and it was happening so nonchalantly. I wanted to scream, "IS THIS NORMAL FOR REALITY TV?!"

Getting out of the small sedan, I rushed through the drizzle for the welding shop to which we had just driven only a few blocks from the hotel a few minutes earlier. Inside, Keith and Jeremy were working on a variety of welding projects. Kind of wished I was at least doing something like that. I've loved the freedom of building what you need when you need it, ever since I took a welding class back in high school. Coming from a long line of builders and engineers, it's in my blood. Instead, I was here to be crew boss, playing the impatient heel to their team—Hollywood scripted tension moments for drama's sake.

On the show, viewers saw me coming into the shop, impatiently asking Keith and Jeremy when they'd be done. By now, the completely fabricated storyline was that I was putting my, and my investor's, money into this treasure hunting expedition and I had to start showing some finds to my investors. I really had to bite my lip and not laugh, as I'd not, and would never spend a single cent on a treasure hunting venture, and that in contrast, it was Discovery Communications paying all of us on that set.

According to that same script from Discovery Communications' Los Angeles office, twiddling around in a welding shop wasn't what my imaginary investors wanted from their treasure hunting team. They wanted to see gold and rubies and all these amazing finds according to the scriptwriters at MAK and production board at Discovery Channel. I could see a reality TV production team putting us in interesting situations aside from the actual searching for treasure, but I couldn't understand why they were telling us how to act, how to speak and what to do. Most importantly it was that every second that the cameras were rolling, every scene was being choreographed and directed by Clancey and Ruggles. There was not one iota of fly on the wall journalism—real true-life documentary film-making.

It was one thing for them to direct us back at Catalina Island, but that, I thought, was just to make sure Discovery was happy with how we looked and interacted together on camera. This was supposed to be the real deal. Instead, they were directing me to ride my crew's ass as if to create the façade we were running late, and money was running out. It would always be about how funds were running out. It was hard to not laugh when the showrunners directed me to harp on this.

Discovery, on average, pays a field production between $3 to $5 million to complete a production. Not much when you realize they're looking to make around $150 million by the time they begin broadcasting overseas in various languages. From that initial investment by Discovery, field production companies pay the crew and cast, pocketing as much as they can, hiding money in such expenses as their offices, vehicles and other items and needs, such as food, with business lunches and dinners, and even hiring a second company that provided the gear, that second business owned by the initial production company. So, though we were being paid by MAK Pictures and Discovery Channel through Tent City Productions, LLC, and the camera gear was being rented by MAK Pictures from Tent City Productions, LLC, it was still MAK Pictures getting that money. It's just the way it's done in LA. Production companies make their money off the investment by expensing as much of it as they can for their own desires that relate to the final product—and keeping the money in house.

I wasn't spending a damned thing on this adventure. None of us were. Instead, I was being paid to be here and talk in front of the camera. At first, it was funny, saying and doing things I'd never, ever do or say, because it just doesn't happen in real life. When viewers later posted on social media and a variety of forums that the dialogue seemed scripted, guess what: it was—they were very astute!

Sadly, the rest of the audience were following along with earnest interest in our team finding the treasure. Even the ones who posted that they felt the whole show, or even parts of the show, were fake, would still post that they hoped it wasn't and they we would find something of worth. What else would they do, if not told by Discovery in a disclaimer that it was all a totally scripted drama?

We are an amazing species. We have something I don't think any other does. It's something that makes itself apparent in some, more than others. It's what I think separates the survivor from the fallen, at least in battle anyway. It's what keeps people going towards a great goal: Hope.

What's twisted is that this innate quality within humans can be played upon by certain factions. Communists and socialists use it to sell their delusionary utopia that always ends in the loss of freedom and some dictator in power that outshines in depravity any previous military dictator or political leader. In media, using words and imagery, through the cliffhanger, hope is manipulated to keep you coming back for the next episode. Through your repeated viewing of the show, the network can gain numbers for its ratings and by so doing they can pad their media kit that's sent to prospective advertisers. This can be millions, and hundreds of millions dollars in advertising.

Now this is just business, and that's fine. When a network sells itself as the last true broadcast network out there, and does provide programming that delivers that much needed record of history and human experience, so much the better. But, when a network broadcasts fake documentary (fakeumentary), without any disclaimer and is doing so to manipulate that innate quality of hope in humans, to overcome a person's disbelief and get repeat viewers, because the audience emotionally connects with a character, or characters depicted by the actors on the show, that's pure fraud.

Hope doesn't just affect the audience. As a certified clinical hypnotherapist, one who used hypnosis to survive eleven months in a communist re-education, and later heal the traumatic effects of five years of combat in Central and Latin America, I was well acquainted with how film and TV, and propaganda for that matter, works: remember, it's only an image on a screen; but have you ever wondered why you have emotional responses to something you're not physically experiencing yourself?

TV, film, radio, and even books and articles are created to render a variety of emotions out of you. In all these, it's with the intention that the content will bypass your subconscious fail safes and get you to believe as real what are only words, images and sounds. In Hollywood, it's done with good scripts, good acting and excellent post-production. In fakeumentary, it's done in a fraudulent manner, using cheap actors, poor scripts and the powerful lie: it's real and "true-life."

Anchored off one of Ilhabela's bays, *Saco do Eustáquio*, the crew and cast moved about the stern of what we had come to call The Wedding Cake. So full of holes from *toredo navalis*, shipworms, the Alpha Crucis' hull looked like a white wedding cake ready to sink. First time I dove over the side and had a close inspection, I was amazed it hadn't sunk long ago with that amount of damage, along with all that rot the owner had covered over in new white paint.

Figure 5. Snake Island doesn't have white sandy beaches and excellent seafood restaurants, but where we found the bonafide galleon anchor does—Saco do Eustáquio.

Over the side went Jeremy, and me, Mehgan and Bryan. In two teams, we moved along the bottom on SCUBA. What with how shallow we were, only ten feet, it was a constant hassle keeping neutral buoyancy. Many times, I just went negatively buoyant, and moved along on my hands and knees, trying not to kick my fins, else stir up the sand and material. It was no easy feat, and often the water just went murky, as Derrick Nevot moved along with his housed camera and caught the action.

Mehgan and Bryan were off toward the ship's anchor we had learned about only a few weeks later. Clearly from an old galleon, it was dragged up by a shrimper's nets and dropped off here, just a few hundred feet off this resort beach that drew thousands every year from all parts of Brazil.

Figure 6. Mirante Restaurant lunch break, on the beach up from the site of the fake Snake Island offshore dredging scene, l-r. the author, soundman Heron Alencar, actor Jeremy Whalen, director/showrunner Ty Clancey, and co-showrunner/executive producer Andy Ruggles.

Jeremy and I would trade between moving the nozzle of the dredge he and Keith had built. A vacuum cleaner had more suction than this joke. For someone who was supposed to be a longtime welder and fabricator, I was surprised. This should have been an easy build. In the last two years, working on a variety of placer mining operations back home in Alaska, I'd used a variety of models from two-inch to eight-inch. This abomination that should have had enough suction to keep me from running my hand across the front of the nozzle, had barely enough to stop my hand for a millisecond.

On a treasure forum, a commenter wrote about how ludicrously dismal the blast of water was on exit. It would appear in a scene where I was supposed to be top side, watching to see what artifacts and debris it was pulling up and dropping into a classifier. All that was going through my mind was, there's no way anyone is going to believe we're doing anything other than filming a fully scripted movie—the dribble coming of the suction dredge outflow was laughably weak.

Even the design was nuts. To get that amount of suction going to get material up from the bottom takes some real venturi force. That's why when you're suction dredging for gold, you have a length of sluice for the material to run, and it's parallel to the outflow of the dredge. Here we had an exit nozzle going directly down at the classifiers perpendicularly to the direction of the exiting water. It was all I could do to not laugh uncontrollably when I asked Keith and Jeremy after our first scene with this it, "Did you guys really design this?"

Jeremy gave me one of those kinds of looks that made me roll my eyes. "Well, something's beginning to come clear," I said.

We did a number of other scenes, most famously the one where Mehgan and Bryan floated on the surface after supposedly finding the anchor, and told those of us on the stern that we had positive proof to make landing on Snake Island worthwhile…all in a bay of Ilhabela, visited by tourists daily.

After shooting a few more scenes with the team on the stern, all of us going through the material that was supposed to be pulled up by what Jeremy incorrectly called a dredge pump (anyone who has actually used one knows the system is called a "suction dredge": a dredge pump is specifically the pump, the motor, that pulls water in order to create suction for moving material through the Venturi principle. Yes. It's the same physics you fellow aviators understand with regards to an air foil).

Back at the metal shop on Ilhabela, I was curious as to why Jeremy was building a suction dredge with such a small jet. Down at the bottom running that dredge it was clear how much that too small jet didn't do much. It was so pitifully week that in first and second episode of season two, viewers can see Jeremy fanning and feeding material into the nozzle. I almost choked on water laughing when I saw it happening live. Just for edifications sake, when you're running a proper dredge, material really moves and it's more trying to make sure the material isn't going up so fast that it blocks the tube. Watch Discovery Channel's other show, BERING SEA GOLD, and you'll get a more accurate idea of what a real dredge is and how it's supposed to move material.

Excited about the anchor, a real find, I asked Ty Clancey and Andy

Ruggles when we were going to go deeper and do more research on the galleon anchor.

"We're not doing that," they both said as they looked up from the show script.

I laughed and asked, "What do you mean we're not going to do that?"

"We're shooting off Buzios the rest of the week," Clancey said.

"This is a pretty important find. You didn't learn about it until just a few days ago, right?"

"Just not part of the show—we've got other content to shoot."

Shocked, I just stood there and looked at him, and then realized, finally, what I'd gotten myself into, and that the non-disclosure agreement included in my contract meant that I would never be able to tell anyone what was happening. It's no wonder no one has ever spoken about what really happens in reality TV, until my words now: only because I actually read my contract again.

All this and how the weeks had been passing made me say to Keith Plaskett as we broke and headed the short fifty yards to shore for lunch at one of the best places on Ilhabela for Brazilian seafood, the *Mirante* Restaurant, "You know, we will NEVER, EVER find treasure on this show…"

He stopped and looked at me. He didn't shake his head. He didn't nod. He just raised his eyebrows and smiled, which made me shake my head and laugh.

"You know you can kiss your archeology teaching career goodbye if Discovery doesn't put a disclaimer on this show."

He looked like a deer caught in the headlights.

Figure 7. Keith Plaskett "Cappy", with a new teaching contract at the Trujillo National University of Peru.

5 CONE OF SILENCE

With what you're learning and how deep this goes, it may seem amazing to you that no one has come out before me to tell you about how twisted "reality TV" truly is. Discovery Communications and its type have more secrets than the CIA, KGB and FSB put together. They use the same tools of intimidation to keep these secrets, and with Discovery Communications, it's through its in-house corporate law offices.

It's how they make money off people who continue to be held in high regard by viewers, especially overseas, because the audience often doesn't get latest skinny: how many of these reality TV stars are either one step from being arrested by law enforcement, or are already in jail? The latest skinny I had gotten on another Discovery Communications moneymaker, DUAL SURVIVAL, was that it's co-star Joseph Teti had been received a restraining order from Discovery to not appear within 300 feet of any Discovery Communications building.

When the first season of TQ:SI began broadcasting, Bryan was not happy: ironically, the crashing wave jump and ensuing sea urchin encounter were all Bryan—my disbelief was all real, too. He would be posting several gripes publicly that just set off Discovery. He soon received a quick talking down by Mark Kadin, who then wrote to all of us, that Bryan had been set straight and sent out an email to all of us:

From: Mark Kadin
Sent: Friday, July 31, 2015 8:26 AM
To: Bryan Grieg Fry; Cork Graham; Mehgan Heaney-Grier; capt keith plaskett; vanjerm (Jeremy Whalen)
Subject: Treasure Quest Update!

Hey Dream Team! Hope you are all well and enjoying the shows. We're very excited so far, and I am extremely grateful to Discovery for showing so much support and really believing in this. I can't believe the amazing timeslots that TQ lives in...after Bush People, Naked and Afraid and Deadliest Catch! Honestly, that's truly as good as it gets, and it shows their dedication to making this their next hit.

I have heard from several of you, and been checking out some Facebook posts, and it seems like there may be some rising tensions within the group. That is certainly normal, but I want to remind all of you of some really important things. You are a TEAM. Whether you like it or not, the success or failure of this show is wrapped up with each and every one of you.

If we are fortunate enough to make it to another season, I would like you all to be involved. But that is only predicated on a few important points. In emails or Facebook posts, do not divulge any information about how the show was made or voice any displeasure about Discovery or the series. If you want to call me or email me and yell at me, you are always welcome to do that. But the WORST thing you can do is act rash and post something that will get you in trouble. Discovery takes their NDA clauses very seriously, and especially on a show of this magnitude, they will not hesitate to take action. Honestly, it's just not worth it. We all have an excellent opportunity here, and let's not let petty differences stand in the way of future success. It's not about pointing fingers at the other guy. You are all individually responsible for making this right with each other. That is what the team mentality is all about.

Please know that we are doing our best in the edit to make this the best show possible. In all honesty, in my over 20 years of doing television, this is the hardest show I've worked on in the edit. The team here is working 20 hour days to meet deadlines. We are trying to be true to the story, and infuse the necessary drama where it needs it. If you feel slighted in the way you are portrayed in some instances, please know that while there may be drama in the short term, our long-term goals are to never make anyone look bad. And remember, the most successful shows have characters that people love AND hate, and characters that they can identify with, no matter if they're on top of the world or down and out.

Lastly, and this is just my opinion so you can tell me to go f- myself, but I feel like there's just a little too much Facebook and twitter activity from you guys about the ratings of the show. That just feels a tad amateurish to me. You should be more excited about finding the gold than worrying about ratings. That doesn't scream authenticity to me. -- Ratings are a fickle beast, and frankly, we're not even close to the status of being a hit, so while I understand the excitement, I would try to keep that to a minimum. When people inevitably start looking you guys up to find out more about you, I don't want the first thing they read to be a ratings post from you. -- Remember, the viewers are on an adventure with you, and we are shrouding this entire thing in mystery. You guys are in danger on the island from snakes and in the water from pirates, so who knows if all of you made it out alive?   Frankly, if it were up to me, I would have put in your contracts that you couldn't post on Facebook or twitter for the six weeks the show was airing, but I'm more of a stickler on keeping the mystery going for viewers.

So take that how you want to, but that's where I'm coming from....unless you know people with Nielsen boxes and then all bets are off!! Tell them to watch the damn show!

Please feel free to reach out with any questions or concerns. Remember, I'm on your side no matter what and we're in this together. So let ME solve problems...don't feel like you have to air those problems publicly.

Thanks guys, and a big thank you for helping on all the pickups. It's absolutely huge that you're doing those.

Good luck tonight! Enjoy the show.

Best,

Mark

What Bryan, and the rest of us didn't understand, is that the very moment that Discovery Communications broadcast the first episode, they had broken the laws of the US, and would soon be breaking the laws of other nations by releasing a totally scripted show without a disclaimer stating that this show was far from real, or true. There is no legal contract that is binding, if the contract is to keep a crime quiet: such as the total fabrication of a TV show fraudulently offered to the public as true news— this falls under false advertising. When we later headed to Argentina, they would breach item 12 to such a degree, I would be amazed that they would so recklessly do so on such a much larger scale:

12. Foreign Corrupt Practices Act:
Participant hereby represents and covenants that Participant has, and all of Participant's representatives engaged in carrying out the services contemplated by this Agreement ("Representatives") have, complied with and will continue to comply with all applicable U.S. and non-U.S. laws, rules, regulations and decrees, including, without limitation, the Organization for Economic Cooperation and development's Convention on Combating Bribery of Foreign Public Officials in International Business Transactions, effective February 15, 1999, the United States' Foreign Corrupt Practices Act, as amended, and other laws to combat bribery, conflicts of interest and corruption of governmental officials or employees, or political candidates or parties (each, a "Governmental Official"). Participant hereby covenants that neither Participant nor Participant's Representatives will directly or indirectly make, give, promise or offer any

payments or anything of value to any Governmental Official, or authorize the taking of any such action, for the purpose of influencing any act of such Governmental Official to obtain, retain or direct any business to any person or entity or gain any improper advantage, and Participant represents that neither Participant nor Participant's Representatives have taken any such action. Participant covenants that neither Participant nor Participant's Representatives, in connection with this Agreement and any services to be provided by Participant to Company or Company's affiliates, will engage, employ, retain or pay any other person or entity to provide consulting, lobbying, facilitation or similar professional services involving potential contact with any Governmental Official or anyone who is reasonably likely to be involved in influencing any Governmental Official, without Company's express written approval. Participant will keep books, accounts and records that accurately and fairly reflect in reasonable detail its transactions and disposition of funds paid in connection with carrying out the services contemplated by this Agreement. Any breach of or misrepresentation in this provision shall be deemed to be a material breach of this Agreement.

You can imagine the questions running in my mind as to who was paid *"propina"* (bribes) in the Brazil government, and what stories were told to the representatives of the Chico Mendes Institute for Biodiversity Conservation, Instituto Chico Mendes de Conservação da Biodiversidade (ICMBIO) in Sao Paulo? By the questions I would get from the biologists who took us on the island, I got that they were being told we were searching for archeological record, basically, they were getting the same story I got before I signed my NDA. I had yet to start the treasure hunt that Aaron Burk had invited me on before my casting—Discovery Channel was helping me keep my promise to never, ever go on a treasure hunt again...Who would have thought that a little bribery in Brazil, would just be the pinnacle of what was to happen in Argentina with regards to illegal activities.

I'd learned long ago in Central America that there are no secrets, especially when I'd end up on the receiving end of ambushes set by FMLN guerrillas, who had forewarning of our operations due to corrupt officials and just the average soldiers who didn't know when to keep their mouths shut. In Brazil, operational security (OPSEC) was hilarious.

The whole island of Ilhabela knew there was a production team from Discovery Channel shooting a show. How Discovery expected to keep it quiet was ridiculous, as they had to hire locals as local fixers to get anything done. Productions don't get completed under a tightly controlled cone of silence. People talk. What's entertaining is what they say.

At the hotel buffet breakfast, which must have been a great price deal for MAK Pictures, as everyone on the crew and cast ate there, our local producer, Flavio Somogyi, our Hungarian-Brazilian, another French speaker who was more than entertaining, asked me how I first learned about the Treasure of the Trinity.

When I told him that I had only first heard of it upon being cast for the show, his eyes went wide. He said he was told that I had been searching for this treasure for twenty years, and that it was something that gnawed at my psyche. I sighed and broke out in a big laugh.

It was almost like my own new personal narrative: "Nope. Never heard of this treasure until getting on this show. I will say that I find it to be an interesting theory the producers and writers were coming up with. I guess if I was really on a treasure hunt, I'd search in this area. I say, this area being Ilhabela. I mean, after all, there's so much pirate treasure history in this area."

It was a horrific history at that. Only a few years earlier, people exploring a cave found a number of skeletons left from a group of pirates who had been chained together, and left to die of thirst and starvation.

Many would assume that based on the broadcast of the show, we were spending a gawd-awful amount of time on Snake Island. It would be a couple months before we'd actually set foot on *Queimada Grande*. Makes sense really, when you consider how dangerous Snake Island really is. I've told many that if we were on that island for the months and months it seems on the show, we'd all have been killed: cast and crew. It's no joke, and just because Vice did a piece on the island, that led to the idea of TQ:SI, and just because the reporter who stayed on the island for VICE spent a night on the island, you'd be out of your mind to spend more time. For the biologists who are studying the island, it'd be insane to stay there more than a few days. They often just go for a couple, to capture specimens and get off the island.

Discovery Channel was just being smart production-wise: by shooting all other footage before we actually landed on Snake Island. If we just happened to all get whacked by a bunch of crazy deadly snake, it wouldn't affect the broadcast of the show. And, if we did get greased by those wonderfully lethal little buggers, so much the better for ratings—reality TV is after all, aside from those true history enthusiasts fully taken by Discovery's lack of disclaimers, directed towards those who like watching a dramatic train wreck.

Until then, the island of Buzios, off the eastern coast of Ilhabela, would suffice for the topography. For most of the show, it would suffice for the landscape on Snake Island. Other parts not shot later on Snake Island scenes would be filled in with the terrain on Ilhabela. It was good to be out of the hotel and working on something other than looking for something to do.

"Can we land there?" asked Ty Clancey, hiding his light complexion and

Irish red hair under a large hat, as he clutched one of the rope loops on the large, orange Flexboat RIB.

Daniel Carvalho, captained his rigid inflatable boat flawlessly, holding us in a pattern just off the rocks like a well-experienced chopper pilot would keep his bird in a perfect hover. "I can put two or three of you off at a time," he said.

"Who's off?"

I would jump up onto the rocks, as would Bryan and our director of photography, Scottie Mckibben. For a wannabe hippie DP, who missed the Sixties by fifty years but had his long hair in a man-bun, he had a set of balls handling that Sony camera the way a machine gunner would move from boat to rock and rock to rock with an M60 and a full ammo can. I grabbed my light pack and machete and followed him from the gunwale to the rock face and scrambled up and away from the waves that continued to try and wash us off, or at least puncture the Flexboat and crush its hard hull.

Throttled into reverse, Carvalho moved the boat away from us under the much-needed thrust of the twin Evinrudes. Then he pulled off the maneuver two more times, getting Bryan, Heron and Bruno off, and then, Jeremy Whalen and our drone camera operator, Derrick Nevot, from Miami. His gear was the most cumbersome, as it required the large Pelican hard shell cases for travel. Equipment light enough to float on a small propeller is often fragile.

While the crew readied to video both our land team and Mehgan and Keiths' dive team, Clancey and Ruggles talked amongst themselves for a few minutes over a by a rock outcropping. They called us over and then said, "We've planted something here."

"Ok?" Jeremy, Bryan and I responded.

"We want to capture your responses, so we're not going to say much more…Go find the treasure!"

The three of us began looking around. Both Bryan and I looked around the mound of rocks that was half way up a rock slide cutting through the island's jungle canopy. Here and there, Jeremy moved with his metal detector. As we scrambled across the rocks and looked in the nooks and crannies of the rock pile, it was clear Clancey was not happy. More than that, it was looking like he wanted to explode. I didn't know whether it was because of our actions or that things were just not going well for him this day.

"Enough! HERE! Look in here," he said, jerking his finger at a tiny cave belong a collection of large boulders. "Get in there Jeremy."

Figure 8. Notice how the fake rock stands out from the ones around it? If it had been placed there centuries ago, it would be covered in moss like the rest...

Jeremy came over and laid his metal detector down and shucked his pack. Doing the same with my pack, I trailed him as he entered the hole. Clancey directed Bryan to another part of the rock pile and said out of the corner of his mouth, "What kind of treasure hunters are you?"

I laughed and wanted to respond with something like, if we were actually searching for treasure, it would have been the team that would have led us to here, instead of the film crew. Based on that research, we would also be very well of where what we're looking for would be. It wouldn't have been us looking for who knows what. We'd be having some type of idea of what had led us here. Even an Easter egg hunt offers kids a better idea of what we were after. As if on cue, Jeremy said, "Cork. Look at this...Just look!"

Jeremy was squatted next to a rock. On the rock were a number of symbols that would cause curiosity and titillation across Internet treasure hunting forums for months. I didn't want to just yell out, "So that's what you brought in the extra, large Pelican case!"

Instead I played along with the charade. "What do you think it is, Jeremy?"

"Those look like Jesuits symbols..."

Figure 9. Excellent carving by the Discovery artist, Sebastian Baille—crew forgot one detail: no moss on the rock, and totally different composition.

Clancey motioned for Mckibben to follow the action with his camera. What the audience got in the TV broadcast was Jeremy and I talking about the rock, as if I was an expert in Jesuit history. What was happening between takes was Clancey reading from his script about the history of the Jesuits, and my excitement learning all this for the first time, with, "Wow! Really?!"

I am, after all a history buff, and as writer I'm professional historian, anyone who considers himself a journalist or writer should. Isn't it sad that so many are not, and it appears as if all they're trying to get is get their name in print? If only journalists would just do their job. I had learned this long ago when I was a freelance combat photographer shooting for the Associated Press and Reuters. That was until one day I came back to see my photos with a story that had nothing to do with my photos.

All this was truly turning into a Hollywood production, clearly not the reality TV/documentary I had thought I had signed on for, when Aaron Burk introduced the project to me by asking if I wanted to go on a treasure hunt. It was all really beginning to gel in my mind now. I come from a documentary background. Many don't know that when I started out as a combat photographer, covering the fighting between the Khmer and the Vietnamese and Hmong and the Pathet Lao, which also led to my imprisonment by the Vietnamese in a roundabout way, and then my first year in Central America, I was also getting freelance jobs running a Betacam for broadcast companies like ABC and the new and burgeoning CNN. I must say now, that though my politics doesn't jive with Ted Turner, he still had a good eye for news, and respected the profession, much unlike so many now in the possession of the control of news service, executives who will sell their first born for a buck or an option.

Turner, even years after I shouldered a camera for his company, has written back to me every time I've written to him, which started with me sending him a copy of my Vietnam prison memoir. He, like the dearly missed Charlton Heston, who represented the elegance of Old Hollywood, have something that is sadly become harder and harder to find in our society, and that is class. From the many who have billions, but don't have class, it's clear that class has nothing to do with money: it all has to do with how you're brought up—being brought up by the government and your childhood peers, instead of your parents, is a big part of the problem.

This is a problem that is hitting our society even more rapidly than I thought possible, and it's helped on its way with the media copping out of being the stalwarts of society, where news becomes fake news, and those individuals who should have been behind bars are being touted as celebrities on reality TV. Teti, Whalen, Hayden, Wyatt, these are all reality TV personalities who are in prison, or likely to be in there soon. Not that this will stop Discovery Communications from making a quick buck off them while they crash and burn. Now if my words seem harsh or inflammatory, keep reading, the plot thickens…and I didn't write that script: It's all Discovery Communications. And the commonality, through all this? CEO David Zaslav, the media poster boy of how if you don't get caught you, you get rich…and they'll even give you a medal.

David Zaslav, and his ilk, were far from my mind as of yet, as I was all too preoccupied with not coming back in body bag from Brazil. Though I should have been more attentive to the dark conspiracy brewing at the hands of Jeremy and his younger brother, James Whalen, otherwise known Kendall D. Mckibben, I was preoccupied with Major Danger in front of me as we walked up the hill on Buzios for the fourth week of production. We hadn't even made it to Snake Island, and I was already concerned that we were going to have our bones broken, or be bit by a viper, as a result of Dr. Feel Good's actions.

What I thought were ego-inflated movements of Paul Bunyan's shoulders swinging like Alaska spruce in a stiff northern wind, were really far from that. It was clear that all the recreational drugs, alcohol and especially the injuries and the venomous near-death experiences had been taking their toll. As a former-longtime resident of San Francisco Bay Area, I had often seen the survivors of the Summer of Love, who surprisingly hadn't died before they all thought they were going to, and even rejoiced by saying, "Don't trust anyone over thirty." They often looked like the Cryptmaster, and the Cryptmaster's wife, hollow shells of their former gorgeous and handsome youthfulness, living out of a shelter, their broken and used bodies sitting on a San Francisco corner, repeating their post-1960s East Indian yoga meditation mantra, "Change, change, got some change, mister?"

All that swagger, all that chest out, and shoulders swinging wasn't just to show how self-absorbed Bryan was: he needed to do it just to navigate across the land. It was an eye-widening scene to observe, after the first time I was right behind Bryan as we moved uphill. Being that he was uphill of me, and considering I'm six-foot, and he's a few inches taller, those extra inches seemed liked the Philistine Giant to my King David, as I immediately looked left and right for a safe place to leap, after the first time his sweep of the legs wasn't enough to get him to the next step. He was a like a little toy soldier with stiff legs that a child would have to amble along a table to make it look as if it was walking. Terrifying, not just because he could drop his easy 230 pounds of muscle and bone on top of you, but that if there was a venomous snake hiding out of sight, but well within an agitated response, there would be hell to pay.

Bryan had made it clear that the golden viper was just one of the many venomous snakes and spiders in brazil. He had made quite a show of talking about the banana spider that gives you an unretractable penis erection before you die, but it was the collection of vipers, who I felt were as much a threat on the mainland and near offshore islands, such as Ilhabela and Buzios, where we were shooting ninety percent of our production.

Jararacas (*bothrops jararaca*) are the golden lancehead viper's nearest cousin. While the golden lancehead (*bothrops insularis*) has a much stronger and faster acting toxin than the golden lancehead, the jararaca is just as deadly. It's the difference between getting hit by .375 H&H magnum and .30-06. They'll both kill you deader than dead. It's just that the .375 is likely to do it quicker. Both vipers deliver a hemotoxin will leave you in a mess of pain, bleeding out of orifices, while your blood gels into a red mousse. As Bryan our local self-confirmed atheist enjoyed saying, it creates the most amazing stigmata.

Dr. Feelgood should know, his carelessness with a Stephen's banded snake put him in the hospital with a very good question as to whether he'd soon end up in the morgue. As it was, his whole system was reworked in a horrifyingly painful manner. On production, along with whatever mood adjusting chemicals he was taking to get through the day, he was taking hormones because his system was that fried by the venom—certain snake bites can ruin your whole day and effect the rest of your life. Add spinal meningitis at 18 months, and a fall that broke his back that led to a taste for painkillers, not to mention the twenty-five other snake bites had turned him into a dead man walking, and I don't know about you, but I'd do everything to make sure that kind of bad luck doesn't rub off on me due to proximity.

As we moved through the jungle on a farm uphill from the town of Ilhabela, on the island of its namesake, it was clear that the weeks were taking their toll on everyone, but especially on Dr. Feelgood. Keith and I had talked with Clancey and Ruggles about his condition, but it just fell on deaf ears. They pushed all of us, which is fine, but the more they pushed Bryan, the more it endangered all of us. What was getting Keith and I the most was that not only was Dr. Feelgood dealing with the balance impairment resulting from all his near-death experiences that Discovery thought made for good backstory, but he was adding to that impairment through recreational drugs.

There's a scene in episode three where Dr. Feelgood is clearly becoming agitated by everyone, and he said, I have an issue with balance, so what? I thought myself that day, he said that, so what?!

Shortly after that scene, we were moving up another incline and Bryan almost lost it completely and would have surely come rolling down on Mehgan. She and I traded glances, that look of, oh shit, I almost got a quick ride to the emergency room!

A few days later, we were underway in the SS (Suicide Ship) Wedding Cake, in rough seas. It would lead to some exciting footage of me yelling, "Standby!" and pointing out the window of the cabin as Keith piloted, which were used in the promos for show. What I was pointing at was Dr. Feelgood who had gone up to the bow and was reenacting the romantic flying scene from TITANIC, except it wasn't Leonardo DiCaprio and Kate Winslet, it was just Dr. Feelgood up there on the bow, all by himself. All around him, were the rest of the Brazilian boat crew doing their best to stow all our diving gear that had been used in another diving scene around on the other side of Ilhabela at the galleon anchor site in Saco do Estaquio.

As Keith and I both watched Bryan out there, his wings outstretch all I could say was, "How the hell did he get LSD?"

"That guy is gonna die…" Keith answered.

I looked over at Clancey, and said, "You better get that idiot inside! With all the metal he's got in his body, he's going to direct a lightning rod straight down at us and blow up this ship better than a mortar round…"

Clancey's eyes went wide, and he ran up to the bow and talked Bryan back in.

When we got back to port and I was sitting at my hotel room desk after dinner, I said fuck this shit, and wrote an email to send out that night…

From: Cork Graham

Sent: Sunday, February 22, 2015 5:34 PM

To: Eric J Christensen; Krystyna Laba; Mark Kadin; Ty Clancey; Cynthia Fraser; Andy Ruggles; Carl Nicolaou

Cc: Capt. Keith; Cork Graham

Subject: YOUR EYES ONLY: CREW & CAST RISK due to Bryan Grieg Fry's recreational drug use.

Importance: High

Greetings, All —

I wish I didn't have to write this email, but the events of the last few weeks are of great concern: I've come to the conclusion that the recreational drug use and yahoo attitude by cast member Bryan Grieg Fry is putting himself and the production crew and cast in danger.

Events:

1.   Back in California, during the shooting of the sizzle, Bryan asked me to join him in the use of marijuana and I kindly declined.

2.   Within a week of arrival Brazil, while checking out the night life of area, Bryan was publicly asking patrons of a bar if they could set him up with marijuana: island telegraph got back to the local fixer, who then asked us who has been at the bar that night, "who was it that was saying they were working for Discovery and wanted pot."

3.   Within the same week, he was asking our local fixer if he would set him up with marijuana—again putting the fixer in a very compromising situation

4.   A week later Bryan told me that he had gotten himself squared away with all the drugs he needed to carry him through his work time here in Brazil

5.   Bryan has made it public the extent of his drug cocktail to deal with a variety of repercussion due to his broken back and snakebite that nearly killed him—my question is how addicted is he to these prescription painkillers…and more importantly how is he taking it upon himself to mix and match to fit his own high?

6. *Within the following week, while caught in a lighting storm, Bryan was pulling a "Titanic" on the bow of our large boat—Captain Keith and I were yelling at him to come in and not act like an ass, endangering himself or others trying to save him should he be hit by lightning, or fall over the side during rough seas: earlier that day he was giving off indicators of someone who was "on something".*

For the record, I've worked for almost 10 years as a drug and alcohol rehab counselor for the Native American community, with a variety of commendations for my work, and so recreational drug abuse isn't my thing. Still, if someone wants to use any form of controlled substance (alcohol, pot, etc.), that's their responsibility within the safety of their own home on their off hours.

What I have major conflict with is when this use of a controlled substance bears on a project; whether through active use during work, or while still under the influence of said drugs while later at work. Also, when the use or reputation of use effects the completion of a work project, I consider it an affront to my livelihood and safety. Considering Bryan has the traits of a sociopathic, egotistical moron; the fact that he thinks he's somehow gotten something over on society by getting his "stash" in a country that is daily reporting on a major drug war within its borders should be of MAJOR CONCERN to anyone associated with him and his arrogant devices.

Personally and professionally, I can't be associated with someone who thinks that he's above the law of a foreign country and is stupidly arrogant enough to put not only himself legally at risk for illegal drugs, but could also possibly put those around him in danger.

In the weeks we've worked, I've noticed a number of mood swings that clearly coordinate with effects of drugs on emotional behaviors, especially when put under stress as during the last week when he was put under major stress while working in conditions that also put me in danger because I was deferring to his more rapid actions, that should have been slowed for the safety of the team, instead of emboldened to make himself look more like an Indiana Jones wannabe. Thankfully, I recognized the oncoming effects of heat stroke and pulled myself into a cave to cool my core temperature—saving myself from being hammered with the full and deadly effects of heat stroke.

In OTFs, Bryan has described himself as a going after snakes in JOURNEY TO SNAKE ISLAND as if going through a scene in the movie HURT LOCKER. The irony is not lost on as me as the main character in the movie, played by Jeremy Renner, was a COMPLETE YAHOO, who put his EOD team in danger because of his antics. We already have a real explosives specialist on our team, Captain Keith Plaskett, whose job in the Navy was to find and disarm enemy explosives and I'm sure he would agree that in the manner that Bryan has been yahooing his way around on this assignment of clearing and making sure his "snake mines" were cleared, it was in rapid and self-absorbed manner that would have had any member of his team booted. Teams are supposed to work together, especially in a dangerous environment, especially a place as dangerous as Snake Island.

During this same week, the next day after the heat stroke event, as a matter of fact, Bryan was totally in his own world yelling out while snorkeling and we were still shooting a scene on rocky coastline—the guy is totally self-absorbed, amplified by whatever he's on at the time. In case you haven't read his new autobiography, this is a guy who admires Hunter S. Thompson, not just for his writing, but also his well-publicized record of playing an amphetamine against barbiturates in his own recreational drug use: a frequent topic of conversation with Bryan often centers around his pride in past use of a variety of drugs in a recreational manner that would kill an elephant. Bryan fashions himself the "Hunter S. Thompson of the snake world": both in risk and drug use.

We haven't even gotten to Snake Island, and I'm with good reason, questioning Bryan's trustworthiness as a person to put my life on the line with while we're perusing an island covered with some of the deadliest snakes in the world, snakes he's supposed to be protecting us from. I already have no interest in following him into deeper areas of Buzios Island, and a potential run in with one of the much larger lancehead vipers that cover Brazil, because of his recreational use of drugs (who knows when and how much), because I don't trust his professionalism, nor his awareness of surroundings: not only that, his self-important attitude, mixed with an unhealthy attraction to risk, make him what we used to call during the war in Central America, a "Lead Magnet". These are the guys who think they're above risk and end up taking a bullet, but also bring down a few of those around them. Once these guys were recognized, they were "shit-canned" and sent home on the next flight available.

I am stating for the record, that I will not go onto Snake Island with Bryan Grieg Fry, unless he takes a urine test for controlled substances before we go on Snake Island. If he's on something while we're there, I'm sure that either he's going to get nailed, or someone else, solely because of his arrogant stupidity: his broken back due to fall, and near death experiences from snake bite, should have been an indication of his past lack of professionalism and skill—I'm sure a local, and much more respected herpetologist in Brazil, can take his place should he fail his drug test, as I'm sure he will...

Best regards,
Cork Graham

As the main office was up late reviewing and editing media sent their way, I did not have to wait long for a response. Within five minutes of my email send, Ty Clancey and Andy Ruggles were angrily banging at my door. I learned long ago when I got sucked into a corporate executive job at a computer security software company during the golden tech bubble years under President Clinton, that one way to get immediate response from anyone in power is to copy as many people in a message string as you can. It's the corporate form of throwing an HE grenade into a room and seeing who comes running out.

The two of them were seething as they stood in front of the door. I looked at them, as Clancey asked, "Why did you send this without talking with us about this?!"

"I did come to you and you didn't do anything about it. The guy's dangerous."

Ruggles broke in, and hissed, his face in a twist, like a baby who needs its diaper changed immediately. "We are sooo fucked!"

"Do you know you've probably destroyed any chances of this show being finished by sending this email?" Clancey said, like he wanted to punch me in the face.

"I'm sorry guys, but you left me no choice," I said, calmly.

"FUUUUUCKKK!" I didn't know if Ruggles was actually talking to anyone, or just expending energy to release the emotional vise he was turning the screws to on his mind.

Then both went into it, "We are so fucked!"

It was hard not to laugh at how their duet was turning out, but I did my best, and said, "What are you going to do about Bryan?"

"We'll take care of it...Please...PLEASE...don't go to MAK with an email without talking with us first. You know you make us look like idiots—It makes us look like idiots. And you sent it directly to Discovery—do you know what you've done? We look like we don't know what we're doing down here..."

I remained quiet in the hopes that the weight of Clancey's words would really sink in.

In the morning a special meeting was held in the production office set up at the hotel. Gathered around were Clancey, Ruggles, Ruggles' girlfriend and MAK's field producer, Cynthia Frazer, and the cast. Clancey began with, "Someone contacted Discovery and MAK and said things that put this production in danger. If you have a problem with something, please come to us first."

"What happened?" Jeremy Whalen asked Clancey, as he glared at me, clearly looking more for an opportunity to lay into me, instead of getting an answer. "So, what you're saying is that this whole production could have come to complete halt, and all of us who are supporting our families would have been out of a job—who was it?"

"It doesn't matter who did this," Clancey said. "We'd just appreciate you coming to us first."

I listened and made a note about how much it seemed that if there were no witnesses, Jeremy would have been across that large meeting table in a heartbeat to attack me. Rage lit his face with an expression that told me that contrary to the feeling Jeremy normally tried to convey to those he meets the first time, there was a mountain of anger deep inside him that went back in his personal history. What it was wasn't clear, but it was clear anyone who set it off better be prepared to defend themselves.

Though it was clear that Keith hadn't just kept the contents of my email to himself, but that he had told Jeremy, it was ironic that it would be Jeremy who had the most anger at my actions. He was, after all, Bryan's major enabler. When we first arrived in Brazil, Bryan was so excited to share that

Jeremy had brought him THC-laced oil for his vaporizer, something that was clearly pre-planned through communications prior to our arrival in Brazil, as Bryan didn't smoke tobacco cigarettes. When Bryan had told me that he had gotten enough drugs to get him through the production, the first person I thought of was Jeremy.

It was funny that I wasn't the only one who kept quiet during Clancey's speech. Bryan was doing everything he could to keep from eye contact. It went on for about twenty minutes, Clancey trying to express how important it was that we take care of any conflicts on our own down here, that we should all feel comfortable enough to come to them with our problems.

When we got out of the meeting, Keith and I were on our own as we took the stairs downstairs. "Was I wrong in my observations?"

"No. It wasn't like we hadn't already told them about how Bryan was acting. They didn't do a thing."

For a group of people who envisioned themselves artists and unique, I found the people in the new media, not like I had remembered in the old media. They might as well have taken a normal corporate job like everyone else who took a job just because of the pay, and did everything they could not rock the boat, as is often the case in the government and corporate world, where innovation is suspect, and where even the most idealistic true believer ends up hiding in their cubicle, collecting a check and waiting for the end of the day and dreaming of four-day weekends.

I would learn how big a monster Discovery Communications is, and how you're rewarded in a corporation that big, by becoming the epitome of the grey man, or woman. Attract attention, rock the boat, and you're gone.

6 AND THE OSCAR GOES TO....!

Just before midnight June 19, 1986, I woke from my cot at the Army base at San Miguel that the commander had been kind enough to offer me, as I had missed the next chopper flight to La Union. San Miguel's 3rd Brigade base was the biggest in the area, and the demarcation point for the major Fenix offensive in Morazan that had been counting major coup against the FMLN, specifically the ERP (People's Revolutionary Army), a group well-known for its use of IEDs, car bombs, kidnappings and murders of civilians.

What had not been fully known to the Salvadoran military was that the ERP in the previous months had been heavily supplying and preparing for what would be one of most effective operations of that time. Trucks from Nicaragua, under the pretense of doing a pit stop in San Miguel to refuel, were bringing in arms and ammunition that would soon wreak havoc on the base.

I should never have been there in the first place, but I had an important meeting at the US embassy with Ambassador Ed Corr and was on my way back to where I was working. I wasn't working with the Salvadoran Army this month. My plan was to return to the Salvadoran Navy SEAL base at *Punta Ruca*, next to *La Union*, and getting onto my evaluations and research. My work was already on my mind, so much so that the first shots didn't register, but the satchel charges did.

Almost immediately after, the Salvadoran lieutenant, who had invited me to use his barracks while he was on duty that night, came running with an extra M16 and harness full of loaded magazines, and couple grenades, while he yelled at me above the exchange of gunfire and explosives to follow him.

"¿Dónde estan los boinas verdes?" I yelled back, my heart trying to pound its way out of ears as I moved from shock to fear. The lieutenant told me that

the 7th Group military advisors from MILGROUP had made their escape through a tunnel which had been built for just such an event. There were only two Americanos on that base, now, me and a contractor on the other part of the base. The FMLN made it clear in their last major attack that they were out to get any Americans helping the Salvadoran military.

Well-planned out, it was all happening so fast. Mortars were falling around the base. While one team had been sent to assassinate the MILGROUP green beret advisors, another team had been sent to take out the helicopters and their pilots, who were sure to come running. This endeavor was much more successful than the attempt to kill all the SF guys. With explosives and hand grenades, they took out the choppers and shot pilots in their seats as they tried to take off.

Putting me with two soldiers defending a corner of the building, the lieutenant ran off to check with others in his platoon. Then another mortar round hit the barracks. It burst into flames. Many soldiers were killed in there as they burned to death, unable to get out in time. Of the 150 soldiers killed that night, fifty of them then died in that barracks' inferno.

We all saw a sapper suddenly appear from the ground as he tried to remove his explosives. Painted and greased in black, he was a like a featureless silhouette of a man, seeming to materialize from the ground. He took bullets from us, and the explosives satchel he was unable to throw at us exploded.

It was mayhem lit by flames as buildings burned, and soldiers were killed by guerrillas dressed in shorts and T-shirts, and flip-flops and sneakers, like fresh recruits. They had smuggled a pistol in a gym bag onto the base and had shot soldiers for their weapons. Soldiers were then shooting soldiers. I ran to help one of these guerrillas who I thought was just another army recruit that had been shot. If not for the quick thinking of one of the other two soldiers with whom I'd been positioned to defend the corner of the building, I would have taken a point-blank round to the chest.

The guerrilla fell to the ground as if a puppet whose strings had just been cut. His brains spilled to the floor and I ran back to the corner. Reaching the corner, and then feeling the full effect of the realization that we had been majorly breached, the Gs running around the base, causing soldiers to shoot soldiers, the worst "friendly fire" I'd ever seen, I felt that the only ones I could trust at that moment, other than the lieutenant who had given me a rifle and kit, were the two men whose names I didn't even know. Many of the soldiers killed that night, were killed by those who started shooting at anyone who had a gun, shooting first, rather than get killed by Gs posing as soldiers.

Figure 10. One of the choppers destroyed the night of June 16, 1986 by the FMLN.
©AP/WideWorld

Constant small arms fire incoming, we returned with our own in ever-increasing volume. Bullets chipped at the walls around us, and the air stank of burning rubber, wood, and the smell of cordite. A thought hit me to check behind us. I thought I saw an armed man moving behind a corner. I slapped the soldier closest to me, and after indicating over the gunfire and explosions that I was going to cover our rear, I made a run for the other corner and fired a burst at a G running for the other building. It looked like one of the rounds hit him, as he stumbled before he got to cover.

Turning back to the other guys, who were just spraying suppressive fire, I made it almost half-way back to them. Then it all stopped for me. Time. Lights out.

When I regained consciousness in the hospital in San Salvador three days later, they said I was the lucky one. One of the other guys with me at the corner lost his arm. The other lost his life. The corner was dismantled by the blast. Some said it was an RPG. Others said it was one of the sappers. I believe the other report. It was a mortar round from an 81 mm.

Wounds peppered my body, but it was the traumatic brain injury (TBI) that put me down. They wanted to keep me longer, but I left the hospital in a week and took the next helicopter on which I could grab a ride from Ilopango to eastern El Salvador. During the refueling at San Miguel, I was able to see what I had survived, and snap a photo of it from an eagle's point of view. For the next fifteen years I would have crippling migraines that would hit me as thought a railroad spike driven from temple to temple. Pain could be so extreme, I'd drop to my knees. Then all of sudden, they stopped. They just disappeared. The traumatic memories? They are here with me forever...

Figure 11. Corner of the white building destroyed by 81mm mortar round, and the barracks beyond that had burned with recruits trapped inside. Photo taken by the author on his flight back from the hospital in San Salvador.

Heat, humidity, jungle, all these make great mental anchors for those who have been tempered by war in the tropics. For those who've fought in the Middle East, it's the desert and all that's dry. For those of my dad's generations in the Korean War, it's the numbing cold that those who keep those memories have them like a sharp icicle driven into their hearts and minds.

It's no wonder that those who were tempered in the desert seek to live in lush landscapes, or the humidity of the tropics. Though I was born and raised in the tropics, and then especially after the fighting I'd seen in the tropical latitudes that made me dream of handcrafted log homes, caribou, moose, and the snows and cold and living in the north whenever I'd get that opportunity. Some might say I was running away. In truth, I was running toward something good when I moved to the North.

But, back in the tropics once again, in Brazil this time, for a period longer than a one or two-week vacation in Cozumel or visiting family in the jungles outside Guayaquil, memories started to flood my mind. It also helped that the director and showrunner were always asking us to pull up memories to bring emotions to our scenes. Basically, we were being paid to attend acting class, specializing in method acting and the teachings of Lee

Strasberg—he played Hyman Roth in THE GODFATHER PART II.

What was also needed to really make a post-traumatic stress healing event was the bringing back of the stress. There was the innate stress of just working on a project and trying to make sure that everything went well on production. Added to that was the stress of actual physical danger.

Threat to life was an ever-present component throughout our stay in Brazil. This was clearly by design, as Discovery was trying to keep our emotions on almost constant alert, because even though they couldn't keep us on Snake Island the whole time we were on production, they could at least keep our emotions bouncing off the wall, where they wouldn't tell us what was going to happen until midnight. In the middle of the night, a slip of paper would come slipping in under the door, as if quietly left by Santa's little helper. A few of the cast would joke that they lay awake, on the edge of their bed, pillow under their chin, anticipating the next day's call sheet. Me, I was happy to be asleep in my bed, getting whatever rest I could from the days of climbing rocks and keeping eyes out for all the things that could kill you, far and away from Snake Island.

When the day finally came to go to Snake Island, it was a day of relief. We'd been shooting for two months in and around Ilhabela. To learn Portuguese, I'd light off that island for Sao Paulo on weekends. Every one or two weeks, I'd call my mom, to see how she was doing, but also to hopefully keep from totally screwing up my Spanish. Ilhabela, no matter how beautiful, was feeling like a prison, where all we did was work on the production, and downtime was an illusion.

Our first warning in Santos was that the place was rife with crime. We had already heard about the robberies and people just shot for killing sake in Brazil. Stress of going to Snake Island really took effect not just on landing, but the night before when cast and crew got the medical briefing.

Our scenario was three-fold. If we got bit by a golden lancehead viper, we had one hour to get medical attention, else we'd lose an appendage. If we didn't get to a hospital in six hours, we're dead. Don't get bit.

"What about the medevac to the hospital?" Mehgan asked.

"There's no helicopter evacuation," the doctor answered.

The look on Mehgan's face was priceless. Did the gravity of what she had signed on to just hit her?

She went on about how we were promised a full chopper medevac by Discovery during our chem test in LA. The medical team and the administrator for biological conservancy reiterated there would be no helicopter evacuation. If someone was bitten by a viper, they would be traveling back to the mainland on the very boat we would be coming in on—Danielle Carvalho a boat tour operator who had been our speed ride from our hotel to the production sites around Ilhabela and Buzios, would again provide our transportation to and from Snake Island from Santos in his orange and white Flexboat. Imagining one of our production laying on the deck of that boat, screaming in pain as the hemotoxin went about turning their blood into Jello, was very disquieting. A shiver went up my spine as I imagined that person might be me.

Keep in mind we had yet to shoot the scene at Butantan Institute in Sao Paulo—that was real fear we experienced in those scenes, because even though we had already completed our scenes on Snake Island, the memories of what had happened there were fresh in our minds, especially when Bryan mixed blood and golden lancehead venom in a Petri dish in episode 2 of season 1.

Still, the shiver at what I could only imagine, yet, wasn't enough to wipe the smirk off my face as I looked at Mehgan who looked like a deer caught in headlights. From day one, starting with her making it known how many movies she'd worked on as an extra and stunt freediver, and how she carried a SAG/AFTRA card, she was our little princess. Now, she was a grunt, just like everyone else in that room that was going to the island—real danger has no respect for titles. Surprisingly, she never complained to her SAG representative—especially regarding life-threatening situations, such as July 23, 1982, when Vic Morrow (one of my favorite childhood actors because of the TV show COMBAT!), was decapitated by the rotor blade of a Huey, killed along with the child actors he was carrying in the scene, SAG/AFTRA is supposed to help prevent something like this from happening.

Flavio Somogyi, our Brazilian fixer, who like Heron Alancar, were old veterans of the film business down here in Brazil, starting with such great films as THE EMERALD FOREST, directed by one of my favorite directors, John Boorman, looked at me and couldn't help keeping down his own chuckle. I grinned back at him, as he looked at Mehgan and me. I already knew he wasn't going to Quiemada Grande. I'm sure he made it clear at the beginning of production that that was the agreement.

Figure 12. An end to our first day on the real Snake Island.

To first set foot on a land that is shrouded in such death and darkness is truly a surreal experience. At first look, the rocky coastline of Snake Island appears devoid of life. But then, after you move away for the waterline and take it all in, there's life all around. It just takes a moment to get out of your inner-screams of not wanting to get killed to settle down and notice the things happening, by taking a knee, or grabbing a seat—after first checking to see there's nothing that can bite or sting you on that rock or by that tree.

After two months of play acting as if we were searching for treasure on one of the ten deadliest places in the world that you'd never want to visit, according to variety of Internet blogs, we were finally play acting our search for treasure on the real Snake Island—Brazil's Queimada Grande. Its foliage was a testament to how quickly things grow in the tropics. As one who was raised in Vietnam, and later worried that I would end up with a variety of cancers of having drunk water that came from Saigon River, whose upper reaches were sprayed with the horrific weed killer called Agent Orange, I had seen how quickly the jungle came back after the war, when I was taken across the country during the communist mock trials in 1983 and 1984, and then when I went back to Vietnam, in 1995 and 1999, to finish the epilogue for my Vietnam prison memoir, THE BAMBOO CHEST.

To see Queimada Grande, which had been basically napalmed to kill everything on the island in the 1950s, so that habitat and farming could be initiated on Snake Island, I was amazed. There was no evidence such drastic pyrotechnic measures had been undertaken. There was life all around, flora that was so unique and interesting that aside from the more famous vipers, it drew a variety of scientists from Brazil and other parts of the world in order to collect samples and study them in their original habitat.

One of the scientists told me that he was designing a coagulating bandage like the one designed during the latest war in the Middle East. Golden lancehead venom was a major component of the bandage, because of how its hemotoxin so rapidly and efficiently coagulated blood. More importantly, the bandage would be organic, so it would just become part of the patient's flesh. I'm sure the payment Discovery Communications paid for permission for its cast and crew to get on the island was a boon toward that research.

Over the next two days, they had us moving across that island to get footage to splice into all the rest of the footage shot on Ilhabela and Buzios. It wasn't even a situation of really acting as if we were looking for treasure that whole time on the island. They just wanted, aside from real footage of Snake Island to splice into the majority of fake scenes, to get the real experiences of us being wide-eyed and head on a swivel as we moved along the island checking for venomous snakes to our left, our right, the branches above us, and the ground around us.

There were two events that still stick in my mind as to how dangerous it was on that island. On the show, I'd referred to how the snakes were like landmines, deadly little tools of terrorism placed with the earnest interest of those to kill and maim, the final objective being terror and intimidation. It's a very effective tool of terrorization. The man-made metal, plastic and wood ones, at least those don't normally move on their own.

The golden lancehead vipers, though, they were always moving. Clancey wanted me to do an OTF (On The Fly) by the old lighthouse. When I made my way there from the makeshift camp the biologists had set up for us, there was a small tree halfway between, which was bare when I made the walk from camp. It was only a thirty-yard walk. After shooting my OTF, while I made my way back, I glanced and saw that a viper had climbed that small tree to be well within striking range, just a little lower than my shoulder up that tree. I was sure that snake had not been there when I made my walk from camp.

Immediately giving the bush a wide berth, I yelled to everyone, warning them about a new danger that had just appeared by the trail within such a short time. It was clear that our movement was getting the snake to also move. Everything was in flux. One moment you think you're safe, the next you're not.

Figure 13. Say, hello, to my little friend...

On Wikipedia, they state that there are three to four snakes per square meter. This is incorrect. Because of how the snakes can be in one place one moment, and another place the next, area populations could be anything. Sometimes we'd look at a place and see no snakes. We'd move to another area, and there'd be many more than the Wikipedia quote. One trail we walked on there were eight vipers all collected within a square yard, in all variety of elevations in the trees and brush. Stress reached its peak at that moment, as Ruggles kept telling us to walk back and forth through the same trail so that the camera teams could more footage—I thought it was nuts.

All this back and forth just continued to build the stress for everyone who was going back and forth. For Keith and me, who have dealt with combat-related stress since our teens from two different wars, it was just continuing to build and add to the post-traumatic stress that is always with you.

From our conversations, it was clear that Keith continued to deal with his post-traumatic stress the way in which he had learned so many years ago. He drank. The more stressed he became, the more intense the drinking became.

For me, meditation, self-hypnosis and introspection were the tools I'd learned to use when I was in prison in Vietnam, and worked on my PTSR (as long as we keep the "D" for disorder, in PTSD, those dealing with it will continue to feel as victims, instead of just those who've had experiences that have required certain tools and understandings in dealing with those responses to traumatic events "R," and be empowered by the challenge required to live full lives with the post-traumatic response to past traumatic events) resulting from my childhood in Vietnam. But, on this production, I learned something about acting and healing PTS that I didn't realize before.

Rainy days were often clubhouse shoot days. When the forecast was for rain, our little elves would slip a call sheet under the door telling us to be ready for an indoor location. This morning I woke to a call sheet telling me that I was to dress nicely, as if going out to dinner. I showed up at the hotel lobby in a black dress shirt and jeans. Evidently, it was only to be my day of shooting—everyone else was to be off. I was working pretty much every day. There were times when one of us was acting in another scene somewhere, and other times we were completely off. During the whole shooting schedule, I had something like two days off in three months in our Monday through Friday schedule. A couple times Mehgan and Keith, had a week or two off. It was just like a salaried job. If you appeared in any episode, you got paid for that episode—as you can see in season one, everyone was in each episode, whether they were on the boat, or on land.

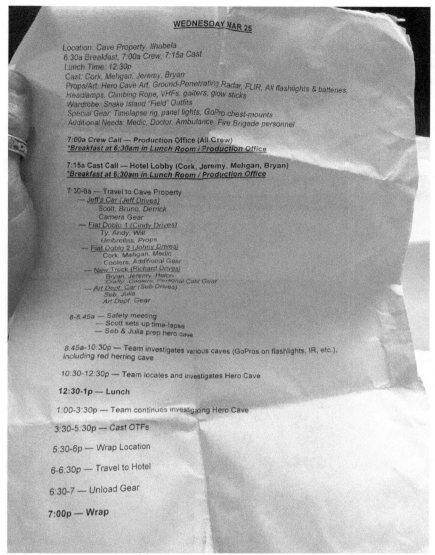

Figure 14. Shooting schedule for the "Hero Cave," March 25, 2015—documentaries don't tell you what to wear, do and say, scripted Hollywood dramas do...

The thing was that this was a true Hollywood drama, and not a documentary trying to catch every chance event and hoping for those events. As had been learned in Hollywood when John Huston directed THE AFRICAN QUEEN, you don't need to shoot everything sequentially. Only documentaries requires that, as it's supposed to be recorded as it happens naturally. When I finally saw the final, post-edit release on Discovery Channel, it was mind-blowing how so many scenes were shot so far out of their order in the story, it was amazing how well it all came together to create Discovery Communications' fraud—no disclaimer at all to warn the viewer.

Outside the clubhouse, rain fell on the small little bay full of sailboats and other pleasure craft. Inside, Ruggles and Clancey conferred as to their next plan of action. For the last three hours, they would ask me what it was like to be hunting this treasure that according to the script I had been searching for the last twenty years. It didn't matter that the first time I'd even heard of this treasure was the day we shot the chemistry tests back in LA, barely seven months earlier.

Figure 15. Such a beautiful view out the window of the club house, while Derrick Nevot catches cloud movement for B-roll.

It was like that. They'd ask these questions as if we were already in character (which we were, considering they were using our real names and real personal stories to add life to the fabrication that arrived every night with the latest script)—it was really beginning to screw with my mind: they would ask us questions, addressing us by our real names, as if we were actually on a true-life documentary, and when we weren't in character, they'd jump us into it, with, "if you had just come back from doing this, what would you tell us?"

"How will you feel if you don't find the treasure, Cork?" Clancey asked, after cuing the cameras.

I sat there for a second. I was really reaching. We were never, ever going to find the treasure, and the thought had been nagging me throughout the production.

Now this is where a reality TV showrunner or director really earns his or her salt. Their job is to get the emotions appropriate to the storyline.

"Ok. Imagine some really depressing point in your life, where you had lost something so important to you, and it had an emotional impact."

I thought about it. There were objectives I wished I had accomplished in my life. There were loves I wished not lost. But, for real heavy emotional impact, I always found myself going back to war whenever I had to bring back some real sorrow. Faces came rushing back. Guilt that I was still alive, and friends were dead, hit me, and I began to tear up as I talked on camera. There were friends that were maimed and crippled while I walked the world lucky and alive that my injuries were miniscule, relatively speaking, and the malaria that still affected me thankfully hadn't killed me. While Clancey asked me how I'd feel if we didn't find the treasure, I felt the full effect of survivor's remorse, something I thought I had well sorted out in my life more than twenty years earlier.

What was just a slight tearing at the corner of my eyes, then turned much deeper as many more traumatic memories came haunting. There was a time I was often asked if I had killed anybody or seen dead people. What haunts me most are not dead people, but the screams and pleadings made by those injured or dying.

There was a time, those ten years after I came back from Central America, when I watched war movies incessantly. A woman who I loved deeply and to whom I proposed marriage but lost due to the both of us being unable to deal with our post-traumatic stress (hers resulting from sexual abuse as a child), was talking with my mother as to why I watched so many war movies. My fiancé at the time said that she didn't know why but knew that I had a need to do so. I'd never realized that I appeared to others as one who needed to. It was then that I realized I watched those movies because I was somehow searching for answers and reasons for why I was dealing with the PTSR.

Though that relationship ended because we needed healing and couldn't find it in each other, it, like any relationship we put our emotions fully into, was very informative. Though it was very painful, I'm very appreciative I had the opportunity have gone through such an experience. A few years later, I no longer had such a need to watch war movies. As a matter of fact, these days I do my best to avoid them. PLATOON and CLEAR AND

PRESENT DANGER were movies that had close bearing to my experiences with regards to the technical experiences, but other than that, war movies just brought up similar experiences that I had no interest in reliving. That's one of the things about bringing up experiences repeatedly, is that the subconscious doesn't know whether you're actually experiencing them then, at that moment of viewing, or that you had experienced them years ago, it just interprets it all to be real, and as a consequence all those emotions you felt during that traumatic event come rushing back.

Don't get me wrong. If these were emotions you should have felt, but weren't able to do, as is often the case in dangerous situations, because you have to have presence of mind over emotions to get things done right in order to get you and your team home safely, then going back one or two times to relive those experiences and find closure and healing through the opportunity to bring it back up and consciously process those emotions, thoughts, guilt, with the aid of a counselor, or your own more experience and thoughtful mind, so much the better. But, to do it over and over, that just leads to a therapist making money off you, and you never really making the closure and moving on with the healing, rewards, and personally strengthening experience of memory processing with present day interpretation. The therapist no longer serves the process of aid to healing but becomes a costly crutch.

What I found interesting about my OTFs when Clancey, or Ruggles would ask me to go back to those personally traumatizing experiences to bring up the emotions they wanted to use to fill their script, was how bringing up those memories which were used to create something for the production were also doing something for me. Acting seemed such a fake and hollow profession to me, I wondered why people with such strong sense of self and who had done some amazing things outside of performance were drawn to the film and theater profession. I wasn't clear on how people like Jimmy Stewart, Clark Gable, and especially Audie Murphy, still the most decorated soldiers in the US military, would work as actors, having lived such full lives privately.

After the umpteenth time of method acting, I had begun to understand completely. Sure, there's the rush of being on stage, the act of having all these eyes on you as you take on a role, but for a combat veteran, or anyone who deals with post-traumatic stress, the calling up of emotions, using a method-acting style of bringing reality to a role, permits you to go back to that traumatic event, not as yourself, but as character, looking at your own life.

It's basically creating a situation in which you can go back to what was a life-threatening or traumatic event in your life, without reliving the real danger, but having the opportunity to process those events through the safety of the present moment. This is like those thrill seekers who go off and put their lives in danger, and get the benefit of having another life-threatening event that gives them the rush that many crave after such events, but also offers the opportunity to process prior traumatic events. Acting permits the same, but more safely, bringing up the traumatic event mentally, instead of through physical reality, which could also lead to more compounding traumatic events to have to process.

I could see how Murphy, Stewart and Gable had that opportunity to vicariously experience some very traumatic events, through a role as a character, and process their own war demons, but at the same time, after the end of work day whistle blew, they could leave everything and go home after a good day's work. Leaving it at the office is a very healing opportunity.

At the end of that day, I shared with Ruggles and Clancey, that I had done quite a bit of work on my PTSR and the various events that had created them, but it was amazing how going through the events on camera, and through method acting brought the healing to a whole new level. It was like an amped up timeline regression that I'd use in therapy to go back through traumatic experiences to deaden the pain and guilt and bring up the rewards of having gone through such self-determining and strengthening events that only those who've been in such life challenging experiences, and especially combat, understand fully, especially if they've done the work of introspection. To go through a variety of experiences, yet not take stock of them is like throwing away a precious jewel, that has taken precious lives to create.

My experiences in Vietnam with a Brit who was thirty years older than me, with many more experiences that age in years afforded, but with such a lack of personal awareness through self-assessment, taught me in my late teens that wisdom doesn't just come with age and a variety of experiences. Wisdom comes through having a variety of experiences and taking the time to be introspective and put meaning and place to those experiences in the mind and take the rewards that those experiences offer, viewed through the lens of taking stock, and emotions powering those interpretations toward self-development. There are many that are drawn to a variety of life experiences and get nothing out of them, must like a nymphomaniac who gains no real pleasure in the act of sex.

Unlike what would later happen in the next season shot in Argentina, this production in Brazil was actually a psychologically strengthening experience. When we would go home from first season, I would feel on top of the world, having excised several demons from my time in Central and South America during the 1980s that had somehow remained hidden from view all those decades before...

Sebastien Baille and his wife Julia Diehl are amazing artists who harken from France and Brazil, respectively. They were hired through Julia's cousin in Sao Paulo, one of our local fixers. Everyone who has seen both seasons of TREASURE QUEST: SNAKE ISLAND has seen their work. Every one of the finds on the show, except for a few that I will go into later, were created by them. They have been in the film, TV, and theater business for years, creating props for a variety of shows. Some of the work you'll recognize were the Jesuit symbols carved into a rock found in the hole amongst the boulders on Buzios, that was supposed to represent Queimada Grande. There was the Jesuit ring with the symbol that was supposedly used to leave an imprint in sealing wax on letters. There was even the rusted, iron key ring that was supposed to have been the anchor point for the block and tackle to move the Treasure of the Trinity to Snake Island, which provided no small bit of humor, when Jeremy grabbed it and yanked it right up.

On the show, it was described as an anchor point, immovably embedded in rock. For the rest of the scene, it was all we could to keep from moving it, while we brushed away dirt and debris that had been placed by Sebastien in order to make it look like we had just found it using the metal detector.

Here's a side note for you metal detector aficionados, who know what a real metal detector sounds like when it's picking up various types of metals. As experienced metal detector operators, have you wondered why the sounds you'd hear during the show didn't match with those you've heard while using your own metal detectors? It's because in post-production the editors have no idea what a metal detector running over iron, or some other metal, sounds like when it goes over gold, or silver. Often, it's because when we were videoing, the metal detectors were off and we were just swinging it back and forth, acting as if we were searching.

Figure 16. More of Sebastien and Julia's work: the infamous ring with the Jesuit symbol.

It's funny how Hollywood thinks this is funny, or that they think it's fine to offer a show as reality TV, especially from a network that markets itself as the "last true documentary network" out there. After the humor died, though, the ludicrousness of it all hit. I'd seen men and women maimed and killed trying to report and document true reality, and to see the word "documentary" thrown around with what we were producing for

Discovery Communications was too wild to comprehend—at this point, I was still under the impression that there would at least be a disclaimer that would legally be required for something of this magnitude. After all, this was being put out as historical record, and there would definitely be real archeologists looking at this show and thinking that what we had found was real.

It was all adding more and more to the stress of what if? What will happen once this totally scripted show was released, and yet, they're using our real names and personal histories in order to validate this charade for ratings.

Ruggles and Clancey were adept at reading us as we plied through these waters, waters I'd never even thought possible only ten years earlier. After all, wasn't there an FCC rule against fake broadcasts of news? At least Orson Welles opened WAR OF THE WORLDS telling everyone it was a dramatic show. It's just that those who listened in later didn't get that disclaimer. There would be no disclaimer on TREASURE QUEST: SNAKE ISLAND from Discovery Communications—ever.

Figure 17. Fake treasure chest remnants, another of Sebastien and Julia's masterpieces, with my SOG Knives Super Bowie for size comparison: 12.88 inches total length—my last option bear protection knife back home in Alaska.

In a terrain of large boulders that create amazing formations with large and small caves, almost cathedral like caverns, our team of actors moved along the landscape, fully into the character of these intrepid treasure hunters depicted in TREASURE QUEST: SNAKE ISLAND. Ahead of us moved Sebastien and Julia, their little bags, kits of movie art magic, slung over their shoulders.

While Clancey and Ruggles directed the crew to shoot us moving around the hallowed boulders, the art team was busy working away in a small cave that would become the focal point for the end of first season. Within a short time, we were at the open of that cave which would in the script lead to season two, if all went well with audience ratings.

Sebastien gave Clancey a knowing look as he exited the cave with Julia. It was always so funny, as if the art team and showrunners were playing an Easter egg hunt game with the cast. Sebastien is thin-boned and smokes a lot of cigarettes in the very French way of keeping lean, so he would often move among tiny caves and passageways with no too much stress. In a very Celtic way, I'm broad-shouldered, and added onto that were forty pounds extra weight I'd gained when I came back from a very active day and night job, to one in a corporate office in the banking and government firewall security software field, where I over ate because I hated my job so much— but the money during the first Silicon Valley software gold rush under Clinton was amazing, so I stayed in it longer than I should have, at great physical and emotional cost.

One scene that they used to dramatic effect during broadcast, but was totally fake and humorous, was when I was moving along a crevice on my side and for a moment I got stuck because I was wearing my backpack. Discovery added a jump to of a snake, and spliced in a wild line recorded months later, from the safety of my home in Alaska, with my saying there's a snake next to me. There was no snake next to me and when you see all that light around me in the scene, you can see that I wasn't stuck. It was too funny. Almost as entertaining was a health and fitness trainer trying to promote his business by using broadcasts on Twitter, and that scene, to try and get me to go on his health program to lose weight.

When I was really stuck was when Clancey tried to get all of us to enter the cave where our art team had placed the remnants of wooden chest. It was probably some of Julia and Sebastiens' best work, not just in having created it, but having placed it in the cave to make it look like it had been covered in centuries of dirt and debris. It was also the scene where I had reached my limit of claustrophobia that make me search out wide open spaces after my eleven months, seven in solitary, in a communist Vietnam prison.

While we filmed that scene, I was looking around and noticed the constellation our art team had carved out of a boulder with a hammer and chisel. When we filmed, even though it was weird playing a character that had our real names and real person histories, there was a role that the production team was good at getting us, or at least me, into, and that was the curiosity of how everything was developing. When I first saw the constellation of Eridanus that had been carved into the rock wall face by our art team, it was a complete surprise.

Clancey was the one who had caught my surprise and his burst of frustration that it was lost because the rest of the camera teams was focused on Mehgan, Jeremy and Bryan working on the fake chest remnants, as not easy to hide. Sheepishly, he said, "Damn, we missed that...Could you do that again?"

"Crazy! I was really in the moment, there—you really got me there. I felt like I was really on a treasure hunt!"

"Could you do that again?"

"Sure...we're actors, right?" I said, and grinned.

We did it again, and I think it came across well. Inside, it didn't feel the same, as coming across the divots the first time. "Still, I pulled it off enough for them to use it in the broadcast."

Figure 18. Mehgan Heaney-Grier framing the Eridanus constellation our set artists, Sebastien Baille and Julia Diehl, so expertly chiseled into the rock wall.

After about another hour of retakes capturing Jeremy talking about the chest, we went outside for a bit more content. This would become what I would consider one of the best bit of acting I've done on TV or in film. This would be the how-do-you-feel-about-letting-your-team-down scene. It was a pretty quick scene. Clancey asked me again to bring up a moment in my life that was so emotionally impacting related to letting my team down.

As a scene, it was to be that moment when we were to have found the treasure site we'd been looking for all these three months…and twenty Hollywood years…and to realize that the treasure was supposedly already found and taken who knows how long ago. I didn't know, and frankly I don't think the production team did either, that this was to be a scene which would be used to get those who had been on the sidelines about the show to invest emotionally and get them to want to see a second season. There was a lot riding on this.

Since this scene was me leading a team, that I was supposed to feel bad about our not achieving the goal of finding that treasure, Clancey asked me to bring up the feelings of letting my team down. I went back to that moment back at the corner during the overrun by the FMLN at San Miguel, and other moments when I'd lost close combat buddies. Aside from not achieving an objective because the odds overwhelm, I think it's the moment of seeing combat buddies dying that are the most emotionally impacting. To go over the memories and the emotions from that time can be very tiring. Who wants to go over emotionally painful events, again and again?

But, I did, though I was getting to the point that I was doing so much work on the past, that the past wasn't hitting me with the same impact it was when I started processing those memories through method acting for the showrunners. Tears came back again, a flood of screams for help, friends calling out to their wives, and mothers, as they sought relief for the pain or the fear of their rapidly arriving departure from the world of the living.

To the audience it was just a scene of me expressing how much I had let my TV treasure hunting team by leading them to a cave in which the treasure had already been stolen, who knew how many years ago. To me it was five years in combat, and even a moment in northern Thailand, when I was only eighteen years old, and saw a person, a young boy, a Hmong, die in a refugee camp on the Lao border.

The week of the broadcast, I saw how emotions can carry people, and an audience, and why Discovery Communications will do anything they can to bring drama to a scene, no matter how contrived. A fan of the show posted a bit of moral support, by having typed on the Treasure Quest: Snake Island page, the week of that last episode of season one, "Don't cry Cork. You'll find the treasure!"

I didn't know what to feel: elated that I could have easily brought those same emotions to a character an honest TV or film drama; or, guilty that I had been party to a network that advertised a true-life adventure that was totally scripted and used the moniker of "reality TV" in order to bypass a viewer's healthy critical thinking, and jumped right into their emotions to capture that audience, those ratings numbers, for financial gain, through fraud—it was depressing.

ARGENTINA

7 THE PUSHERMAN

You know the dealer, the dealer is a man
With the love grass in his hand
Oh but the pusher is a monster
Good God, he's not a natural man
The dealer for a nickel
Lord, will sell you lots of sweet dreams
Ah, but the pusher'll ruin your body
Lord, he'll leave...he'll leave your mind to scream

—Steppenwolf

Rolling deep green seemed to stretch for miles, defining this meeting of steep, humid mountains that marked the Honduras/Nicaragua border. As the Huey dropped down into what seemed like a tiny eye of a landing pad in the face of a giant monster of the Honduran jungle, I stared at the wounded Contra fighter screaming up at me, almost looking like was trying to pull the IV from his arm in his fury of pain. The night before he'd been the unlucky recipient of three rounds to the abdomen. It was lucky that the rest of the platoon hadn't been greased by the Sandinista special forces unit. They used their Spetsnaz training well.

"What the hell am I doing back here again?" I thought to myself. In the months since I took a sabbatical, with the intentions of continuing my studies toward becoming a heart surgeon, all prepped with my previous years in Central America, that started paramilitarily as a field corpsman or combat medic, I thought I was done. But, the war wasn't over, and it kept nagging at me. There were always openings for those with my experience and knowledge.

The anti-communist guerrilla locked those eyes of pain with me. The anger at myself for not staying away and out of all this hit me at that moment. I could have been back in school, like all my friends back in the states of the same age. I could say it was because I knew too much, and it would have been unforgivable for me to follow all that pro-communist propaganda that lulled the minds of those who'd never left the US and seen up close the gains the communists had made in the last ten years, to be right at the doorstep of the US. Many had already ridiculed the idea of the Domino Effect, but it was right there as plain as day for anyone willing look at some unpleasant realities—the final insult would be the media incorrectly stating that the Soviet Union collapsed all on its own. What they seemed to have ignorantly forgotten was that the free world had been in fighting it tooth and nail in far more conflicts than Korea and Vietnam, starting with President Woodrow Wilson sending the Polar Bear Expeditionary Force from Troy, Michigan to Archangelsk, Russia to fight Bolsheviks in the North Russia Campaign of 1918.

The chopper jolted to a landing and as I rapidly tossed my flight bag onto the light brown clay. I grabbed the WIA's hand to keep him from falling off the stretcher as the two door-gunners and I pulled him in with the medic. Jumping to the ground I cleared away with the rest of the passengers, a contra commander with a prothesis for an arm (A mortar he and his team were running during a mission had exploded—he at least lived, albeit missing an arm), by the *nombre de guerra* of "Captain Mike," and a doctor who had flown out from Tegucigalpa with me.

That night, after an inspection with the commander of this secret FDN base on the border of Nicaragua and Honduras, a well-received, and very tasty, and much needed protein, of tapir that had been hunted with dogs and AK47s by a group of indigenous peoples at the base (the Sandinistas didn't only treat the Miskito Indians poorly) stewed in canned tomato sauce, I was again asking myself, "What in the hell am I doing down here, again?" Nobody cared back home in the US—and why should they? Both administrations, Reagan and Bush Sr., had been kept in a quandary of not sending troops down to Central America (though there was major troop buildup in bases like at Palmerola in Honduras), as had been done in the 1920, though this was much more serious, simply because no president after Vietnam wanted to have to deal with the public relations nightmare of sending troops to another country. As far as they often said, this was a South of the Border problem. Too many people were trying to make money and live the Wall Street dream depicted in Oliver Stone's big '80s film. I thought after all the years I'd spent down here and took a sabbatical of a year from, I was done...

Figure 19. Always wondered whether this wounded Contra had made it...

Conversations were still running around in my mind on the flight from Houston to Bueno Aires. Krystyna Lab had been the Discovery Communications lawyer during the negotiations the initial round for our contract. But, when I told them I wasn't going to go for a second round of production on the same contract, I was in conversations with a Bob Thompson. It was a whole different feel to the production from that point on. I wouldn't know how much until we started shooting.

While talking with Thompson, he told me he had been involved with the initial negotiations with MAK Pictures on the start of TQ:SI. I found it very interesting. What I found most disconcerting was when he said, "You must be really excited to be on this adventure. Do you think you'll find treasure this time?"

"What?" I asked, a bit perplexed and a bit more suspicious. Was Thompson trying to test my keeping of Discovery Communications' secret, that this whole show had been a completely fabricated, totally scripted show posing as a reality TV/documentary from day one? Were they testing me to see if I was honoring the cone of silence they thought binding by the non-disclosure agreement in the employment contract?

"Uh, yeah..." I let escape from my lips, as I remembered the dinner at which I had learned the whole secret, the real secret to the Treasure of the Trinity, Snake Island, and how it all came together in Discovery Channel's 2015 new hit series, TREASURE QUEST: SNAKE ISLAND.

Almost eleven months earlier on May 6, 2015, I was in Los Angeles doing a bunch of OTFs, some of which appeared in the show, such as me talking in front of some rubber plants, to make it look as if I was back on Snake Island, but I was on a ranch in a suburb of LA, that served as a backdrop for a variety of TV shows and movies. As a treat, the executive producer, Will Ehbrecht took me for steak and lobster at Duke's Malibu.

After a few drinks at Duke's, I asked him how the show came to be. It was a question that had nagged me since that day I had my realization and told Keith Plaskett, that we would never, ever find treasure on the show.

According to Ehbrecht, Eileen O'Neill, who was president of Discovery Channel at the time, let it be known that she was furious at the way in which A&E, through History Channel, was kicking their butts in audience ratings with CURSE OF OAK ISLAND. She asked, why didn't Discovery have a treasure show?! More importantly, she ordered a request for proposal (RFP) for such a show. And to make it even more interesting, put it on that island off Brazil that Vice had just done a real documentary on. Yeah, that island called Snake Island.

Normally, Discovery and A&E, and all these networks with reality TV shows get an onslaught of show ideas—many they flat out steal, and more atrociously than they did with ideas from my Vietnam prison memoir. I can't tell you how many horror stories I've heard from friends, and those who knew I've worked for Discovery, of sending in their show ideas only to see a much too similar show appear on a network to which they'd submitted a written proposal to or did a pitch to in person. Theft is rampant in Hollywood, New York and Silver Springs. If you're going to come up with a show these days, you might as well come up with the money, too, and take it directly to Amazon, Hulu, or Netflix.

Figure 20. Ehbrecht was right; you've got to hit Duke's when you're in LA!

Internet broadcast is the new frontier that Satellite was when Ted Turner first led the campaign that all these other networks jumped on. Satellite is an elephant on its way to the elephant graveyard, the signs starting when channels like Outdoor Channel, Sportsmen's Channel, Pursuit, and all those others who started double-dipping from the advertising dollars, and then also charging content providers to broadcast their shows, but only giving them small advertising windows, keeping the larger slots for themselves to sell to the very large advertisers the providers hoped to get advertising from.

It's the old scavenging the bones at the elephant graveyard model that has overtaken satellite broadcast over the last twenty years, and especially now, as many have become fed up with having to pay for program packages that often contain channels and programming the customer will never watch, but still must purchase with the whole package. Why pay for channels and shows you'll never watch, when you can go to places like

YouTube Red, Hulu, Netflix, or Amazon and pay for only the shows you want to watch? That's the beauty of a truly free market: the market will dictate the market, not the government or the corporations.

O'Neill should have learned her lesson by her other fiascos like MERMAIDS: THE BODY FOUND, and then a show that came out while were already in Brazil, and O'Neill had by then been replaced by Richard Ross, previously of Disney. That show was EATEN ALIVE. What made that show so important to us on set, was that MAK Pictures was the field production company hired to produce it for Discovery. The irony was not lost on Bryan, our herpetologist, when we were shooting in Brazil.

MAK Pictures will do anything to fill a production request, the president of Discovery Channel will do everything to please the CEO of Discovery Communications, and the CEO of Discovery Communications, David Zaslav, will do anything and everything he can to keep the board members rolling in money to get his cut. For a network that sells itself as "the last true documentary network" that's a tall order. For Michael Moore to become the richest documentarian, he had to fudge the facts and bring up the drama and emotional impact. Zaslav must have been paying attention when he came on board at Discovery, and opened the Hollywood office, which then hired several women who would rise to prominence in the reality TV industry, such as O'Neill and Nancy Daniels, to build that drama in order to draw the female audience he craved.

When you track David Zaslav's negotiations and mergers all that come to mind, is greed over facts and principles. The latest to hit the shelves was the merger between Discovery Communications and Scripps Networks Interactive which was described by THE HOLLYWOOD REPORTER as bringing "together two big cable networks groups known for non-scripted and lifestyle content, with the companies eyeing $350 million in cost savings." What a header for a network that offers mainly scripted offerings.

Some might say that the scripting had only happened on TQ:SI, but I live in Alaska, and the joke I came up with was: move to Alaska and get your own TV show. But, I've learned that scripting has become the norm, and not the exception it was when my friend Mykel was hitting winners with his wife Ruth England Hawke on MAN, WOMAN, WILD. That wasn't a scripted show. The talent led the production, because they had to, in order to be true to the format.

Nowadays, Hollywood has taken so much power, and fully vested into the understanding that reality TV is an opportunity to make an amazing amount of money by locking non-actors into poorly paying, highly dangerous acting jobs, that no self-respecting SAG/AFTRA representative would knowingly advise a union member to take.

Unbeknownst to me, when I was being cast and then hired for the role of team leader, I was truly being hired for a role not as a team leader running an expedition, but being hired to play the role of a team leader on a show that was to be run from Los Angeles, with content shot one day, being reviewed by the MAK Pictures executive producers, Mark Kadin and Wil Ehbrecht, and guide and edited by suggestions from Joseph Boyle, the Discovery Channel executive producer running the show.

It always perplexed me as to why I was on a show that was clearly greenlighted not just by Eileen O'Neill, but also Richard Ross when he came on. Imagine my thoughts when, after knowing the real story of how TQ:SI came to be, that Richard Ross told the NEW YORK TIMES, in a January 3, 2016 article that, *"'When I came here, there was a lot of history of focusing on History," he said. 'I kept hearing, 'The pitch for this show is competitive with History.' I said, 'Stop talking about that. I really don't care.' If we think of ourselves only in the scheme of beating History, that's small ball. We have to think about what Discovery can be.'"*

I'd never laughed as much as I did reading that. It's ALL about beating A&E for Discovery Communications, and especially, Discovery Channel! As I prepared for the second season of Discovery Channel's TREASURE QUEST: SNAKE ISLAND, I'd learn how well Discovery was using TQ:SI to count coup against A&E.

The wealthy, I mean the really wealthy, the power elite of this world, are a different crowd than you and me, not financially, but morally and ethically. I'd learned this a long time ago, when I was only in my mid-20 and came home from a war I was convinced was going to take me out before the age of thirty. I'm sure there are few who wished that happened, especially when I started talking about that period of my life.

There's that old saying, "what do you get the richest man in the world?" Or, woman for that matter. You get them power. See, having a lot of money is nothing in regards to power. This is the reason the wealthiest live in a world different from the rest of the common man and woman that are the majority. And how do you get power? Well, one way is to get money, and these people, like David Zaslav, have a lot of money. But, once you have a lot money, then you realize that even though you have more money than others, there are still many who have more money than you. Remember that old cartoon depicting a fish eating smaller fish, and then that bigger fish being eaten by a bigger fish?

This is what has been happening in the network business for decades. I saw this all the time in the software tech field during the 1990s when I was in the Silicon Valley, watching companies I was employed at being acquired by bigger fish. Then, that bigger fish was then acquired by a bigger fish. This is the big fish, little fish world of corporations.

On a TV channel to TV channel plane, this acquiring is as simple as getting the field production team of a competing show. Can you imagine my surprise when while chatting with the new showrunners David Carr and

Tom Dorman, they told me that their last job was CURSE OF OAK ISLAND? I almost choked on my coffee when they told me.

First, I was already surprised that Ty Clancey wasn't along for this adventure, but Clancey has much more experience in the true Hollywood field of directing films and TV dramas. Just IMDB him on the internet. The difference is striking. While Carr specialized in reality and alternative TV shows like TREASURE QUEST: SNAKE ISLAND, CURSE OF OAK ISLAND, and ANCIENT ALIENS, Clancey directed episodes of GIGI: ALMOST AMERICAN and GIGI: ALMOST AMERICAN Season Two, plus several commercials back in Spain.

Perhaps, what was a just another job directing a TV show, suddenly put its full weight on Clancey, that as a fully scripted show that broadcasts without a disclaimer is basically deceiving the audience, and definitely defrauding the advertisers. What advertiser would want to be associated with a show that is being advertised as a true-life documentary, but is anything but true-life documentary?

Figure 21. Left to right camera operator Ariel Benarroch, Showrunner David Carr, co-showrunner Tom Dorman, soundman Brett Ulery, director of photography Scottie McKibben—shooting at the pools where a variety of scripted money shots were collected, such the gilded tin can Inti mask recovery scene, and the real, Incan fetishes illegally purchased and smuggled by James and Jeremy Whalen from Peru.

Curiosity was getting the best of me as I went down this Discovery

Communications reality TV rabbit hole for the second time. I'd already known about this new actor that had been hired to replace Bryan Grieg-Fry. They said he was to be our new survival expert and security guy. Really, I said, when Ehbrecht told me over the phone that the guy's name was Brett Tutor and he was PJ in the Airforce. *Really?!* I thought. That's impressive. I'd known SEALs who went into the Air Force because they were up for new and different challenges that compared well to their completion of BUDS/SEAL training in another branch of the military. What most impressive is the PJ's sense of service in how their whole job purpose is to defend, provide medical aid, and rescue those in harm's way, most often downed pilots.

I'd personally met and had great times with PJs when I did a talk at Osan Airbase when I was working as an instructor for the Korean Army in 2007. I was truly impressed. These were people who had goals and let nothing get in the way. If I was a pilot shot down in enemy country, I'd feel a sense of assuredness that the right people to get me back would be the PJs. These guys don't quit. If they failed a first round, they'd come back and do in the second.

Something just didn't jive with what I knew about PJs. First, I did a search on the internet and found that there was a Brett Tutor, who was an actor and stuntman who has hosted a show on home improvements. There was nothing about the Air Force and especially nothing on having anything to do with survival training. I sent a link to Ehbrecht, and said, is that your guy? He returned an email, saying, yes. I was astonished.

I had suggested Mykel Hawke, not knowing that Mykel, and like me now, had been blackballed from ever working at Discovery Communications again—just a few months ago a producer suggested me for a new role on a historical fact-finding show in Paraguay (I was promised this one was real, this time) and Discovery Channel producers told him, *NO, he's suing us*, which made me laugh. Bonafide survival expert and retired US Army Special Forces captain, who had combat time in Afghanistan, and later as a security contractor in Africa and Colombia, Hawke is the real deal. When MAK Pictures told me they already had someone, and it was Tutor, I had to find out something more, and had Hawke do a background check. Within five minutes, I had that he had enlisted in the US Air Force, tried out for PJs, washed out due to an Achilles injury, and then left the military. It was hard to understand. I've got a friend, a US Navy SEAL, who tore his Achilles heel. He worked in the civilian world as surgical tech, and in the Navy as a platoon leader and corpsman, who soon after he had his Achilles reattached and it had healed, he was participating in Operation Anaconda in Afghanistan.

When I was auditing the Salvadoran Navy SEAL's training program in 1986, as part of an assignment for the US State Department, I had hyperextended my left knee the first time in life, during hand-to-hand combat training, with our hands tied behind our backs. I got the first guy down, but when I put the second volunteer down, I didn't get my left knee out in time and his full weight came down on it, as we both went down. My knee swelled up like a watermelon. The Salvadoran base commander told me if I didn't get through the three days of hell, fashioned after the program the US Navy SEAL advisors from MILGROUP, I had to go through to complete in BUDS, they wouldn't give me my diploma. US Navy SEAL CMDR Dick Flanagan, who was MILGROUP commander after COL Jim Steele had rotated out, was going to give me my diploma that day of graduation—it was part of a US Navy/Salvadoran Navy tradition going back to the first US advisor killed in the war, LT CMDR Albert Schaufelberger, whose death I read about in Newsweek when I was just about to make my foray into Vietnam.

As it was, the Salvadoran Navy commander for the eastern region, Capitan Melchor changed the ceremony slightly, stopping CMDR Flanagan from handing me my diploma. Instead, Capitan Melchor handed me that diploma, and offered me a salute and words of gratitude that I hadn't been blown up at that base overrun in San Miguel, and that I was able to complete the course.

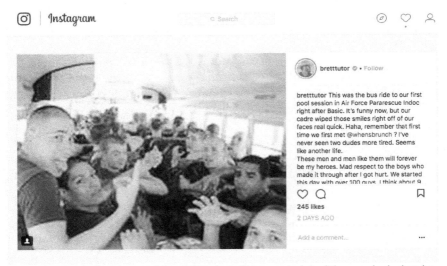

Figure 22. Here's the Memorial Day 2018 photo Tutor posted, and then yanked when he was called out for stolen valor.

I've known many members of the special operations community over the years, who've been challenged by physical duress to get their diplomas after going through a ration of crap, who have even taken two attempts to finally get that Special Forces or Ranger tab, or that SEAL Budweiser, but I've never seen someone who really wanted it just give up.

When we first met at the airport in Buenos Aires, I was apprehensive about Tutor, but he seemed a nice enough guy from Austin, Texas. It was clear that this was going to be a different show all together from what Brazil had been. It seemed as if the whole budget was either smaller, or Discovery was spending more to get local government hands greased.

On Ilhabela, we had a hotel and it was by the resort island beach. There was good food of various types. It was a place to recover after a long day, or night, of shooting. We got to San Ignacio, and I felt as if I was stepping back thirty-one years to Central America during the war. Remember, Argentina had gone through an economic crash in 2001 that left Argentina in a Mad Max-type post-apocalyptic society, where people where armed and thieves were coming up to people getting gas and shooting them for their vehicles and money.

Through loans offered by the International Monetary Fund (IMF), Argentina enjoyed a heyday of false wealth, so inflated that Argentines were flying to Miami to shop. When the IMF came to collect, the wealthy elite, who had funneled as many of the funds as they could to their offshore banks in Cayman Islands and Switzerland, took a long vacation, many of them not returning for more than a decade, if ever. Left with the debt was the average Argentine citizen, who was just making ends meet. I liken the transfer of wealth like that illegally put upon the US citizens by the socialist government of Franklin Delano Roosevelt, who made it illegal for private citizens to own gold: a few days after the wealthy elite in the US had transferred their gold to safe deposit boxes in Switzerland.

Argentina had yet to return to its former glory days before socialism and getting on the global dole, so much so that though it was 2016, I felt as though I was travelling in a tense nation ready to explode, a nation that was battle weary and always ready to grab anything it could. With a society that thinks bribery of officials and theft by government is just the way it is, is it any wonder that such places draw so many production companies trying to do here, which they can't do in other areas of the world, where the word of law is more respected, and officials look at their public offices as an opportunity for service, instead of as a chance to pad the bank account?

There's a great book on what happened in Argentina, and how easily it can, and has already happened, elsewhere, titled THE MODERN SURVIVAL MANUAL: SURVIVING THE ECONOMIC COLLAPSE by Fernando "Ferfal" Aguirre. Referred to me by a friend in the prepper community when it first came out, I was surprised at how much of the book was still applicable to travelling around parts of Argentina in 2016, especially the further away you got from Buenos Aires. In a perplexing nostalgia, it reminded me of Vietnam in 1983 and 1984, when it was as though you were going back ten to twenty years the further you moved away from Saigon.

Though Ty Clancey wasn't on for the second season, Andy Ruggles showed up. So was our DP Scott Mckibben and our excellent drone camera operator, Derrick Nevot. It was an interesting contrast to see two worlds in photography: McKibben from southern Appalachia, and Cuban-American from Miami Derrick Nevot. Nevot and I didn't learn until second season that we both attended West Miami Junior High, separated by decades. I laughed when I saw them at the airport in Buenos Aires.

"What the hell are you guy doing here?!"

Nevot shook his bald head and said, "I swore I'd never come back after Snake Island."

"It's like an addiction, or the mafia." I laughed again.

With our new cast mate in tow, we all took our luggage to customs, as we were having to take a limousine from the international airport (EZE), over to the national airport (AEP) by the water, in order to make our connecting flight to Puerto Iguazu, where the last big production filmed was THE MISSION, with Jeremy Irons and Robert De Niro. It gave me time to see what Tutor's background entailed.

At AEP, he admitted that he was on his last legs in the home improvement business that he had basically inherited from his grandfather, and doing it was just killing him. If he had all the money he would need, he would just act on TV and film. That's all he wanted to do.

When I asked Tutor about his survival and security experiences, he said he had gone to school to become an EMT and went through a SWAT course. Having my own experiences in combat medicine in the Central America War, and having several friends who teach CQB and SWAT tactics, and survival, who are still working in law enforcement, or in special operations, I was floored. "So, how did you learn about this role?"

Figure 23. This photo says it all: anyone who has been through a SWAT course or picked up an AR15/M4 in military training knows this is how you hold a bolt-action .22 Chipmunk on a ranch, not a fighting weapon—Discovery hires a lot of guys who like to pose with guns, but clearly don't look like they know what they're doing. Oh, and it's not a "toy."

Figure 24. Another poser with a gun, "Studman," who doesn't know how to handle a firearm—check out which shoulder he's slung the single-point sling on. One reader's comment: "What's he going to do—take over the picnic at the park?"

"Oh, my Hollywood agent learned about it, and put me in for it."

I immediately flashbacked to Mehgan, remembering how she became a cast member. Her agent and manager pushed and pushed and that's how she ended up on the show. It was all becoming clear. Every show needs a foil. Mehgan now had hers. Mehgan was our cheesecake, and for the female audience that CEO David Zaslav so yearned for, we had our beefcake. It was too perfect. As we talked I was taken by how much, if he were a horrible stereotype of a woman, he would have been labelled a ditz.

As I got to know him later, part of that airheadedness stemmed from his inability to truly find himself. I find this in many actors, which I think is why these types yearn to act, as if to try and find themselves in a character and find that grounding they so lack in their real lives. I find it more and more in actors I've known during these days. Those of an early time, like Charlton Heston, who still fills my memories as a person who was squared away, and acted as a professional, and not as a form of never-ending therapy and need to find him or herself.

More and more it was becoming clear that TQ:SI was being more and more populated by people seeking to find themselves of bolster their self-image, than people who had real-life experiences like Keith Plaskett and myself. Acting on camera and controlling the image from the other side of the lens can be very addicting.

As Nevot and Mckibben mentioned, they were surprised that they were here again. I wasn't too surprised. There's a part of shooting a camera that kept me going back to it for years after I thought I had lost any interest. Traumatic experiences have a way of doing that to people. For us, in Brazil, especially the rush I'm sure those manipulating the cameras in the jungles, while venomous snakes and insects filled the landscape, had experienced, it had a way of exciting the senses and drawing out the endorphins.

Travelling to other countries has this effect. Imagine what it's like to travel to another country, where you're almost on a vacation, but you're not; you're working. It's not like moving to another country and working there as a resident. Foreign locations blur the line between working and vacationing.

That's one of the reasons it was so attractive to Jeremy when he was always trying to find out when the next season was going to happen. For him, though he was living in South America, having moved from Peru to Salinas, Ecuador, travelling to Brazil, then Argentina were opportunities he couldn't have afforded on his own. Being paid to go to another country is very attractive. Even Plaskett was excited to go to Brazil on Discovery's dime.

When I saw Jeremy in Argentina, it was very interesting. There was a new edge to him that was telling, but I didn't yet know the significance. He wasn't the insecure fish out of water new actor, trying to bring something to the production. It was as though he was beginning to believe his own press. To watch someone with an addictive, obsessive compulsive personality, it's very interesting to watch. Whalen is good at hiding it. He has a good sense of control. I wouldn't know how well he put on a charade until much later.

Figure 25. If you're going to pose with a firearm, at least look like you know what you're doing: 1. This is how you efficiently control an AR15/M4, with your shoulders in front of your hips, in a fighting stance—else your muzzle bounces all over the place. 2. A single-point sling is slung across your chest to your non-dominant side: Single-point slings are a poor choice by the way (more of gun gamers tool for 3-gun competition than a practical sling for combat), a two-point sling is much better. 4. If you're going to do a Hollywood pose with a gun, do it in a war.... Kit courtesy of Aero Precision (6.5 Grendel), Smith & Wesson (M&P 2.0 9mm), High Speed Gear (war belt), Comp-tac Holsters, Bushnell Optics, SOG Knives (Bowie 2.0), and Blackhawk (single-point sling).

What struck me most about Jeremy Whalen when I first met him, was though US born and raised, he reminded me so much of the hustlers I'd run across in my travels through the third world from the 1960s to the 1990s, when those places were truly THIRD WORLD. He was like those kids who would hit you up when you got off the plane and headed out the gates of an airport in Southeast Asia or got off the train or bus in Latin America. It was a shocking realization when it hit me who he reminded me of.

From then on, I was normally on guard, and NEVER letting him in on my private world of any worth, except for passable rapport. These kinds of people don't take secrets, and important parts of information, and keep them as tokens of faith in friendship. These people take information and have an almost uncanny way in which to process it all, and like a cash register, giving you an immediate bank balance.

It helped only a little that I'm one of the few people to have been on both sides of an interrogation table, and had been instructed in, and had to use, the techniques of studying micro-expressions collated by Dr. Paul Ekman: Like shooting firearms, skills fade rapidly when you're not actively using them daily. Pleasant life experiences since leaving the world's areas of strife have that way of letting us become too relaxed, fat and happy, and finally lazy.

With this calculating ability clearly learned at a young age, Jeremy had been able to first ingratiate himself to Keith Plaskett years ago, through appearing a pal, and more importantly for Plaskett, a drinking buddy. Relating through drugs with Dr. Bryan Grieg-Fry, he was able to keep contact, even long after Bryan unfriended all the rest of the cast after he blamed us for reporting him to Discovery Channel for speaking on social media, contrary to the Discovery contract's NDA.

I just wasn't aware of how much was going on behind the scene with Jeremy and his lackey, younger brother. Jeremy Whalen would be a wonderful poker player if he did that as a full-time profession against the average player. He's so good at telling you one thing, and then saying another behind your back. The epitome of this was when Keith Plaskett told me about a conversation that had occurred between Jeremy and the governor of El Oro, Ecuador, Esteban Quirola. Esteban Quirola was a friend of Keith's and of course, Jeremy worked his way into getting an introduction by Plaskett, which led to them hanging out as is normal between friends.

As a friend, Quirola told him about a new roadway construction that was going to be conducted in the province. Quirola suggested he put him in for a position as a project manager, or foreman. This is no small deal. Do you know how many Ecuadorians would jump at this with the economy that had been screwed up Correa, much like his brother in socialism had done in Venezuela, while stealing from their countrymen?

Keith said, that after the meeting, Jeremy said, "Can you fucking believe that?! He offered me that job! Who does he think he is?"

It was an eye-opening into the ego-based mind of Jeremy Whalen. It's the mind of a person who has no true sense of self, and such a lack of self-confidence, that he would toss an opportunity for financial security for his family out of a need to show he's better than everyone, i.e. he doesn't need any help to get where he wants to…but, as I was learning, he had no qualms about lying, stealing and most of all manipulating, to get something that would have just as easily been given as a gift.

This guy got off on manipulating people. I think he got more joy out of the act of getting things over on people than the actual prize, whether it was the girl, the pay, or the acting role on a show that would become Discovery Channel's new hit series for 2015. When Keith finally realized too late what lack of character Jeremy Whalen had, he began confiding in me. Sadly, it wouldn't be until it was too late.

What I would learn beyond these little vignettes, like a glaring a gift horse in the mouth with Quirola's friendly offer, was how Jeremy really got on the show. I had suggested a friend of mine who was a six-pack captain in Alaska, and had been a US Army combat medic in Vietnam. But, MAK Pictures said they had decided on Plaskett's friend Jeremy Whalen.

How he came to be TQ:SI was through calling…calling…and calling. He hustled Ehbrecht and Kadin so hard, they must have thought immediately they had the perfect actor, one who would do anything they asked—the perfect psychopath, who has no conflict breaking any rules or laws to achieve their ends. Also, in the conversations, Jeremy tried to push himself as a treasure hunter, perhaps an even better treasure hunter than Keith. Mind you, Keith Plaskett captains a research vessel and has been at the deep seas archeology field for years, and even teaches at school in Peru. Jeremy Whalen, had a metal detector and freedove and spearfished, slithered his way into other treasure hunting expeditions as a deck monkey.

When Plaskett told me that Whalen had weaseled his way into my press contacts at MineLab and sold himself as this great treasure hunter, I made it clear to the marketing department they should be talking to Keith Plaskett, not Whalen: Plaskett was the real treasure hunter. This is the way it has always been with Whalen. He's a scavenger and opportunist, that would deliver him as the character of Jack Dawkins in our little theater of life, our own Artful Dodger. He learned at a young age, for reasons of family history most would be aghast. You'd need to in order to have fine-tuned the skills of a confidence man like he had become.

●●●●○ Verizon 📶   5:38 PM   ◤ 90% ▰

‹ 1   **Cappy Keith K...**   ▢◁   ✆

> Also, talking with Minelab this week to see about you getting speaking gigs at conventions: total bs Jeremy hijacked them (you're the one who should be doing them and for a lot more $$$)--I set up the relationship for us to even be using them on the show.
>
> 10:21 AM ✓✓

> I will check on the model... yes Jeremy is trying to steel my Identity...
>
> 1:35 PM

Figure 26. After returning home from Argentina, and once it really sank into Keith Plaskett that Jeremy Whalen had not only used him to get on TQ:SI but was now even trying to take his identity in the treasure hunting community—much like I'd learn about the psychopathic tendencies of Joseph Teti toward Mykel Hawke.

Whalen headed out on this dark voyage of self-discovery as a teen; he went to Peru on a student exchange program. Initially, listening to him tell his story, it was actually very impressive, but then I remembered he got that money by selling drugs. In Whalen's also telling of how his father didn't just give or loan him the money, in the first place, it clearly rubbed him the wrong way. Considering what his father committed earlier in 1982, it was clear to see why he felt his father owed him that much. That passive aggressive reference about his father should have been a warning sign, not just about Jeremy Whalen's victim attitude that often affects psychopaths, but that I had somehow, perhaps because of my being overweight, reminded him of his father and not in a good way—weight and references to family, and angry sodomy would be language references in the cyberstalking email and internet attempts at defamation Jeremy Whalen and his younger brother James Kendall Whalen, aka Kendall D McKibben, would commit. What is telling, is how it came to be. There was a bunch of dark family activity going on, and Jeremy Whalen wasn't just off for a high school adventure. He was running away when he went to Peru the first time.

How this sick and twisted bit little piece of family history would affect me, wouldn't be clear for a couple years, when I finally dug deeper than I really wanted to go. Jeremy came off as the helpful team player when in reality, his idea of being a team player is really to play team members against each other. Funny, how people will always tell you everything you need to know: you just have to give them time, and you really need to listen. Do you know what the worst enemy for an interrogator is, and especially a field interrogator?

By the time prisoners of war are transferred back to base, they've already got the fully crystallized script in their mind, and someone who might have been a guerrilla officer, could have easily worked up a legend that might get him or her past an interrogator in a room. The worst enemy of any interrogator, either in the field or back at base, is not the lies, that and legends created by the prisoner. It's the truths we don't want to believe.

Take for example, a woman, and you're a man. She's pretty. She's young like you. She seems so innocent. She even tells you that she comes from a small town, from a nice family, that all they wanted to do was raise corn, chickens, beans and live peacefully on a small *campo*, a little *finca*. She looks terrified. She looks like a little girl who was forcibly taken from her family's home and turned against her will into a fighter for the ERP guerrillas, one of the communist factions fighting under the FMLN flag.

You get into conversation, and your Spanish has been good enough now that she asks you from what part of El Salvador you come from—you're after all wearing the uniform of a military unit from her own country. It's a personal ego stroke, her thinking you're Salvadoran. But, as it goes, you notice that she's doing the same thing to you, that you've been doing to her. You don't want to think that she's that well-trained. If that were the case, she wouldn't be that innocent little girl that you had thought you had. She would be that woman, who had been a communist since her early days in college. No way would she be some poor *campesina*, victimized by a war that had taken most of the older generations in just the first six years of the war before you arrived there in 1985.

Figure 27. Jeremy Whalen, James and their dad, Myron, on Jeremy's high school departure for Peru the first time in 1987—bit of that anti-establishment, young punk, black suited anarchist demonstrator attitude in Jaime, as Seattle has been known more globally for of late?

Further intel gathering by interviewing the rest of the prisoners, kept away from each other, and who been taken in this camp that was nearly annihilated by your team, brings the bittersweet fruits of staying on the course and doing your job. You're pissed now as you put her on the chopper, to where she will be scrutinized even more, by interrogators with the time, and hopefully with the information collected in the report you send back with the prisoner on that UH-1D.

You're pissed, but you smile and try to comfort her, by saying it will all be okay, though you know full well that this woman wasn't a recruit forced into a war—the only question you have in your mind now is whether they'll be able to convince someone with her background to defect and become an asset. She in reality was a commander who had been recruited by the Cubans long ago, trained in Vietnam and Havana, and had been coming back and forth with arms she accompanied from Nicaragua.

And she was poor by no means, coming from a family who could have sent her to any school in the US or Europe. Sorbonne, Harvard, Yale, Berkeley, take your pick. Angry laughter fills your mind as you've already learned from another of the prisoners that you've talked with that she was one of the commanders running recruiting programs that forced young girls and women into their guerrilla army, killing, maiming or torturing Salvadorans as a lesson to those not on board with their communist front.

Not only that, she was party to the strategy of using car bombs and IEDs to create mayhem in metropolitan areas of El Salvador. She was well-read and improvised on Maoist and Vietcong tactics that she had learned when she was sent to study insurgency tactics and strategies in Cuba and Vietnam. Terrorist and homicidal maniac, Dr. Ernesto "Che" Guevara would have been proud. Anything for the cause.

When I pulled the finished report from my battle board, slipped it in an envelope and zip-tied to her collar, as she sat in the chopper, I told her, "Don't worry—you'll be okay." I moved away from the helicopter that took the prisoner away, I'd tried to keep that lesson hard to my heart for decades. It all has to do with not being prejudiced toward an outcome, nor judgmental about a person or situation. It's hard—we're humans, after all. We have prior beliefs based on prior experiences, and we're so different, yet so similar.

See, even the worst of us still have a subconscious hope that people are essentially good, and if we're bad, it's only because we've lost our way. It's a strong basis for the socialist ideology that has overtaken our society, where people would prefer to accept the rewritten history, instead of the actual events that had been recorded at the time. It's for this reason that many below the age of thirty don't think socialism and communism are bad, or even believe that six million Jews were murdered by the German Work's Socialist Party. Isn't it just so much better and comforting to think that people can't be that bad.

Well, the problem, for interrogators, and people who just want to get to the bottom of things, is that this subconscious need to see the good in all, even if we don't want to admit we do, is that it lulls us into a lazy complacency, for no other reason than we might have to get along with bad people, really bad people, just to get on. In my case, I ignored so many things about Jeremy Whalen, that verged on personal suicide, or at least stupid ignorance, and perhaps some bit of laziness. It's the hope and knowledge that if you have to really deal properly with a bad person, it's likely not going to be a comfortable event.

It's so much easier for us to just let bits of information come and go, and not get too involved or preoccupied with certain facts, no matter how ugly, and counter to the benefit of doubt we prefer to offer our fellow humans. This innate quality in good people is what Joseph Teti used against my good friend Captain Mykel Hawke and led to his years of hell dealing with the repercussions as the result of a multitude of Teti's manipulations and evil deeds, one of which led to the death of a chopper pilot, a cameraman and a close combat buddy of Mykel's by the name of Michael Donatelli.

In Brazil, while on the bus to location on Ilhabela, Jeremy told me about his first machete. His father had brought it to back to him from South

America when Jeremy was a teen in Washington. He talked about how he had walked up the coastal streams by his house and went about chopping spawning salmon in half with that new gift from his father. A wildlife conservationist since I was kid, and especially since working in the field as an outdoor writer, I was appalled. Basically, Jeremy was saying he was breaking wildlife laws in his home state of Washington, while expressing his anger at his father for what his father had done.

When he told me that, I made a clear note to myself the way someone who hears that a person is killing and mutilating or performing just about any form of cruelty to animals. Researchers since the 1970s have found cruelty to animals as indicators of delinquency, violent and criminal behavior. More importantly, this has been a sign that the child has been the victim of, or observed, abuse at an early age. What type of abuse would be made clear in a couple years when I started delving into what happened, starting in Brazil and then exploded in Argentina.

Normally, when people tell personal stories like this, it's to share something of a private nature, that will somehow bring a bond between the teller and the listener. This is genetic, going back to sharing a campfire and stories among tribal members. It builds rapport. This is good.

There's another reason it's done. It's not to just to build rapport and put an enemy or potential enemy at ease, make them a comrade, it's done to collect information. It's a very old technique and well described in psychologist Robert Cialdini's excellent book on persuasion.

There's a chapter on the act of gift giving and reciprocity. In that chapter, Cialdini writes about the act of giving, and how manipulators will give gifts with the understanding the universe hates a void, and the automatic reaction for most people is to respond in kind. Like everything in life, there is nothing good or bad about the act of giving. What paints the act is the intent in which it's done. Does the giver give, simply because they enjoy giving and find it an enjoyable act of sharing and bringing together? Or, is it a tool used to get something out of another, that gift given in response that the initial giver is giving to get in kind, or more?

What with all the other parts of Whalen's demeanor, it was clear from day one that he was giving with the intent offered of the later. During our break, while waiting to see when there would be a second season request coming down from Zaslav and Ross, Jeremy contacted me out of the blue, and mentioned how much he loved my Vietnam prison memoir, but unlike just about everyone else, he didn't mention the unbelievable adventure of my time in Southeast Asia, or the lessons I learned in prison, he mentioned how much he enjoyed my writing about food. He even said, I should write more about food. This was something that would stick with me when I trying to find out more answers about what Jeremy was doing behind my back.

For now, he was calling and focusing on what he enjoyed about my writing on food, but his real reason for contact me was to check in and see if I knew what he and his brother were up to, as any predator up to no good would (cowards don't proceed into unknown territory—they're not explorers and adventurers, they're just cowards and vermin, dangerous pests). Also, he was trying to get something out of me. He was complimenting me on my writing not to just say he enjoyed my writing, but to give me a gift and the return gift he expected was again, if I would give him a copy of an imaginary letter I sent to manufacturers to get equipment to do a trial and evaluation for my articles and firearms and outdoor writer.

It was so transparent that I thought he couldn't have gotten so far with his style of persuasion, but evidently, he had. It just wasn't clear yet how much he had achieved. He had already played his cards earlier that year on one of a bus trip from the hotel to the set, when he told a few of the crew and some of the cast that he was a drug dealer back in high school in King County, Washington. It wasn't just the fact that he was saying he dealt drugs back in school that I found interesting. It was that he bragged on never getting caught—psychopaths, predators, reach high levels of dark maturity through ill achievements. If he had been caught and punished at an early age, research shows, he wouldn't have developed into the predatory criminal he had become.

Reciting a story about how the school's undercover narcotics officers, known as a narc in those days, was very enlightening in deed. Seems one day, after many days, the narcotics officer, whose cover was as one of the students, pestered him for a sale of drugs. The way Jeremy put it, he had a feeling this one day was the day to not bring his stash of marijuana to school, as he normally did to fulfill his daily sales. It also happened to be the day that he was brought into the principal's office and they made it an event of also having him open his locker for inspection.

Playing mum to the idea of drugs and his pride as the most successful dealer at his school, the principle and the narc had nothing to hit him with. What kind of person would Jeremy Whalen become if instead he did get caught and learned his lesson at a young age? Perhaps he would have turned out to become a person who added to society, instead of preyed upon it, gloating in his ability get one over on the establishment. From what I would later learn, he has all the qualities of your typical anti-establishment criminal, who blames society and the establishment for all the ill will he has experienced in his life.

What it all comes down to is that he's a victim, as you'll see in what his father had done, and victims take strength in feeling that they are somehow better than, and being put upon by, the establishment. The crowning glory for these types of victims, the thing that keeps them going is their ego being fed by every twist and turn in which they stick it to the establishment and authority. For some twisted reason they think it really matters every time they achieve some ego-based attack on the establishment: the establishment is uncaring, simply is, and just keeps moving, until it changes into something, hopefully better at least as good as it was to the citizens. As Jeremy has said many times, he lived in South America, because he doesn't do well in the US. Frankly, I don't think he does well anywhere, because every nation has an establishment and a society. It's just that in Latin America and pretty much most of the third world, you can get away with a lot more than you can in a modern society like the United States.

Can you imagine having to spend day in and day out with a guy who tries to come off as your friend yet can only envy the success and fame in your life? You're somehow in the way of where he wants to be, but he never put in the time, nor paid the price, and clearly never would have the personal life story he envied—beware of when a predator puts his sights on you: he'll want to skin you and put that skin on himself like a coat. To say it's like carrying a target on the back of your head everywhere you go, where your psychopath will stop at nothing to get you out of the way, and put himself, or herself, in your place, is an understatement.

Back in Brazil, Jeremy seemed a little insecure and not really knowing the temperature of the water he'd worked so hard to get into. On the show, he had the role of deckhand and the lofty title of treasure recovery specialist. I had a laugh with Keith about what that meant. It was so ambiguous and meant really nothing. Evidently that title got to Jeremy's ego, and low and behold he was already planning to be the co-team leader, as if this wasn't supposed to be a documentary, and was instead Mark Burnett's SURVIVOR and he was going to get everyone, except himself, voted off the island. The big question that really needs to be answered is when did this change occur—when did it snap?

Aside from what we were told at the beginning of season one, our titles were pretty much defined: Keith was boat captain, Mehgan was archeologist and dive master and Jeremy was to be the guy who could build anything. But, for some reason, everything that Jeremy built either didn't have enough oil (dredge pump non-starting in Brazil because they ran it almost dry), or actually never really worked, except through the magic of post-editing (the piece of tubing mounted on the back of an outboard to send clear water down the bottom on the Parana River was achieved through splicing a topside scene of Jeremy running the outboard, and an underwater dive scene shot with Mehgan and Keith in a lake with much better visibility).

But, how did Jeremy become co-team leader? The natural progression would have been for the real treasure hunter, Keith Plaskett, to become co-team leader, not Jeremy. True to the definition of a psychopath—one who'll stop at nothing to achieve his goals, and using his drug dealer skills initially honed in high school—Jeremy had been wheeling and dealing with Mark Kadin and Will Ehbrecht behind everyone else's back, trying to make his position that much bigger.

It's important to understand what really turns on a drug dealer, especially a successful drug dealer that Jeremy Whalen and his brother have been. You might think it's the drugs, or the money. But really, it's the power. It starts off by giving away samples and giving personal strokes to the potential customer, and then once the potential becomes the reality, the position of power is locked in. It's kind of like big government getting as many people as they can on social welfare program and the dole, and employees of the government. It's power in its truest form: talk back, or rebuke government, and you're out. No more pay or retirement checks.

For the dealer, it's no more supply, and you're not part of the cool, in group. It's power in its truest from. It's the dynamic of the supplier. If you become the main, if not the only supplier, of something that person, group, or entity needs, then you have power over that entity for which you provide.

In high school and in Peru it was drugs, at Discovery, it was Jeremy providing research for TQ:SI. As a resident of Ecuador, he was able to visit the local university libraries and consult with various history professors. With this information, he was able to feed the facts-deficient writers, who then went about bending those facts to fit the script. Of course, like when he used Plaskett to get on the, show, Jeremy would name drop to bring more importance to himself at MAK and Discovery. By doing so, he then made MAK Pictures, and by default, Discovery feel more comfortable breaking more laws.

The Nazis did it with the German people by getting them to first break the windows of shops, and then working themselves up the next stage, and then the next stage, until good people had become monsters, lining up Jews, the infirm, Slavics, and the rest of the politically unreliable and ethnically impure for entry into the gas chambers. Drug dealers do it by getting customers who would never use hard drugs onto pot, then cocaine and finally heroin and crystal meth. To get someone straight onto hard drugs is pretty hard but increasing them from something seemingly as benign as marijuana to much harder drugs in varying degrees is much easier: here, try this…and then this…and then this.

To get someone who would never break the laws of a nation, even a corporation that includes such a clause in their contract against such activities, to do something as rash and stupid as break international laws that relate to the stealing of national treasure is not something that someone just says to themselves, *hey, I think I'll commit acts that will get the FBI, and INTERPOL on the hunt after us*, is a stretch. But, when you've got the pusherman who has decades of practice coercing people to do things they wouldn't normally do on their own, and makes it appear as not so bad, things can change, and then it becomes very easy to take risks they'd never have contemplated taking previously because the reality is, it is so dangerous...

8 THROUGH THE LOOKING GLASS OF THE MAGIC BUS

Reality TV. It was all becoming too weird. I noticed it taking hold on us back in Brazil, as I felt myself being drawn into the character of treasure hunting team leader, conscientiously trying to make sure his team didn't become gravely injured. Now, it was taking on a whole new feel, like a bizarre gaslighting experience played on yourself by your own mind. Mehgan, Jeremy, and now Brett, were being possessed as if by a demon by their TV characters. Our local guide on the show, a local naturalist, and tour guide, who captured the most amazing wildlife photography in the area, some of it published by various publications around the world, was Emilio White: like a mix between Ilhabela local fixer Jeff Cavendish and wildlife enthusiast Dr. Bryan Grieg-Fry, just a lot more mellow.

Out of all us, he seemed to be the one least hit by the character he was playing on TQ:SI. I attributed it to his being able to go home to his wife at the end of the day, and truly leave his job at the office. We, on the other hand, were either squirreled away in our own hotel rooms trying to reach out to the outside world through the worst Internet connectivity I'd experienced since the early commercial days of the Internet, or trying to get to the nearest town with a population just over two-thousand.

I'd joke with him when during filming, asking him how in the world he had gotten on this kangaroo production. I'd laugh when he told me it was a friend and neighbor who told him, and suggested he try out. He was perfect, Julio Noguera, the local fixer told him. But now Emilio was really questioning his decision. This was someone who had worked with Jeff Corwin and Sir David Attenborough. We shared American Revolutionary family history. About the time my direct ancestors, Scots-Irish immigrants David Graham and his son Andrew were Colonial militia sniping British

111

Tories at the battle of King's Mountain in North Carolina, his ancestor, a sea captain, was carrying slaves to Brazil in the hold of his ship, and so then brought the very British name of White to Argentina. The name had some prominence, enough for the label of *Peronista* to be considered a derogatory name in his family. Apparently, his grandfather had had bad dealings with the Peron government, as many did during those times when Argentine President Peron and Adolf Hitler were best buddies.

While Emilio fared better making that separation between character and reality, Mehgan, Jeremy and Brett were falling hard. Mehgan was all about being a nurse, or field medic, now that she had taken a quick seminar in mountain medicine back home in Colorado, during her off time in the real world. She was all excited to show us what she'd learned.

She had drugs galore to deal with variety of potential ailments due to bacteria, parasites, and just plain injuries. Her mother was an RN, she said, so she was able to get what she needed, putting together a pretty large bag, any combat medic, or field corpsman would have envied. I didn't know whether to admire it or be concerned. If we were to get into a situation where we actually needed all that she had brought with her, I'd hope the medical support we had been promised and would be required in a union production, if this had been a union production, would be at hand.

She was pulling out all the medical terminology she could muster from just that course. It kind of reminded me of the combat medicine training I went through when I was auditing the Salvadoran Naval Special Forces course in Punta Ruca, La Union in El Salvador during the war. The difference was that most of us had practical experience soon thereafter, as we were also being sent into the field on operations to protect the base from possible mortar attack by the FMLN during the training evolutions, so the importance of what was being taught wasn't so theoretical and almost fanciful as was in Mehgan's describing in her explanations of what she had learned—beware actors who blur the lines between their TV and film roles and their real lives.

At one point, I just made a quick quip that I hoped we had our set medic, Dr. Gustavo Peterman there ready to go if the situation really hit the fan. Another time, I did everything to keep from laughing, nervously probably, as I thought she might actually have to come to our aid during an emergency. For some reason her just taking a mountain medicine course a few months earlier, a much too large pack of importance she had put together with the help of prescriptions through her mother, and that she was so getting into her role as our own little Laura Croft, Tomb Raider, made me think of a moment from my past when I thought I had given war up and took a much needed sabbatical to San Diego State, which was a half-assed effort toward medical school, but turned into a nice little break of partying as a brother in the Alpha Tau Omega, my combat-stressed subconscious leading me to become a blackfoot, an ATO, because of the creed formed at VMI in 1865, by founders Otis Allan Glazebrook, Erskine Mayo Ross, and Alfred Marshall in the aftermath of the American Civil War. These were words which appealed immensely to someone like me, who had just returned from having observed and experienced wars and a communist Vietnam political re-education prison during the previous five years, starting as an eighteen-year-old photojournalist covering a group of Hmong infiltrating across the Mekong into Laos in 1983:

"To bind men together in a brotherhood based upon eternal and immutable principles, with a bond as strong as right itself and as lasting as humanity; to know no North, no South, no East, no West, but to know man as man, to teach that true men the world over should stand together and contend for supremacy of good over evil; to teach, not politics, but morals; to foster, not partisanship, but the recognition of true merit wherever found; to have no narrower limits within which to work together for the elevation of man than the outlines of the world: these were the thoughts and hopes uppermost in the minds of the founders of the Alpha Tau Omega Fraternity."

But, what hit me on this surreal, reality TV acid trip with our own little Florence Nightingale, weren't such noble ideas, but the story of an ATO brother, as Mehgan went on and on about such serious items and topics as emergency medicine, tourniquets, antibiotics, various forms of painkillers. A story often told at the frat house was of a brother drunk out of his mind, the girl he had just hooked up with, the two of them passionately going at each other, and then he reaching for a pair of scissors, which made her scream at the first snip of her pantie strings, and he responding through his drunken laughter, "Don't worry honey, my father's a doctor...my father's a doctor!"

All that ran through my mind as Meghan went on and on, were the words, "Don't worry, my father is a doctor!...Don't worry, my mother's a nurse..."

And while Discovery's TREASURE QUEST had Mehgan's psyche in its clutches, it coiled around Brett Tutor as well, taking him down a road as the actor believing his own inner press about his role as the survival and security expert. He went so far as to say in his introduction on the first episode that he was a survival expert and had even done security overseas. This was to imply that he had been a security contractor, because other than an overpaid bodyguard, that was the only other option for such a label. I warned him not to make such a claim. As one who found a way to use my training and experience after leaving Central and South America during the 1980s, I got work as a security consultant in counter-piracy and smuggling interdiction in Indonesia and the Philippines during the early 1990s. Many of my friends and former associates would find such a claim by Tutor to be blasphemous, nearing on stolen valor for military veterans, but not so offensive as his trying to make a mountain out of a molehill of his non-important Air Force Pararescue attempt.

The more I looked at his stack of self-help books, and also noticed a strong quality of narcissism (actually very prevalent in actors—it's all about having the camera on oneself, right?), I realized something a bit disturbing. A friend on set even mentioned it, by stating, "Interesting mix of being lost and a narcissist? Reminds you of a lost kid, whose demeanor calls out to you for help, but you know you'll get burned if you do."

In 2018, after the broadcast of season two of TQ:SI, and his inclusion as the new actor being groomed for the Ty Pennington slot on TRADING SPACES, he would write what was a very confusing description of his time as an Air Force recruit. It was so confusing that I would have to have my birthday brother, Hawke, who has become the poster boy for bulldogged stolen valor hunting after all his experiences with such Discovery and National Geographic posers as Joseph Teti, Grady Powell, who said he was on combat on missions, but his DD214 says no CIB (Combat Infantry Badge), Tim Ralston, who said he was a an Airforce PJ, but turned out to be in air traffic control—you'll remember him as the one who shot his thumb off on DOOMSDAY PREPPERS.

Tutor would say on his bio page at bretttutor.com:

"Brett enlisted in the U.S. Air Force at age 21 and was put in charge of a 60-man basic training squad on his first day of training. He was accepted into the Pararescue Special Operations program but was unable to complete his training or be deployed after tearing his Achilles tendon during his first year with the elite team."

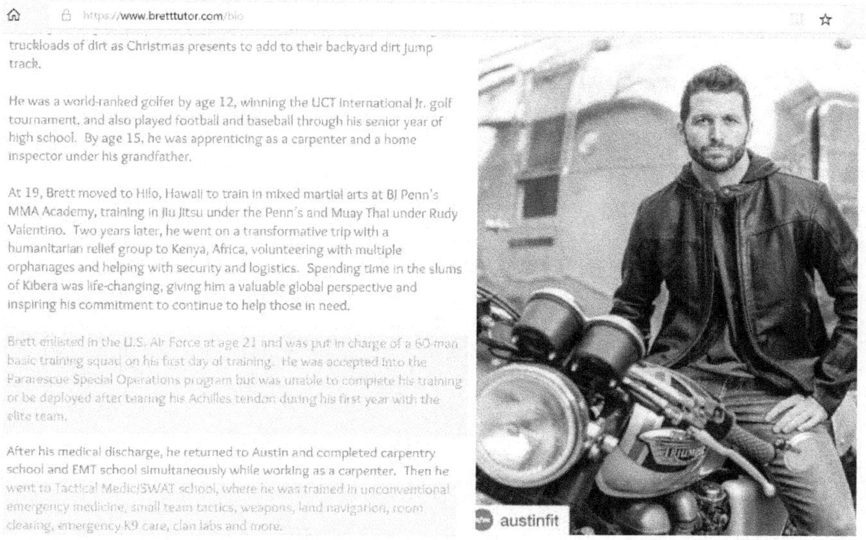
https://www.bretttutor.com/bio

truckloads of dirt as Christmas presents to add to their backyard dirt jump track.

He was a world-ranked golfer by age 12, winning the UCT International Jr. golf tournament, and also played football and baseball through his senior year of high school. By age 15, he was apprenticing as a carpenter and a home inspector under his grandfather.

At 19, Brett moved to Hilo, Hawaii to train in mixed martial arts at BJ Penn's MMA Academy, training in Jiu Jitsu under the Penn's and Muay Thai under Rudy Valentino. Two years later, he went on a transformative trip with a humanitarian relief group to Kenya, Africa, volunteering with multiple orphanages and helping with security and logistics. Spending time in the slums of Kibera was life-changing, giving him a valuable global perspective and inspiring his commitment to continue to help those in need.

Brett enlisted in the U.S. Air Force at age 21 and was put in charge of a 60-man basic training squad on his first day of training. He was accepted into the Pararescue Special Operations program but was unable to complete his training or be deployed after tearing his Achilles tendon during his first year with the elite team.

After his medical discharge, he returned to Austin and completed carpentry school and EMT school simultaneously while working as a carpenter. Then he went to Tactical Medic/SWAT school, where he was trained in unconventional emergency medicine, small team tactics, weapons, land navigation, room clearing, emergency K9 care, clan labs and more.

Figure 28. Brett Tutor must have excelled in posing at modelling school...

Yeah, wrap your mind around that. There's boot camp, otherwise known in the Air Force as BMT, which stands for basic military training, which goes for 7.5 weeks, and then there's Airmen's Week. After that, it's off to Indoc. If you wash out of boot, you aren't even in the Air Force, much less a part of Pararescue. So many questions. I even gave him the benefit of the doubt, that he wasn't that smart. Hawke said, "Naw, he's just crafty, like all these stolen valor guys, if you read it again, he's inferring he was with the US Air Force's PJs, which was just as bad as actually saying he was a PJ."

At first introduction at the airport, I was pleased to be working with someone who appeared to be doing some introspection and self-assessment by the number of self-help books he had brought on the plane. I suggested Kindle, but he said he still liked reading paperbacks. In time, I'd see that carrying all those books around seemed more to show off to people, because when I pressed him on what he'd learned, it didn't seem like he grasped any of the ideas that these authors were putting forth. Acting in itself draws a whole slew of people really into themselves. To have one who had no true self-identity, especially if he was selling himself as the survival/security guy, and finding his new identity in that role, made him as dangerous as Bryan, but at least Bryan "knew his shit" as we use to say, he just liked pushing the envelope in his morbid obsession, when there was no envelope to push.

CERTIFICATE OF RELEASE OR DISCHARGE FROM ACTIVE DUTY

1. NAME (Last, First, Middle)	2. DEPARTMENT, COMPONENT AND BRANCH	3. SOCIAL SECURITY NUMBER
TUTOR BRETT MICHAEL	AIR FORCE - REG AF	

4a. GRADE, RATE OR RANK	b. PAY GRADE	5. DATE OF BIRTH (YYYYMMDD)	6. RESERVE OBLIGATION TERMINATION DATE (YYYYMMDD) N/A
AMN	E2		

7a. PLACE OF ENTRY INTO ACTIVE DUTY	b. HOME OF RECORD AT TIME OF ENTRY(City and state, or complete address if known)
FORT SAM HOUSTON TX	GEORGETOWN TX

8a. LAST DUTY ASSIGNMENT AND MAJOR COMMAND	b. STATION WHERE SEPARATED
342 TRAINING SQ [AET]	LACKLAND AFB TX

9. COMMAND TO WHICH TRANSFERRED	10. SGLI COVERAGE NONE
NOT APPLICABLE	AMOUNT:

11. PRIMARY SPECIALTY (List number, title and years and months in specialty. List additional specialty numbers and titles involving periods of one or more years.)	12. RECORD OF SERVICE	YEAR(s)	MONTH(s)	DAY(s)
1T211 - PARARESCUE HELPER, 2 MONTHS.	a. DATE ENTERED AD THIS PERIOD	2007	FEB	27
	b. SEPARATION DATE THIS PERIOD	2007	JUL	10
	c. NET ACTIVE SERVICE THIS PERIOD	00	04	14
	d. TOTAL PRIOR ACTIVE SERVICE	00	00	00
	e. TOTAL PRIOR INACTIVE SERVICE	00	06	18
	f. FOREIGN SERVICE	00	00	00
	g. SEA SERVICE	00	00	00
	h. EFFECTIVE DATE OF PAY GRADE	2007	Feb	27

13. DECORATIONS, MEDALS, BADGES, CITATIONS AND CAMPAIGN RIBBONS AWARDED OR AUTHORIZED (All periods of service)	14. MILITARY EDUCATION(Course title, number of weeks, and month and year completed)
AIR FORCE TRAINING RIBBON. NATIONAL DEFENSE SERVICE MEDAL. GLOBAL WAR ON TERRORISM SERVICE MEDAL.	BASIC MILITARY TRAINING, 6 WEEKS, APR 2007.

15a. MEMBER CONTRIBUTED TO POST-VIETNAM ERA VETERANS' EDUCATIONAL ASSISTANCE PROGRAM		YES X	NO
b. HIGH SCHOOL GRADUATE OR EQUIVALENT		YES	NO

16. DAYS ACCRUED LEAVE PAID	17. MEMBER WAS PROVIDED COMPLETE DENTAL EXAMINATION AND ALL APPROPRIATE DENTAL SERVICES AND TREATMENT WITHIN 90 DAYS PRIOR TO SEPARATION	YES	NO X

18. REMARKS

Member has not completed first full term of service... NOTHING FOLLOWS..

The information contained herein is subject to computer matching within the Department of Defense or with any other affected Federal or non-Federal agency for verification purposes and to determine eligibility for, and or continued compliance with, the requirements of a Federal benefit program

19a. MAILING ADDRESS AFTER SEPARATION (Include Zip Code)	b. NEAREST RELATIVE (Name and address - include Zip Code)
	Brtt

20. MEMBER REQUESTS COPY 6 BE SENT TO TX DIRECTOR OF VETERANS AFFAIRS	X YES	NO

21. SIGNATURE OF MEMBER BEING SEPARATED	22. OFFICIAL AUTHORIZED TO SIGN (Typed name, grade, title and signature)
BHt	ARTURO TREVINO, YC-1, DAF CHIEF, SEPARATIONS Arturo Trevino

SPECIAL ADDITIONAL INFORMATION (For use by authorized agencies only)		
23. TYPE OF SEPARATION	24. CHARACTER OF SERVICE (include upgrades)	
25. SEPARATION AUTHORITY AFI 36-3208	26. SEPARATION CODE	27. REENTRY CODE
28. NARRATIVE REASON FOR SEPARATION		
29. DATES OF TIME LOST DURING THIS PERIOD (YYYYMMDD)		30. MEMBER REQUESTS COPY 4 (Initials) Brtt

DD Form 214-AUTOMATED, FEB 2000   PREVIOUS EDITION IS OBSOLETE.

SERVICE-2

Figure 29. This is the general discharge form from the USAF that earned Brett Tutor a stolen valor place at THIS AIN'T HELL: If you get one, it's likely because of an inability to live up to standards, drug abuse, or assault and battery: so many redactions for a "general discharge." https://thisainthell.us/blog/?p=79931.

As the show continued, I'd see how the lost narcissist was trying to make his TQ:SI role become his personal identity—it was method acting in the opposite direction. Months after production, along this theme, he would take a high country long range shooting course from MagPul, trying

116

to get a little experience in what knowledge he tried to sell on TQ:SI. A check on IMDB states that he played a SWAT lieutenant on a film called DISARM. Begs the question of whether everything he does is in order to fulfill a role, or later back up a role, instead of actually going to do what he trained for, i.e. actually work in SWAT unit at a department, or served as a PJ in the Air Force.

What I really should have paid attention to was how deeply Discovery's fully scripted reality TV show had sunk its fangs into Jeremy. This was one TV fable-charged ego that could wipe out a legion. Unknown to me at the beginning of Season 2, was that Jeremy was becoming the team leader, in a move by MAK Pictures to get rid of me, after using my personal history to get the show off the ground. Now, someone who was hiding out in South America was suddenly feeling his oats, inspired by his closer relationship to Discovery, and feeling the spirit of a ship's captain taking him over. An uneasy feeling was overtaking me that negotiations and plays of power were occurring behind the scene on an unknown level of intensity: if they were so willing to do so with me on my pay raise to initially get me on the show, then it was probable they would do the same with others, such as Jeremy— the question was how far would MAK/Discovery go? The question I was also having was whether Jeremy Whalen was starting to fashion himself after Captain Ahab, Captain Bligh, or LT CMDR Francis Queeg.

All this charade was taking its toll on us, especially as the days turned to weeks, and weeks to months. You might think that you're one big happy family when you're part of a film or TV production. Everyone says they missed everyone from production while they were home. They say, "Love you!" It's the Hollywood thing, where you second guess adoration and connection of the "love you," with the alienation of them really meaning, "Fuck you!" The reality is far from the maddening crowd. Look at it from the needs and wants of everyone involved. There's only the screen, and it can be partial. It's one thing to play a character on a film or TV show. It's another to be playing a character that is told what to do, and what to say, but you're using your real name.

Though nobody on a reality TV show would want to admit it, it subconsciously weighs you down, heavily. It wasn't as noticeable on the first season, but by the time we had arrived in Argentina, it was full-blown. Basically, it was the cast believing its own press.

There was Mehgan Heaney-Grier who was beside herself telling us about she had been flown out to Los Angeles for an event orchestrated by Instagram. Huffington Post had an article on it titled 28 BADASS WOMEN YOU SHOULD BE FOLLOWING ON INSTAGRAM, by Taylor Pittman on October 26, 2015. When Mehgan told us about it, was as if she were amazed, too. I was truly blow away because what had put her on

117

the map publicly was this fake show in which she played at danger.

Back on Ilhabela, during the close of production, while we were shooting our OTFs and wild lines, Will Ehbrecht, who had come down from production, brought a copy of USA TODAY that mentioned our show for the first time. There were smiles all around, but I'd never seen a person so excited as Meghan was to see her name in print. It's was as if she had won the lottery. I'd never seen a person light up so much after learning that she was in the press. She blurted, "This is big!"

Apparently, my enthusiasm wasn't enough for her. I'd had my fifteen minutes of fame when I was released from Vietnam in 1984. To this day, Discovery has yet to come close to providing such publicity and fame. I'm not jaded, I just also remember how quickly the spotlight can turn somewhere else, and what was international news one moment, is a distant or forgotten memory. When I think of fame, it needs to be accompanied by a lot of dollar signs to make me take notice, else it's just a hassle: there are enough famous TV and film stars out there who can testify that fame and fortune don't always walk hand in hand.

"I mean this, is really big!" she said again, clearly not satisfied with my response. I just smiled, and looked at Ehbrecht, who had his own reserved smile.

It hit me then that I'd never seen anyone get so excited about such publicity. It was as if her world changed it and it was full of unicorns farting multi-colored sprinkles. She was a sight to behold, and a bit shocking that it took me aback. I thought I'd seen a lot in my 53 years on this planet. Her eyes were so wide with excitement, I thought I was looking at someone who had just stepped on the tail of an pissed off viper. The sight was so startling that that I later shared my amazement with Plaskett at how I'd never met a glory hound of this intensity before.

This business really turned her on. She was made for this world of illusion, positioning, and pretense, which was why I was so amazed that she would share something that nobody would ever share with the world if they were so concerned with their image. But, share she did on the Magic Bus...

The Magic Bus, or the sodium pentothal bus, as I'd sometimes call it was the min-van that would take us to and from the set location. Sometimes the rides would be short, other times they would be long. Longer rides permitted passengers to settle into the ride and the need to communicate. After hearing some of the most startling admissions, on the Magic Bus, I'd often wonder why so many felt compelled to share such private information.

It was easy to understand this personal sharing in Central America, while working with tight teams, whose next day could likely have been our last—where we trusted, and relied on, each other with our lives. Here, on a production which was like a working vacation what with how many were here from the US, not just for the money, but to go to a place that travel expenses were covered by the Discovery Communications, was a delight—there was as much trusting and bonding as would be got on a cruise ship. When Keith Plaskett and I were chatting about whether the new President at Discovery Channel Rich Ross would sign off on a production that his predecessor had okayed, and the unlikeliness what with how no administration likes to carry on the projects of a predecessor, all he could do was hope and relay how much he hoped that Ross would give TQ:SI the greenlight. He wanted so much to get to Brazil for Carnival, and to have it all covered by Discovery was a dream come true when it finally happened.

Figure 30. Society is really screwed when the lines between reality and scripted TV blur...even Twitter and the Huffington Post were hoodwinked by a TV role #MyStory.

No. The sharing of secrets came about for a variety of more reasons than that which would have come about from a bond built through battle. There were a variety of reasons on this magical mystery tour that started with a trip from the hotel to the set, or a long shoot, and the trip back to the hotel.

With Jeremy Whalen, it started as a fishing trip. He'd let a little of himself out and see if it was enough bait to get a hit. He'd use just enough personal history such, as the bit about his getting out of what could have been a major drug bust at his high school, as a little teaser, like an anglerfish extending and waving a little part of itself, its dorsal appendage to bring in prey. It was enrapturing, the way I might watch a predator in the wild always on the alert for whether someone was aware of what he was doing, and then gleefully engulfing everything as fast as possible.

It had become more and more clear that any interaction with him outside of time on set working and communal activities was suspect and frankly tiring. Can you imagine what it's like being on guard every time you're around someone who's always on the make? In Brazil, I almost always headed to Sao Paulo, or some other destination on our weekends off, just so I could relax.

Here in northern Argentina, no such luck. Keith seemed to hit it right on the head when he said that Discovery was keeping us in a mansion of the very wealthy Bemberg family, whose history went back to the creation of nearest town, Puerto Libertad so to amplify our stress. It was a gorgeous mansion, and the local residence handed down to Peter Bemberg, the patriarch of the Bemberg family that founded the Guinness, Coors of Argentina, under the label Quilmes. He was supposed to meet us at Puerto Bemberg before we wrapped production, but he never made it back from their home in Paris in time.

Keith liked to get out and mingle with the locals, preferably at a local bar or fiesta. The problem was that though he'd been living in South America for the last ten years, he'd only picked up enough Spanish to poorly pronounce swear words and order a cerveza. To get into town, he would have had to have spoken Spanish to the magic bus drivers and then navigated back and forth down a pitted and cobbled country road that was barely passable for 4x4 traffic, much less our van. I hated that road for how much it just shook you to the bone. Every ride to set was as if my belly were about to rip open, spilling my guts out onto the floor of the vehicle. It was a long brace.

We decided that this was all part of Discovery's plan to increase the drama, by increasing the on-camera drama through stress. The more uncomfortable and riddled with cabin fever we became, the better for the conflict of the show. I did my best to take care of it. I live in Alaska—cabin fever can be made a friend. But, it takes some solid self-awareness and a willingness to self-assess the light and dark, the yin and yang that makes up all humans. Keith preferred to perform his introspection through the magnification of the lens of a full bottle of rum. It was a voyage I had no interesting in taking with him as I had found myself attempting to do back in Brazil. Thankfully I went back to healthier tools I used to keep myself from walking a much darker path of remorse, guilt, sadness and just plainly painful memories, when I returned from Latin America in 1990.

As the days stretched the stress built, the truth serum quality of the magic bus began having much more effect. Jeremy used it to get our new survival and security character to open up about himself and share more than he should have.

Brett was from Austin, Texas. Though it seemed like he had done a bit of traveling in Central America and Africa on missions, that seemed more about self-promotional than actually having effect and being philanthropic, he was the most Mr. Hollywood person on the production. It was as if he had just gotten out of acting school and he was on the proverbial road to success. He'd had a bit of success, doing bit parts and some stunt work, being on a home remodeling show in Texas that none of us had heard about, but TQ:SI was clearly his big break.

He and Jeremy hit it off with Jeremy following a workable blood trail into his past as an MMA student back in Hawaii. Air Force recruit who washed out of boot camp, MMA trainee in Hawaii, attended university but never finished, always reading self-help books but never really comprehending the full meaning, Brett Tutor was the proverbial student who never got past attempting. He was an easy mark for Jeremy, most made clear when Jeremy's game of open up, got him to tell everyone how he had played a 911 prank on the local police back in Austin when he was in high school.

As he bounced around in the story, it was hard to keep track of what happened, but what we gleaned was that a police officer had been called out to a bridge, and then went to the house where Brett and his friends had been and was going to arrest them for the fake 911 call, but just gave them a warning based on their young age.

It led to Jeremy telling how had been living in Peru and found himself in conversation with a girl a party that led to him giving her a ride home on his motorcycle. He said he didn't know that the young lady was a girlfriend of the local drug chief, who chased him all the way to where he had dropped her off. When drug lord caught up, a fight ensued, and Jeremy shined on his prowess and defending himself and not getting whacked by a guy who had a reputation for murdering opponents. It was one of the penis comparing stories that little boys like to tell other boys, and Brett ate it up, coming back with his own about his MMA fight training days.

That bus was truly magical. One night, after some major drinking by Mehgan Heaney-Grier, where she was telling everyone how much she loved everyone on the production, as those who have heavily imbibed are prone to spout while trying to keep the world from spinning out of control, I noticed Jeremy out of the corner of my eye. It was a look I'd seen often in predators: four-legged and two-legged. If you've ever noticed a fox, or more like a weasel in the forest, it's that same darting look they give when they're hunting, but also doing their best not to become prey. These are furtive movements, much like Jeremy was making that night we were all riding back in the bus from a night of food and drink at the one of the best steak house in Puerto Iguazu, El Quincho del Tio Querido.

The wine flowed that night and pretty much the whole bus was filled to the gills, which of course made the laughter that much giddier. It also helped that part of the crew had accidently gone through the border and were having a hell of time trying to get back, because we had all come in on work visas, and suddenly they were stuck and had to get a tourist visa to come back—Discovery Communications had the audacity to bring us down on a thirty-day work visa, then paid off local law enforcement to look the other way while they had us get tourist visas to work on for the next sixty days.

I think that night was when those of us who have travelled broadly and understand you don't work in a foreign country unless you have a work visa, found it very disconcerting that MAK had told us that we had ninety-day visa, but instead said in Spanish, we had thirty-day work visas that needed to be used within 90 days. What was worse was that Discovery/MAK Pictures had kept us working over the limit of our 30 day visas, so we had to pay a fine and when we returned to Argentina we were to get tourist visas.

They said it was all okay, and Keith and I just looked at each other and shook our heads. The problem is that you have to go slightly into Brazil to pay online at a hotel that would even help with the process, then return to Argentina on that tourist visa. I would do this a few days later. But, that night the thought that the whole production could be in jeopardy because the crew couldn't come back in put everyone on edge, which of course lead to major drinking by the cast and crew. After the malaria that almost killed me in Central America, alcohol hits me pretty hard, so two glasses of wine is pretty much my limit. Anymore and it's just headaches, pain and jaundice.

Bottles were drunk that night and the repercussions we great. According to Keith Plaskett he heard the screams of a woman in the throes of orgasmic intensity in the room above his. Keith was so sure that Brett had gotten lucky that night with Mehgan. "Wrong room, Keith," I said.

Affairs happen. Though I was slightly entertained by Jeremy having bedded the crush he'd had since he'd first seen her on TV years earlier, I was more concerned with what would later transpire when Keith's fears got the best of him and he let me know that I had to watch my six. After the union of Mehgan and Jeremy hailed the loud banging and outbursts of an impassioned couple, Keith began opening up more to me and said that he noticed a major change in the person he thought was a friend.

I flat out told him Jeremy was no friend to anyone, unless he was going to get something out of them, and that from day one I saw he was just a common weasel who had manipulated his way on Keith's shirttails to this production. Still, even as his world was falling around him, Keith defended Jeremy and said it was all good, and that Mehgan was simply Jeremy's Delilah. Jeremy would never be making such a play to make to get rid of Keith and me, in order to make the show all about Jeremy and Mehgan. I told him there was no need of manipulation by Mehgan to get Jeremy to do anything of the sort. It was always in play, and what happened by their sexual union was a meeting of minds. Mehgan didn't get Jeremy to do anything, other than give him permission and embolden him. Two people married to two other people, how this was going to play out was anyone's guess. I just hoped no one got really hurt, meaning dead. People do crazy things in the jungle.

At first sight on this second season, Jeremy was just a bit angrier, and holding to himself. Still the guy with a calculating look in his eye as if sizing you up. This time, though, it seemed as if he had more cards at his disposal and been up to quite a bit with MAK and Discovery concerning his position on the show. We had yet to see him as team leader, because all those OTFs in which he'd say that he had brought his own money into the hunt, were all shot secretly. There was never any mention of him becoming a team leader during the whole production in Argentina, for very good reasons. Discovery and MAK had planned to get rid of me, from day one, and would do so by having me perform acts that I would NEVER do on my own.

Not until the sexual affair and conspiracy commenced between Jeremy and Mehgan that night did things really move into overdrive. Suddenly, seemingly because he felt more masculine having conquered his crush, Jeremy was seeming on top of the world and what I thought was just common feeling full of self that some actors get when they begin believing that they are their he-man characters on TV, he was turning into something more much more dangerous, especially with the anger he always carried inside of him from some his childhood experience, I had interpreted from cruel and manipulative acts as a teen but had not yet learned of in its full entirety.

One of the craziest things I learned in the jungles of Argentina, was a few days later, after that night of Jeremy and Mehgan's first tryst. Once again, the sodium pentothal bus worked it's magic, by getting Mehgan to incriminate herself with one of the most damning confessions I'd ever personally heard anyone offer, outside of hearing a confession to murder.

Before her marriage, and before Jeremy, there was Mark Louis Rackley, who basically was her doorway into television, starting with Rackley's production partner, Manuel Enrique Puig, aka Manny "Sharkman" Puig. You'll likely recognize him from a variety of freediving, spearfishing, and swim with the alligators and sharks TV content. Puig and Rackley, who was dating her at the time, suggested she train with them in order to set a woman's freedive record. And as it's said in reality TV, the rest is history, actually not History Channel, but Animal Planet's EXTREME CONTACT, where Puig was the beef and Mehgan was the cheesecake.

From what I'd learn about Mehgan's former cameraman boyfriend Rackley, he'd always been into controlled substances, arrests across Florida and Texas. It was one of the arrests in Texas that caught my eye when I began my investigations. On the magic bus, Mehgan had blurted out that she had perjured herself to get her boyfriend off a drug smuggling arrest. I had assumed it was an arrest that included the Sharkman, and I did find that a Manuel Enrique Puig was a guest of the US Bureau of Prisons in Lake County, Florida on August 26, 1992.

But, Puig doesn't seem to have been involved with the drug smuggling Rackley was busted for on August 16, 1994. As the arrest report stated, Rackley was pulled over for weaving on the road in Jefferson County, Texas. When the officer went up to his vehicle and trailer, the officer smelled fresh resin, which tipped him off to the 48.08 pounds of marijuana, which according to Mehgan had been laminated into the hull of the boat on the trailer.

Ironic, considering she refused to be seen on TV drinking a shot of rum to the dead with us on deck in Brazil, when Keith was toasting those men and women who had died at sea and gone to Davey Jones' locker, but she was willing to perjure herself for a repeated drug user and smuggler. For someone who repeatedly said she admired her grandfather Judge Gerald W. Heaney, I was flabbergasted.

It was bad enough she perjured herself to get Rackley off. But, to then admit it to people who were only co-workers on a totally scripted show masquerading as a "true-life" documentary? I can tell you if my grandfather was a US Army second-lieutenant who landed in Normandy with the 2nd Ranger Battalion in 1944, and then ended up becoming appointed by President Lyndon B. Johnson to the 8th Circuit of the US Court of Appeals, he'd be beside himself to learn his grandchild had perjured herself to get a repeat drug abuser and smuggler off. Rackley has quite the record, going way back.

"Can you believe what she admitted to today?" I asked Keith as he began his evening's rum gauntlet that would last who knew how long into the night, in the fireplace cove of the Bemberg mansion. If Brett Tutor ended up coming down with a guitar of his own that he picked up at a one of the greatest luthiers in Argentina, Casa Chavez in Posadas, Misiones, that bottle, or a second, would last all night. Those guitars by Chavez, whose family history of luthiers goes back to Spain before 1880, were so beautiful and amazingly inexpensive that Tutor, Mckibben and I purchased one each from the master luthier himself.

It was all becoming so bizarre. First there were my questions about Brett Tutor's military experience in the US Air Force. I had assumed that he had gone through bootcamp and the first thing I learned as a lowly Naval midshipman is to keep your mouth shut unless otherwise ordered by a higher-ranking officer, but it appeared the only ones keeping their mouths shut were Keith and me—except when Keith was beginning to confide in me as he noticed more and more the real reasons Jeremy had him as a friend. Still, he was clearly hoping he hadn't lost a friend to Delilah.

Pondering what could have caused Mehgan to confess such an egregious act, I remembered that she said she was a good Irish girl and had even gone to Catholic school. Confession is ingrained from an early age. That's when I realized that Keith wasn't just making up a story about lover's trysts and collusions for power. She couldn't have publicly confessed to having started an adulterous affair, but it must have been troubling her, what with how she would talk proudly about her husband and married life. So, to release some of the pressure, just like a detainee in interrogation, who needs to release tension through the unconscious bouncing or shaking of feet, or letting little truths out in order to keep the big one a secret, she let the pressure out by confessing perjured testimony that got a repeat drug offender off, instead of admitting she had entered into an affair with a co-star, and that that shady union was focused on taking out anyone blocking their way to stardom.

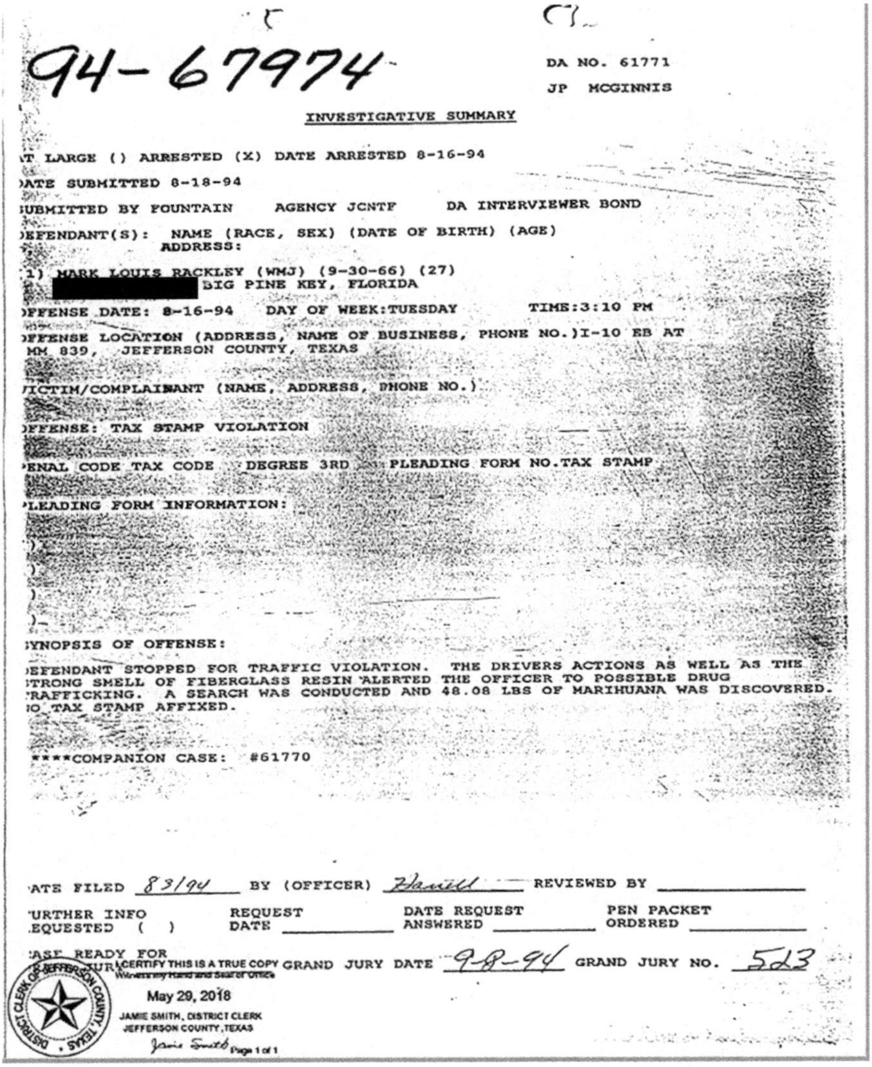

94-67974

DA NO. 61771
JP MCGINNIS

INVESTIGATIVE SUMMARY

AT LARGE ( ) ARRESTED (X) DATE ARRESTED 8-16-94
DATE SUBMITTED 8-18-94
SUBMITTED BY FOUNTAIN AGENCY JCNTF DA INTERVIEWER BOND
DEFENDANT(S): NAME (RACE, SEX) (DATE OF BIRTH) (AGE)
ADDRESS:
1) MARK LOUIS RACKLEY (WMJ) (9-30-66) (27)
[redacted] BIG PINE KEY, FLORIDA
OFFENSE DATE: 8-16-94 DAY OF WEEK:TUESDAY TIME:3:10 PM
OFFENSE LOCATION (ADDRESS, NAME OF BUSINESS, PHONE NO.)I-10 EB AT MM 839, JEFFERSON COUNTY, TEXAS
VICTIM/COMPLAINANT (NAME, ADDRESS, PHONE NO.)
OFFENSE: TAX STAMP VIOLATION
PENAL CODE TAX CODE DEGREE 3RD PLEADING FORM NO.TAX STAMP
PLEADING FORM INFORMATION:
)
)
)
)

SYNOPSIS OF OFFENSE:
DEFENDANT STOPPED FOR TRAFFIC VIOLATION. THE DRIVERS ACTIONS AS WELL AS THE STRONG SMELL OF FIBERGLASS RESIN ALERTED THE OFFICER TO POSSIBLE DRUG TRAFFICKING. A SEARCH WAS CONDUCTED AND 48.08 LBS OF MARIHUANA WAS DISCOVERED. NO TAX STAMP AFFIXED.

****COMPANION CASE: #61770

DATE FILED 8/3/94 BY (OFFICER) Hamill REVIEWED BY ______
FURTHER INFO REQUESTED ( ) REQUEST DATE ______ DATE REQUEST ANSWERED ______ PEN PACKET ORDERED ______
CASE READY FOR GRAND JUR[Y] GRAND JURY DATE 9-8-94 GRAND JURY NO. 523

DISTRICT CLERK OF JEFFERSON COUNTY, TEXAS
I CERTIFY THIS IS A TRUE COPY
Witness my Hand and Seal of Office
May 29, 2018
JAMIE SMITH, DISTRICT CLERK
JEFFERSON COUNTY, TEXAS
Jamie Smith Page 1 of 1

Figure 31. Mark L. Rackley's arrest record for trying to smuggle drugs laminated into the hull of a boat, for which Mehgan Heaney-Grier's perjured testimony factored in his release.

9 WHITES AND REDS, KNIGHTS, KINGS AND QUEENS

What a chess game going between A&E and Discovery Communications in Alice's Wonderland. Eileen O'Neill, whose entry as President of Discovery Channel was the harbinger of Hollywood and fakeumentaries offered as "true-life" documentaries, was no longer President of Discovery Channel, but she had gotten her wish of a new hit series against History Channel's CURSE OF OAK ISLAND. Her about face when she was named Global Group President at Discovery Studios made me smile. I didn't know whether she was honestly thinking getting a show so fully scripted like TREASURE QUEST: SNAKE ISLAND broadcast, was an earnest attempt by her to right a career that had careened out of control with such fiascoes as the MERMAID series of fakeumentaries, or EATEN ALIVE, that led to such total disgust by the audience, or was it just her way of throwing a grenade in the room as she exited the building?

According to a February 20, 2015 article in DEADLINE HOLLYWOOD, Discovery Communications CEO David Zaslav, called her "one of the very best we have at Discovery." If that was the best Discovery had, does that mean, contrary to its slogan of being the last true-life documentary network out there, that it was in reality making money by hoodwinking its audience to a whole new level P.T. Barnum couldn't have even imagined?

Rich Ross was doing a great job carrying on the tradition of counting coup against A&E, even though he stated in a NEW YORK TIMES January 3, 2016 article:

"When I came here, there was a lot of history of focusing on History," he said. "I

kept hearing, 'The pitch for this show is competitive with History.' I said, 'Stop talking about that. I really don't care.' If we think of ourselves only in the scheme of beating History, that's small ball. We have to think about what Discovery can be."

A&E continued to be Discovery Communications' direct rival in the satellite TV business. Of course, it was all about beating History! Doesn't anyone remember the old joke about the two campers who come across a grizzly bear? One camper cuts the Achilles heel of the other, so he can run faster than him and get away from the charging bear. All Discovery must do is out run A&E and they corner the audience, by avoiding the bear and getting the bull market.

Can you imagine what it was like for me to sit around the San Ignacio hostel (where Discovery quartered us because the hotel in town was so bad, that even David Carr and Tom Dorman, who had done ANCIENT ALIENS for History in Bolivia, didn't want to stay there), and look at a whole new crew—except for Derrick Nevot and Scottie McKibben—that was the production team of CURSE OF OAK ISLAND?

There was David Carr and Tom Dorman, both from History Channel's ANCIENT ALIENS and CURSE OF OAK ISLAND, and music videos in Los Angeles. Dorman was a former Marine, so we got along well, like most who come from a Marine family, or were Marines. That's global by the way, especially with regards to British and US Marines. Take the globe and anchor insignia and emblem, for instance. US Marines' eagle, globe and anchor depicts the western hemisphere, while the Royal Marines' depict the other half of the world, in their globe and laurel: put the two halves together and they make the complete globe.

David Carr was the same age as me, so I thought we understood each other from a generational point of view, though we had very different upbringings, mine overseas, and his in Southern California and back east, and while I was being asked to explain myself to a bunch of Socialist Vietnam interrogators, he was in film school and the LA music scene, which of course often leads to producing videos, as it had for him.

With our illustrious showrunners were the rest of the crew they brought from CURSE OF OAK ISLAND. Ariel Benarroch, our Parisian French-Jew, who didn't do time with the Israeli Defense Force (IDF) but was proud of his Jewish grandfather in the French Resistance. I've always found this perplexing. The Jews of my generation who vote for the Democratic Party, though at every turn, the DNC is trying to give Israel back to Palestine. This would have been unheard of in pre-Vietnam Hollywood. It's as though they confuse a kibbutz for an overall socialist government, when a kibbutz was really just a quick fix to get everyone on the same wavelength and working together. It also helped that it created a truly self-sufficient community, that was also able defend itself from attack using a solid civil defense force. Remember, it wasn't just Palestinian guerrillas and Iranian Mullahs back then. Egypt was a formidable foe with tanks, and not until the Six Day War, and Israel's defining moment, that survivability of the nation of Israel was improved.

I've known members of Mossad and the IDF very well. A little bit of Central America history: aside from some training and instruction from British SAS in Belize, and former Rhodesians, specialists in counter-insurgency, Argentine Navy, the other bit of assistance from across the pond came from Israel, through Mossad and the IDF. They provided a number of training cycles for members of the Salvadoran and Honduran forces, and other nations in the area doing their best to keep Daniel Ortega and Raoul Castros' designs from coming into fruition in Central and South America, such as the Nicaraguan Democratic Force (FDN/Contras). Not that it really mattered. The Castro brothers won the war in Latin American by later bankrolling the campaigns of the FMLN in El Salvador, Lula and Rousseff in Brazil, Correa in Ecuador, and Chavez in Venezuela, basically using the free elections system and the promise of access to the government coffers to bring socialism into power in these nations. Basically, they did what every unscrupulous politician does in trying to win the vote in a democracy.

As Alexander Fraser Tytler said, "A democracy cannot exist as a permanent form of government. It can only exist until the people discover they can vote themselves largess out of the public treasury. From that moment on, the majority always votes for the candidate promising the most benefits from the public treasury, with the result that democracy always collapses over a loose fiscal policy—to be followed by a dictatorship."

Benarroch came from an old Hollywood film family, according to Scottie McKibben, and that's why he was in the film business, in no small annoyance to Mckibben. During the wars in Latin America, though a still photographer by trade, I'd freelance as a soundman and cameraman for such companies as CNN—what professional turns down easy money? Cameras and guns aren't that hard to operate when you get the basics down, like any technology designed for a large market.

Shooting a camera is easy in contrast to other professions. It just takes an eye, which many good photographers get from looking at a lot of photos as a kid, as I mentioned in my Vietnam memoir, where I always reviewed the photos in my dad's copies of NATIONAL GEOGRAPHIC, TIME, NEWSWEEK, and PLAYBOY. It trained my eye—all the rest was technical learning. It's like firearms, where you really get your eye to shoot with bow and BB guns as a kid, and then you get older and you get the technical learning that is done in long range tactical shooting. Snipers are not born, but, as Carlos Hathcock, the Marine sniper's sniper, reminded us, they are taught from an early age through BB guns, .22 rifles for squirrels, and then bigger rifles for deer.

Figure 32. First photos of Soviet-made SAM-14 surface-to-air missiles captured from the Sandinistas by the FDN/Contras, an operation that included the capture of a Sandinista major (the village hated him so much they handed him over, too). He stands in the middle, facing the camera, parrot in hand, photographed by the author in 1989.

Both Benarroch and Mckibben had great eyes for images. The conflict was that Benarroch was Hollywood and Paris fashion Kodachrome, and Mckibben was Henri Cartier-Bresson black and white print, Kentucky coal mine and 1960s civil rights movement in the South photojournalism. When their tires hit the pavement of color and color temperature, they were like two ships passing in the night, trying to communicate with two different code books. This was easily seen in the difference of how season one and season two were shot, even though Mckibben was director of photography on both shoots.

It was this know-it-all attitude of Benarroch that was kind of annoying by the time everyone's candle was lit at the both ends by the end of production. I didn't know if it was because he was arrogant because he was from an old Hollywood family, or that he was a Parisian. I love hanging out with French country folk, but there's a protective shield the people from any large city build in order to survive, that can be grating when all you want to do is relax, and not hear a cameraman, who is clearly not the directory, or showrunner, telling you how to act, especially when he's not even doing what the DPs telling him to do—which brings us back to what this book is all about: in what world is okay for anyone to be telling talent how to act, and what to say, if it's truly a "reality"/"true-life" TV show?

David Zaslav, Richard Ross, and even Eileen O'Neill must have been laughing themselves to the bank, that they had achieved such a coup against A&E/History Channel. Here they had not only been winning with a new treasure hunting show to compete against CURSE OF OAK ISLAND, but they had hired the production team from the competing History Channel show. Networks like to think and express publicly that they respect the non-disclosures of completing networks, but we at TQ:SI were hearing from CURSE OF OAK ISLAND about the roman broadsword that could be got on eBay, and that the production crew was surprised and blown away when the cast found a coin that the crew were sure was not planted. Well, they were mostly sure hadn't been planted.

Along with Carr, Dorman, and Benarroch, we got Cathy Grant, and Dan Buchanan from Nova Scotia, and John Adams, from Louisiana. They loved saying "John Adams"—JOHN ADAMS, as if to say, "Hello, Mr. President." Cathy was our line producer, who replaced Richard Kathlean from our first season. Two very different types of personalities for line producers. Kathlean was there to do his job, but also have fun, which entailed all of us crew and cast benefitting from things like hiring a motorized buccaneer sailboat to be our base of operations when we were shooting off Ilhabela. Cathy was a textbook, by-the-book line producer, who met the budget where the accounting met production, making sure everything came under budget.

John Adams was our producer's assistant and Dan Buchanan was our DP's assistant. They pretty much made sure things got to where they were supposed to be at any time, people, things, vehicles, etc.

We were all the pieces in this Alice in Wonderland game of chess. ALICE IN WONDERLAND and THROUGH THE LOOKING GLASS, were both about politics, and there's nothing as political as the warring between two networks. And through this all, there was this slinging of propaganda that was something expected by two Asian nations at war, well-educated in the Sun Tzu's ART OF WAR and Lee Zhong Wu's THICK BLACK THEORY, playing a game of deception. The deception in this world of networks was what CEO David Zaslav called "true-life" programming. What is true-life programming if it's all staged and programmed? How far will a network go to keep the money rolling in? From what you'll see, they'll do just about anything…legal, or illegal.

Remember, according to THE WRAP, David Zaslav made more than $42 Million in 2017. That was $5 Million more than he made in 2016. That's not how much he made up until 2017, that was what he made each year! Keep in mind that the next highest paid at Discovery Communications in 2017 was his international counterpart Jean-Briac Perette, who made only

$8.2 Million. Yeah, only $8.2 Million. With money like this moving around, do you think they pay too much attention to national and international laws, even though they sell themselves as the last bastion of education and true documentaries? Yeah, I didn't think so.

Figure 33. Being at sea in Brazil had a lot more benefits to it than being stuck in a jungle in Argentina—Richard Kathlean's sixty-foot score for the cast and crew, as a comfortable base of operations away from the ready to sink SS Wedding Cake.

How far will they go? To answer that, let's take my friend Green Beret birthday brother CPT Mykel Hawke (RET) and his trials and tribulations that started with a person I'd completely consider a textbook definition of a psychopath, a predator, Joseph Teti, of DUAL SURVIVAL (DS). DS was a major moneymaker for Discovery, starting with the original costars, David Canterbury and Cody Lundin. They were the golden boys of the survival reality TV world.

That was until the public learned that Canterbury had lied a bit about his military record: he wasn't a US Army Ranger, and he wasn't a sniper. So, they got rid of him and then they got Joseph Teti. Basically, Discovery, in their constant disregard for vetting talent, had gone from being in the frying pan with Canterbury, to jumping into the fire with Teti. Adding to the fuel that would light everyone at Discovery up, was that while Teti got the role on DS, he also sold DS's producer French Horowitz and Discovery on a show called LONE OPERATOR (LO), which was to be produced by Joe Teti, with him as the lead.

See, he didn't have the background in survival, so he didn't think he'd get on DS. Backing himself up with options, he pitched LO. When it rains it pours, and he got both roles—too bad he wasn't qualified for either. Three people died as the result of Discovery Communications not vetting its talent, especially for something as dangerous and with so many legal ramifications as a show that included firearms and aircraft.

Many are still blown away that no one ever caught Teti in his fraud and forgeries when he went into the US Army National Guard, which enabled him to later become a member of a Special Forces unit. He walked his DD214 over from the US Marine Corps and enroute rewrote items that made it look like he was qualify in a variety of skills that he wasn't, such as combat diving, and making it look as if he was Force Recon instead of Recon. At face value they appear to be the same, but that's like saying you're a Green Beret, when you're really a Ranger, of saying you're a SEAL, when you're really UDT. All these are important components of each branch, but they serve different purposes.

Now this is where it gets very interesting. Teti said that he completed combat diver's school in Florida, which would have been the Army Special Forces combat diver's school. Thing is he never graduated combat diver school. Some in the community say, no way he could have become a member of Force Recon. Most importantly, with regards to integrity, Teti's combat divers school records state he was failed for cheating on his test. He did take a Navy Diver course at Pearl harbor, which enabled him to become Marine Recon. As said before, Marine Recon is not Force Recon (FORECON). What's worse is that when he went to the National Guard he pulled pay off having graduated from combat diver school, according to his forged DD214!

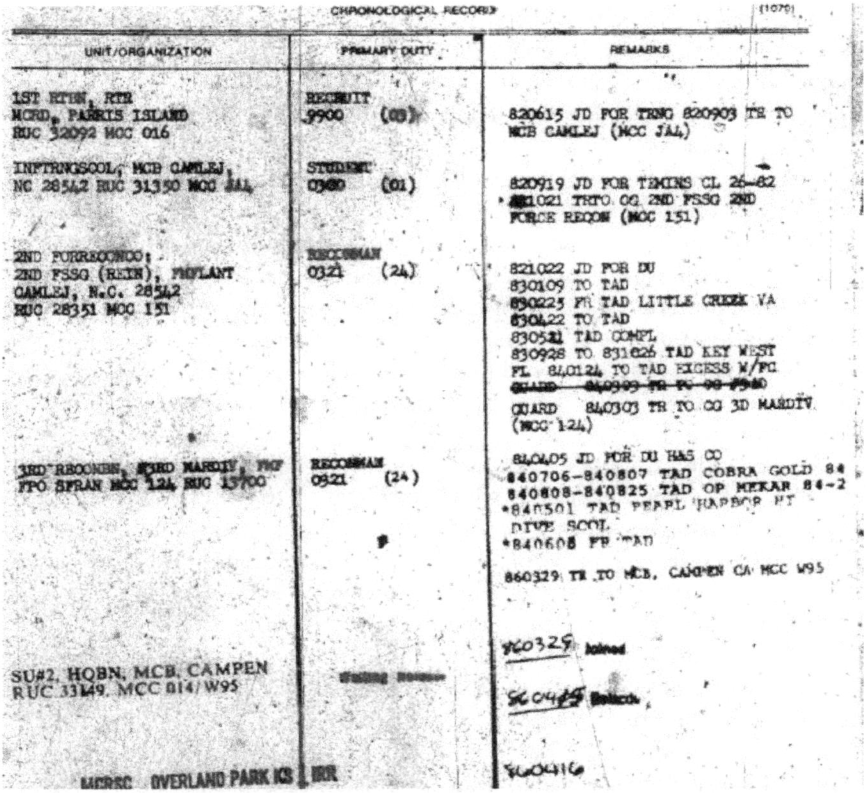

CHRONOLOGICAL RECORD (1070)

UNIT/ORGANIZATION	PRIMARY DUTY	REMARKS
1ST RTBN, RTR MCRD, PARRIS ISLAND RUC 32092 MCC 016	RECRUIT 9900 (03)	820615 JD FOR TRNG 820903 TR TO MCB CAMLEJ (MCC JAL)
INFTRNGSCOL, MCB CAMLEJ, NC 28542 RUC 31350 MCC JAL	STUDENT 0300 (01)	820919 JD FOR TEMINS CL 26-82 821021 TRTO CG 2ND FSSG 2ND FORCE RECON (MCC 151)
2ND FORRECONCO: 2ND FSSG (REIN), FMFLANT CAMLEJ, N.C. 28542 RUC 28351 MCC 151	RECONMAN 0321 (24)	821022 JD FOR DU 830109 TO TAD 830225 FR TAD LITTLE CREEK VA 830422 TO TAD 830521 TAD COMPL 830928 TO 831026 TAD KEY WEST FL 840124 TO TAD EXCESS W/FC ~~[illegible]~~ GUARD 840303 TR TO CG 3D MARDIV (MCC 124)
3RD RECONBN, 3RD MARDIV, FMF FPO SFRAN MCC 124 RUC 13700	RECONMAN 0321 (24)	840405 JD FOR DU HAS CO 840706-840807 TAD COBRA GOLD 84 840808-840825 TAD OP MEKAR 84-2 *840501 TAD PEARL HARBOR HI DIVE SCOL *840608 FR TAD 860329 TR TO MCB, CAMPEN CA MCC W95
SU#2, HQBN, MCB, CAMPEN RUC 33149, MCC 814/W95	[illegible]	860329 Joined 860405 [illegible] 860416
MCRSC OVERLAND PARK KS IRR		

Figure 34. Teti's USMC records showing no Combat Diver School—only Navy Diver School in Pearl Harbor.

That's an actionable offense. It's a felony to bilk pay from the government. Teti was well-known in military circles in the Marines and Army as stated in an article on CCN Ireport, by Monique Marie:

> *"Teti Claims Special Operations for over 20 Years.(Same as Cody claims in the Discovery video introducing Teti as Cody's new partner, LOGIC dictates that Teti's RESUMES contained this information, the TRUTH Captain Hawke has been saying all along).....Teti was National Guard for 8 years, never deployed as SF Green Beret into Combat, got kicked out of most of his Units for Stealing, Violent Tendencies and Lying. Contracted for a year on and off and got fired from all Contracts for Stealing and Lying."*

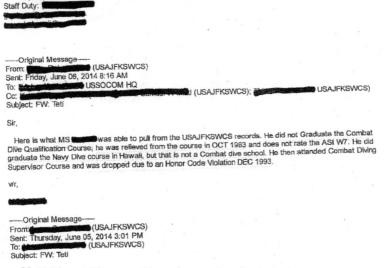

Figure 35. Vetting at Discovery Comm. has much to be desired—so many psychopaths in their employ.

Later in the article:

"Quotes from Teti's Team Commanders and Team Mates from MILITARY TIMES Article:

"I believe Joe is a sociopath [who] could be dangerous to those he believes have injured him," writes Sgt. 1st Class Daniel McClain, Teti's former team sergeant, in a letter to the Special Forces Association that is part of a formal response in an ongoing lawsuit.

"I personally have heard him claim to have burned out a competitor to his Las Vegas cleaning business. And, I witnessed him describing threats he made to others. He seemed to brag about this activity," McClain writes.

"I knew he would always be a problem," writes Teti's former executive officer, Lt. Col. William Sharp, in another letter, part of the SFA's 50-page rebuttal to the lawsuit filed by Teti late last year. Sharp, now with U.S. Special Operations Command, writes that he was preparing paperwork to bar Teti from reenlisting, revoke his security clearance and strip him of his Special Forces tab, before Teti left the unit on his own.

"Teti is far below Special Forces standards, he is an embarrassment to Special Forces and Special Operations," writes Sharp, listing a litany of allegations.

Joseph Teti has slipped through the Legal Cracks for far too long. DCIS should do what is right and prosecute on the known crimes he has committed. Innocent Retired Special Forces suffer while Teti is permitted to continue to profit off of his Lies. Discovery Channel is responsible also for good and Innocent Retired Special Forces Men being made to suffer this injustice just so they can make money."

That's the crux: Discovery Channel making money, above all else. How else can someone who had been so lambasted in the media continue to be put up in front of the public, as though a hero? By default, anyone who is being marketed as an authority on TV, which Teti still is, with regards to the military and survival, even though his credibility is lacking, will be looked at by the public as famous. The idolatry that Moses warned about in the Old Testament, is exactly what this is. If you are a network, who continues to support the image of a person proven to be a fraud and lacking in character, then you, as a corporate entity, are aiding and abetting fraud, and committing conspiracy to defraud your audience, your investors/shareholders, and your advertisers. Most insidiously, during this time and age of FAKE NEWS, you're laying down the shore battery for an invasion of the minds of the populace to believe anything, especially fake news.

In a MILITARY TIMES article dated April 29, 2014, titled DISCOVERY CHANNEL REALITY SHOW STAR TRADES FIRE OVER COMBAT EXPERIENCE, Teti said of his goal for getting on TV:

> *"One, I wanted to be a good role model for kids. My second goal was to represent the special operations community as a whole in a good light," Teti, co-star of Discovery Channel's "Dual Survival," tells Military Times. "I wanted to portray to the public what an average special operations guy is."*

How does Teti, who lied about his experience and knowledge by forging military records to get a reality TV show based on his failed security contracting company, called LONE OPERATOR, and who then was responsible for the death of an honorable CAG member, and supposed friend of his, become a role model for children through Discovery?

Former CAG (US Army's famous Delta Force) member Michael Donatelli, age 45 in 2013, when he was killed in a helicopter accident on the set of LO, was a mutual friend of Joseph Teti and Mykel Hawke. Two other people died in an accident that should have never happened had the producer in charge known what he was doing. From 1985, to 1990, I flew as a passenger on a multitude of blackbirds and UH-1D helicopters. I'm very well versed on standard operating procedures (SOPs) for night operations, requiring the wearing night vision goggles (NVGs), and never using a bare light to illuminate the cockpit or the interior of the aircraft in a manner that would blind us. One of the most glaring parts of the crash that killed pilot David Gibbs, cameraman Darren Rydstrom, and cast member Donatelli, was the amount of light in the cockpit.

Before takeoff, the camera operator asked the pilot if they could try to use the light pad, and the pilot responded, "we'll see, it just really [sigh] blinds me." The camera operator then showed the actor how to operate the light pad. The actor turned it on to the lowest setting, and the camera operator remarked that it was bright but that they would see what the pilot thought; the pilot did not comment. During the initial takeoff and while maneuvering over the dry riverbed, the actor continued with scripted dialogue for about a minute until the pilot intervened to state that he needed the light pad turned off. The camera operator acknowledged him and informed the actor to turn off the light by pressing a button twice. The actor leaned forward to turn off the light, and, 8 seconds later, the camera operator announced, "where did uh, we're going down low," indicating that he was temporarily disoriented and then noted that they were descending. The actor cycled through the light's settings and eventually turned it off while the pilot simultaneously stated, "okay, okay, I can't." The camera operator interrupted saying, "pull up, pull up." The helicopter subsequently impacted terrain in the dry riverbed. Postaccident examination of the wreckage revealed no evidence of mechanical malfunctions or anomalies that would have precluded normal operation.

The pilot recognized on the first flight that he was operating with reduced/no visibility and with a bright light in the cockpit that "blinded" him when it was on but chose to proceed with both flights likely because he believed that was what was required to fulfill the production requirements. Despite recognizing the hazards of the operation and relaying his concerns to the ground crew and camera operator, the pilot was the only person knowledgeable about helicopters. As the pilot, he was responsible for the safe operation of the helicopter and should have initiated the measures necessary to ensure that the helicopter's internal lighting and the lighting on the ground would enable him to conduct the flight in a safe manner.

The accident occurred during the hours of darkness on a moonless night over minimally lighted terrain. According to Federal Aviation Administration (FAA) guidance, these conditions can result in illusions that make it difficult for a pilot to visually determine altitude, depth perception, and orientation, and often create the illusion that the aircraft is at a higher altitude than it actually is. Additionally temporary blindness, caused by an unusually bright light, may result in illusions or after images until the eyes recover from the brightness. Based on the dark night conditions, the minimal ground lighting, the bright light in the cockpit, and the absence of preimpact mechanical anomalies, the pilot was likely temporarily blinded by the light, lost visual reference to the ground, and then flew the helicopter into the ground.

Figure 36. Excerpt from NTSB report Identification: WPR13FA119 ; Probable Cause Approval Date: 06/18/2015.

What pilot flying that close to the ground, with as many hours as Gibbs, wouldn't have turned off all the lights in the cockpit and demanded the cameraman use a night cam and have everyone use NVGs? From reading the NTSB report, the article by VERTICAL MAGAZINE, being a fixed wing pilot, and having acted on a Discovery Communications production, where I acted in scenes due to pressure from the MAK Pictures' office in Los Angeles, thinking that Discovery Communications couldn't possibly respect a psychotic co-stars desires, aspirations, and actions over my well-being, it's easy to see how Gibbs flew past his logged flight plan, under conditions he should have known well, were completely unsafe.

The problem for accuracy of blame is that pilot in control (PIC) is a term not used lightly in aviation, much as ship's captain is not used lightly in maritime law. Responsibility for any accident rests with the captain at sea, and the PIC in the aircraft. Questions about extenuating circumstances come, though, as to how it all could have gotten so far out of hand. Teti, by his direction (hired under his contract as producer and technical specialist), should have known that the conditions were so unsafe as be ridiculously attempted with the lighting arrangement used that night. He clearly did not know the subject he sold himself as being a specialist in.

Figure 37. The night Mykel Hawke's combat buddy, Michael Donatelli died as the result of Joseph Teti's false background. l-r. Dale Comstock, Joseph Teti, Michael Donatelli.

Shame on Teti for basically directing his friend to his death. Shame on Discovery for trying to cover up the fact. When I first heard of the accident from Hawke, I was perplexed as to why Teti was never really mentioned as the person responsible, and initially kept out of the press. Much of the coverage from that time doesn't even mention him at all. What became clear was that hush money was paid to a variety of media.

Once I learned of the level of criminality Discovery will go to cover its tracks on TQ:SI, it was starting to become intimidating. In trying to report Discovery Communications' illegal activities on set in South America, I would learn how much media doesn't like to report bad stories on media. Throw in hush money, and names that should be included in news pieces, end up disappearing.

What could have led Discovery to do such a thing with Teti? Well, remember when he proposed LONE OPERATOR (LO), he was also casting for the role opposite Cody Lundin, to replace Dave Canterbury. Well, lucky devil, he gets a new production AND a new role. Problem is that he screws up his chance as a producer with the crash on the set of LO, and Disco doesn't want to lose on the content all ready to go from having produced the full season of the new Lundin/Teti season of DS. Damage control was in high gear and Teti's name was omitted from several articles about what should have been a major manslaughter case against Teti.

If you're into studying human behavior as I am, there's some interesting psychology going on here. Teti screws up; Disco jumps in to prevent a major financial hemorrhage. Dual Survival is French Horowitz's baby, and there's nothing he won't do to keep from losing his edge as Disco's executive producer with such hits as Flying Wild Alaska, Stormchasers, Yukon Men and Dual Survival. This made him Disco's go-to adventure guy, according his IMDB profile.

I liken him to Joseph Boyle, who was our Disco executive producer, who I've noticed has become Disco's new go-to treasure guy. I'll fill you in him later, but unlike Boyle who never appeared on TQ:SI's set in either season I was there, even though we were Disco's new series hit for 2015, Horowitz was there all the time from what I'm told.

As I said, I'm really into psychology for a variety of reasons, many of them professional. The study of it teaches us about ourselves, and our behaviors with others in all different situations and environments. In my observations of how Jeremy Whalen used certain tools of persuasion, you could see how he used what Robert Cialdini calls the principle of reciprocity: I give you a bit of information, and since the universe hates a vacuum, you give me a bit of information about you. With this information, he was able to formulate a strategy of action for his attempts at ascension.

There's another principle of persuasion, or manipulation, however you'd like to call it, called the principle of congruency, "commitment and consistency" as Cialdini prefers to say. Leonardo Da Vinci said it well, "It is easier to resist at the beginning than at the end."

Had Discovery Communications (DC) been a standup corporation under David Zaslav's command, one that had the strength and fortitude to admit a wrong, cut Teti loose as the dangerous pretender he turned out to be, Teti would have been held responsible in court. DC would have had to have bit the bullet on the fees and fines, and Teti would have been easily prosecuted by the FBI for his forged documents regarding his forged combat diver certificates that the Defense Finance and Accounting Service (DFAS) paid out monthly, all those years when he was in the Army National Guard. It was after all a federal offense, a felony for him to have pulled that pay all those years, all the way to his exit, the day before "stop loss" was in effect.

Pretty crafty, don't you think? Getting out just before everyone was slated to go to Afghanistan? That's how psychopaths are—thought they play the role well, they are not team players and have no comprehension of service, which requires sacrifice. They make decisions from reptilian part of the brain, and are solely focused on themselves, and beware anyone who gets in the way of their goals. You could easily become collateral damage. Psychopaths aren't known for empathy, and even worse, when they get away with something, when they really get a taste of success as the result of immoral and illegal actions, they like to, as Emeril Lagasse likes to say, "Take it up a notch—Bam!"

Well, that's what happens with corporations and normal people, too, in a different way, of course, when the principle of commitment and consistency comes into play. The Nazis used it very effectively to get fine, conscientious German, French, Austrians, Hungarians, a variety of Europeans to exterminate the Jews and others considered undesirable to the National Socialist German Worker's Party.

First, they got your neighbor to say bad things about Jews: "They're taking over the country;" "They're hoarding the nation's money as bankers." Then, they went from deplorably exercising their rights of free speech through verbally expressing their bigotry against Jews in Germany, to vandalizing the property of Jews in German. After vandalizing, comes assault and battery. From there, it's easier to attack and even kill those who were demeaned through the initial acts of verbal attack. It's all about little steps, like the lobster or the frog that doesn't know it's cooked until it's too late.

Freedoms are pulled from free citizens in this manner. Genocide comes about from this. And, corporations slide down a slippery slope of deceit that starts with keeping a psychopath like Jeremy Whalen from getting just desserts from criminal activities, such as smuggling stolen artifacts from one country to another. Previously, it was Teti who kept getting away with murder, and it was all because of greed. Discovery had spent money creating the public identity of Joseph Teti as a survival expert, though he didn't know anything about survival, and had even lied about attending SERE school, which is the only way he could have fully learned about it in the military. Many don't know that just because you served in the military doesn't mean you necessarily know how use a firearm, or if you're Special Forces, you know everything you need to know about survival.

Mykel Hawke went through SERE school, but he freely admits that the reason he's a survival expert is that he studied with several survival instructors over the years before and after SERE. All of them he acknowledges and pays respect to in his instruction, writing and comments. Basically, when it came to actual survival experts on Dual Survival, Cody Lundin was the expert, and he had his hands full dealing with Joseph Teti. By the time Lundin had run his course with DS, he was in fear for his life what with the death threats from Teti, and was, and is, by the publishing of this book, in litigation with Discovery Communications for defamation.

If you remember the scene with Cody Lundin in Hawaii, tossing matches into a pool as he giggled, and laughed, you'd think he was losing his mind. But, as one who had my own Cody Lundin throwing-matches-in-the-pool moment with my backpack, supposedly full of all my precious research in it, rolling off the rock into the river at the falls of Nacunda-I, and the shower scene that was also used to character assassinate me to prepare my expulsion from the show, it's important to know that it's all staged, and fully scripted.

This is the modus operandi with producers and execs at Disco. They have no respect for talent. They hire talent cheaply, like easy money, and like easy money, they blow it. What they want is someone who will do anything they tell them to do. After all, they don't hire talent to be specialists, though that's what they use in their sales pitch during casting sessions. Cody Lundin is a bonafide survival instruction. He's been doing it for decades. Keith Plaskett was hired because he was a bonafide treasure hunter. I was hired because I was a published author with a bestselling memoir about having been on an internationally recognized treasure hunt that put me in a communist Vietnam re-education prison for eleven months when I was eighteen years old.

What they really want is meat for the grinder, to sell a façade. Cody was a survival instructor who said many of the stunts would never be attempted by someone who was truly trying to survive. Plaskett and I often gave suggestions as to what would really happen and how to do it truthfully and accurately. They never took any advice from us when it came to what we were to say and do. It all comes from some scriptwriter that they hid under an executive producer credit at the end of each episode. You'll recognize our scriptwriter on TQ:SI as Executive Producer Anuj Majumdar.

It's no wonder they protected Joseph Teti. Teti never complained or tried to keep the production true to the content. He just did what was required, no matter how fake or outlandish. This is reality TV, remember; this is Hollywood making millions off low, extremely low, overhead.

According to a WASHINGTON POST article on January 2, 2016, David Zaslav said, "The typical Discovery show costs $400,000 an hour to make, while scripted shows, with their cinematic set pieces and Hollywood caliber fashion, can cost $2 million to $4 million an hour."

The average calculation is that $5 million will bring $50 million. If you really have a big hit, $5 million will bring in $150 million when you figure the international returns. Is it any wonder that DC will do anything to protect its investment (and Teti is an investment), even protect a person who has profited from stolen valor, glaringly through his illegally collecting pay from the DFAS, and through a production that should never have been contracted out?

Many who have heard parts of this story ask, when did this all start? I used to love Discovery, History Channel, TLC, and all those great channels, they'd say in the same breath. Initially, I, too, thought the Discovery Channel of now is the same Discovery of ten years ago, that I also enjoyed watching. Not now. It can all be nailed down to 2011. That's when Mykel Hawke and his wife, Ruth England, were brought to the Silver Springs headquarters of Discovery Communications, and was told by Clark Bunting, President and General Manager of Discovery Channel, that MAN, WOMAN, WILD had broken records in female audience draw. It was also the second year that MTV had amazing, record breaking audience ratings with JERSEY SHORE: 6 million in 2010, and 8 million in 2011. DUCK DYNASTY, another scripted reality TV show, would grab 6 million in 2012.

Bunting walked Mykel and Ruth up past the floor that had fifty lawyers, a legal force that would have their importance made clear only a few years down the road, when Hawke and his wife Ruth England would be fighting for their lives in court, as a result of Discovery Communications protecting Joseph Teti. Funny how that works with Discovery Communications. I get assaulted, and then Brett Tutor jumps me while I'm defending myself, and he's groomed by Discovery to be the boy next door on a TLC show called TRADING SPACES. Jeremy Whalen, has brother smuggle graverobbed artifacts from Peru to Argentina in order to salt fake archeological dig sites for TQ:SI, and in a coked up state, commits assault and battery on me in Argentina, and then Discovery Communications rewards him with a new role on Season 3 in Bolivia. What a twisted world, but chickens do come home to roost.

Mykel and Ruth went up to CEO David Zaslav's office, and he reiterated what Bunting had mentioned, how excited they were that Ruth had brought in a such a lucrative female market. Most don't know what advertisers and especially media execs hold up as the holy grail. It's kids ages 15 to 25, because if you get them then, they're brand associated for life. Next is white men, ages 25 to 55, as they're top spenders. But the big school of fish they voyage out for every season, are women of all ages, because they have spending power and numbers irrelevant of age.

This was a momentous time. It was at this time that CEO David Zaslav actively targeted the female market, and to do so, he put major effort into signing female execs that he recruited in Los Angeles. And that's where the slippery slope began, not because of hiring women, but because it led to Eileen O'Neill becoming president of Discovery Channel, and most importantly, Discovery Communications opening an office Los Angeles. That's like AP, UPI, Reuters, Fox News and CNN firing all its heavily experienced hard news journalists and hiring Hollywood film directors and producers to provide content. Seems farfetched, until you realize that's exactly what happened at Discovery.

It all occurred specifically in order to reach that female audience. It's actually a very solid marketing approach when you think about the targeted market and understand the differences between the male and female psychology of the human species. We like to think we work and think the same, but in reality, we don't, for good reason. If we didn't think and act differently between men and women, we'd have gone extinct centuries ago—like the emotion-stirring phrase in JERRY MAGUIRE, that melted the hearts of women around the world, and filled the coffers of TriStar Pictures, "We complete each other..."

There are multi-billion-dollar businesses based on these the differences. One of them is the romance novel industry. Billions of dollars are netted each year. This media was specifically designed to appeal to the emotional and romantic side of a woman. One of the other major industries is the dating industry, specifically the variety of courses and books on the subject of teaching men how to seduce women through using words to create and guide images in their minds, and resulting feelings in their bodies. To get the average man, all a woman pretty much needs to do is have a great body, cute face, and most men are already at a woman's beck and call, as men are hardwired more visually to respond to stimuli, than the internal mental dialogue women have developed over thousands of years to be so responsive to. Hundreds of thousands of subscriptions to Playboy and Penthouse couldn't have been wrong, nor the billions of dollars still collected from porn, whose major audience has generally in the past been male.

What better way to reach the female mind than hire women, and base operations in Hollywood, where there are tons of cheap scriptwriters, showrunners, field producers, line producers, camera operators, all that's necessary for producing and; and they're always looking for work, or their big break? For a society so concerned with their figures and visual appearances, Hollywood is always hungry. Taking documentary work to Hollywood was like giving the keys to historical record to those whose job was to rewrite and fabricate history. When the US Government needed propaganda in WWII, it didn't go to journalists. It reigned in journalists with censorship. When the US Government went to Hollywood, it went to buy the tools to sway the masses, by stirring up emotions toward patriotic action.

When Discovery went to Hollywood, it went with the intention of attracting a larger female audience that would appeal to bigger spending advertisers, using the same emotion-stirring tools. While they did so, they really ramped up the musical chairs, a shell game. David Zaslav is known for firing and moving employee around at Discovery, but it's not to shake things up to get the creative juices going, as often reported. It's in order to make it appear as if things have changed, when in reality they haven't.

It became clear that during Eileen O'Neill's time at the helm of Discovery Channel, the scripting on what Zaslav likes to call "true-life" documentary ramped up exponentially. That's when the "true-life" megalodon, mermaids and eaten alive by tired unhungry anaconda were broadcast. It led to the shake-up that Zaslav is known for, and O'Neill was replaced with Rich Ross, previously of Disney. This was Discovery's further traveling down the rabbit of hole of inviting the fox into the henhouse.

At first, it appeared as if a change of someone at the wheel would bring new blood and creative ideas to the corporation, where the label "corporation" automatically draws the image of a large beast, lumbering too heavy to move out of its own way. True to form under Zaslav's musical chairs style of direction, putting Ross at the helm was as impacting as a BB gun on a large African elephant. While a real documentarian would never consider ideas for dramatization being applied on set by various reality TV networks, someone from Hollywood, well-versed in the tools of drama, such as scripts, and major post-production, what Discovery was doing out of its Los Angeles office would be chilling to anyone calling themselves a documentarian.

While a real "true-life" documentarian would have fired anyone who had even attempted the things that O'Neill had done during her time in charge, CEO David Zaslav gave her a promotion, saying of her in THE HOLLYWOOD REPORTER:

"One of the key pillars of Discovery's success over the past eight years has been our significant investment in world-class content across all screens, and part of that strategy has focused on strengthening our in-house studio capabilities, acquiring more IP across new genres and formats, and bringing some of the world's top production houses into our company. Eileen is one of the very best we have at Discovery. In this new role, she will accelerate the growth, output and development of our production engines, and oversee the strategy and investment in new programming, new content creators, new categories and new technologies."

That translates to: Eileen O'Neill successfully hoodwinked the global audience by defrauding them with fake content, created to stir emotions, and get past the bull-shit meter by advertising it as "reality", or "true life" TV, when there's nothing true or real about, other than the constant "ca-ching!" of the cash register.

Of late "Fake News" has been a rallying point for the public in its disgust at how the news media has been reporting world events, totally missing the point of how the media has been able to dupe the public with its propaganda paraded around as news. *It has only been successful due to the ground work laid on the minds of the masses through the reality TV industry.*

If only it was just a Discovery Communication's flaw that can be easily corrected by Discovery Communications' board of directors jettisoning Zaslav. I thought it was just TQ:SI, and EATEN ALIVE, both field produced by MAK Pictures for Discovery Communications. That was until I was watching HUNTING HITLER, on A&E's flagship History Channel, specifically episode 2 of Season 2, titled THE COMPOUND.

There were three scenes that caught my eye: the scene on the Parana River with Tim Kennedy and a female piloting the inflatable, the scene with Kennedy striping down to his black Ranger panties, and finally the scene with Kennedy and journalist Gerrard Williams, author of GREY WOLF: THE ESCAPE OF ADOLF HITLER. In the first scene, immediately recognizable, is an Argentine boating and sailing instructor by the name of Leandra Burtnik.

Leandra's one of the best sailing instructors in South America. She was also our boat operator, but outside of scene on TQ:SI. Instead, the showrunner had me operate the outboard while Brett Tutor jumped off the top deck of the platform boat and we sped to extract Mehgan in the totally scripted scene where she was supposedly lost underwater, and Jeremy went with his totally scripted for drama blood bucket scene—I never saw a single piranha my whole time in Argentina: the fixer couldn't find one to save his life. We ate false piranhas in one scene.

The next scene was again with Leandra, where Kennedy strips to his Ranger panties and jumps in the river and swims to the bank like he's doing a beach recon. There was no reason whatsoever for this scene to have occurred. Why? This scene was shot near the "Hitler House", which is known also as the Bormann House, as in Martin Bormann, Adolf Hitler's chief of the Nazi Party's Chancellery, who escaped Germany at the end of the war. Seems only the rest of the world doesn't know this: bad people don't always get their just desserts as we wish they would. Or, as Mykel Hawke mentioned when we were going over the evidence of all the criminal, and just plain dirty bag of activities Discovery Communications has been up to under David Zaslav's watch, "The bigger the crimes, the less likely the ones involved will be punished."

Figure 38. Tim Kennedy and Leandra Burtnik.

As said, totally for drama's sake at the other reality TV network, Tim Kennedy makes the swim and short reconnaissance, in a scenario, for information which a quick look at the tourist map for Argentina's Teyu Cuare Provincial Park on the Parana River could have easily provided. But this is supposed to be a remote part of Argentina, right? Like the falls, of

Nacunda-i? Right...The falls in another national park in Paraguay. Bormann's House, of the "Hitler House" is on the park map. It's right next to San Ignacio. As a matter of fact, you can get a tour to take you there from the Rio de Club, a beautiful boating and waterski club, just upriver from the Bormann House that History Channel shot episode 2, THE COMPOUND. I'm sure for lunch Kennedy and the rest of the HH cast had Leandra drive everyone back there, just like she did for us on TQ:SI: the fried local jungle catfish is good.

We had our lunch there often while filming the fake piranha, caiman and Bormann House scenes. Downriver, about four-hundred yards is the Bormann House, and upriver about three-hundred yards was where we shot piranha attack, the get Mehgan-out-of-the-water-with-Brett-on-the-inflatable scene, and the other various scenes at the fake Guarani village excavation. That whole hillside, that was supposed to be an archeological site of an ancient Guarani village, was cleared out by a variety of employees from the Rio de Club wanting to make an extra buck, of which the local fixer, Tambo Film, was all to ready spread around the area. Tambo Film, by the way, based out of Lima, Peru, figures into the Discovery Communications web in a way I didn't know until I investigated further into the final Joseph Teti/Discovery psychotic episode that led to his being prevented from entering ANY Discovery Communication's property. Don't worry, you'll read all about it later in this book—it's a juicy one.

Ñacunday Falls
Paraguay

Figure 39. In the bottom screenshot from HUNTING HITLER, an arrow in the upper part of photo marks where Brett Tutor would months later act as if he had just found a pterodactyl egg-like stone, with a carved circle and triangle, in the upper screenshot form TQ:SI. The Rio Club is just out of screen in the lower left of the HUNTING HITLER screenshot—Great fishing for freshwater dorado up to 20 pounds below the bluffs!

By the end of this book, I'm sure the local tourism entities will be more than delighted to use this copy to put together tours for a variety of visitors who want to get the whole, "let's make fun of the Gringos coming down here to make fakeumentaries for the rest of the world" tour. It's all good money to them, especially as they suffer the effects of the socialist dictatorships they thought were going to be better than the previous military dictatorships. No such luck with the latest administrations, as evidenced by such socialist leaders as Maduro, or Rousseff, running to Europe to enjoy her millions of dollars she stole from her citizens.

The last is the scene, that made me drop my chin in amazement and laugh out loud, was starring Gerrard Williams and Tim Kennedy. If not for having our drivers been Leo Ayala and Omar Armoa, Leo with his trademark Argentine second wife always at his side, a thermos a mate, I'd probably have not keyed on the image of Williams and Kennedy asking Ayala and Armoa if there were any Nazis in Misiones.

In the scene (at about 36 minutes to 37 minutes of THE COMPOUND episode of HUNTING HITLER), Omar does all the talking, while Leo Ayala, his face blurred, works his thermos and sucks on his *maté*...just like we used to drink maté when I'd head to Puerto Iguazu to take a break from cast and crew, who couldn't get away from where Discovery had sequestered us in Puerto Bemberg, because most of the cast and crew couldn't speak Spanish. Armoa and Ayala were our Discovery Channel production "magic bus" drivers, as I'm sure they were for History Channel. Yes, even something as historically important as the hunt for Adolf Hitler has been whittled down to totally scripted reality TV show, written more for emotional impact in order to get that coveted female target market audience than getting the facts straight—as it used to be before when you actually got the facts, but now have to go to H2 Channel, in order to get what was previously offered at the original channel.

Frankly, I find it mindboggling that someone, like Tim Kennedy, who says he was on something as serious as hunting Al Qaeda terrorists would even be on TV, or much less draw so much attention to himself as an MMA fighter. In almost one breath on THE JOE ROGAN EXPERIENCE podcast #027, he talked about how he was excited about being a media recruiting tool for the US Army, as he promoted his latest offering not at A&E, but at Discovery Communications, called HARD TO KILL, and then ironically, mentions the creed of the US Army's Green Berets, the "Quiet Professionals", whose creed states:

> *"I serve quietly, not seeking recognition or accolades.*
> *My goal is to succeed in my mission - and live to succeed again."*

It took me more than 25 years to even talk about what I did in Central America, and when I did, it was at the personal request of my friend and colleague, sniping instructor and book author, and former-MACV-SOG operator Major John Plaster, who told me Eric Holder was railroading a former Green Beret, and fellow paramilitary officer (PMO) by the name of Steve Stormoen. Stormoen was being readied as the unwilling sacrificial lamb in a PR stunt against the previous administration, the Obama Administration even concocting lies to have him imprisoned as a war criminal. Mind, you Obama had killed many more than any president in history using drones. Many nations now think of Obama as a war criminal for his actions during his administration.

Figure 40. Omar Armoa, said, "Anibal Quilvera....[oh, mierda, as he checks his palm for the name given by the director] Anibal Silvero!"

During Central America, there were Salvadoran officers and personnel who committed what would easily be considered war crimes. Their counterparts in the communist front did the same and often worse, but far be it from the FMLN-friendly press to report that. As a matter of fact, NEWSWEEK went so far as to fabricate a lie by using the photo of a group of campesinos sleeping under a tree with a caption saying to effect: photo of campesinos massacred by Salvadoran government forces. My friend, Major John Donovan (Army Special Forces, retired), of SOLDIER OF FORTUNE fame, was there that day in the early 1980s, about the time I was still a midshipman in the US Navy. He was totally disgusted to see what NEWSWEEK had done. "I was there, and you can quote me on that," Donovan told me when I told him I was working on a book on fake news, and how fakeumentaries, such as those done by Michael Moore and Discovery Communications have laid the ground work for fake news being that much more effective on the world's populace.

To go from a time, when combat veterans were returning from Central America, working for MILGROUP, CIA, STATE, and being told to keep your mouth shut, say nothing about what you were doing in Central and South America, even though some of your combat buddies were coming back in body bags, to what the clandestine community has become now, with CIA officers and Navy SEALs publishing books, while barely out service, and Green Berets like Tim Kennedy spouting off about how PTSD is for pussies and that he has killed women and children is truly mind-blowing.

Figure 41. Armoa tries not to look at the "spy cam", while Tim Kennedy walks away and Leo Ayala reloads his maté with his thermos.

Perhaps he didn't get that history memo about the time a number of Jesuit priest and nuns were raped and murdered in El Salvador, and I had to deal with a communist photojournalist from Italy who kept telling me how he would, by hook or crook, get that shot he felt was a true capturing of the "US's war in Central America": a Salvadoran Army chopper flying low over a village in El Salvador, gunning down the unarmed campesinos—just like in Oliver Stone's SALVADOR, except the Italian communist saw a chopper in his creative work, instead of a plane gunning down John Savage.

Tim Kennedy is known as a "businessman" in the special operations community— He stated on his friend Joe Rogan's radio show, that he has the full blessing of SWCS ("Swick"), the John F. Kennedy Special Warfare Center and School, to do what he does publicly. It reminded me that there's nothing new in the world, and that we're just down here reinventing the wheel. Does anyone recall what happened when John Wayne released the movie GREEN BERETS, during the Vietnam War? Or, NAVY SEALs with Charlie Sheen when I was hunting some very fucked up people, who had a license to from the communists down in Latin America in the 1980s?

Each of these special operations groups suffered because of the type of person drawn, specifically those we'd call "glory whores," as compared to those who understand the meaning of service. With Vietnam as an unpopular war after the Tet Offensive, the influx of those volunteering for the US Army, after John Wayne's movie, was a boon in numbers, but not in quality. Many in the SF community say standards we were dropped to fill ranks—"Berets were just being handed out!" was one comment on that time. In the 1980s, well-experienced SEALs were complaining to me about the primadonnas who were filling their ranks after the movie NAVY SEALS released, when it was thought we'd never get into a war— remember, Central America and Latin America were secret wars on par with what Laos and Cambodia were during the 1960s. One chief petty officer buddy of mine, in Seal Team 3 at the time, told me of a kid fresh out of BUDs, who during SEAL training, fired a three shot burst into a van right next to him. The reason given for such a clearly unsafe move, was that the aspiring SEAL was checking his trigger by pulling it—yeah, he didn't get the Budweiser pinned on his chest. This is the dilemma of a military trying to compete with Fortune 500 companies for employees, and using the surreal, bravado, hero-inspiring media from Hollywood, most often filmed, performed, produced and directed by those who couldn't show you how to manipulate a firearm, much less fired one in anger.

Comments by Kennedy, such as:

"So, in 2001, I had a couple of women pregnant. I was a professional fighter, I was working at a bar, I was in grad school, and I was a complete douchebag. I cared more about what pants I was wearing at a party than what was going on in the world. Then I saw some planes crash into the towers. Everyone remembers where they were. I was sitting at a desk at a dot com in commerce before the bubble popped in California. I was working the early shift to answer calls from companies on the East Coast. I was sitting behind my desk watching the live-stream as the second plane flew into the building. There's that moment where I realized that I was a piece of shit. I was a self-serving, narcissistic, ethnocentric fucking piece of shit. I might've had some anger about that, so I walked down to a recruiter's office that day again thinking I was doing something great. I was like the two thousandth person in line, yet again showing what a douchebag I was. I thought I was going to be like the only one there," reminds us that there is a certain type of soldier from which TV and film media, *Hollywood*, attracts. Remember, 9/11 was in 2001…Tim Kennedy joined the US Army on January 4, 2004. As I've said repeatedly about interrogation: you don't have to beat them, you just have to let them talk, and just really listen…They'll tell you everything you need to know.

Figure 42. A&E's Tim Kennedy gratuitous cheesecake moment, that was a totally faked "recon" scene—check the national park map (There's nothing to "find," just using a park trail groomed by the local park rangers and they take you everywhere.)...On TQ:SI, we just tied up the boat and walked ashore.

Just this week, Anthony Bourdain loved by the pro-socialist, one world order crowd, offed himself in France, even though he previously said he had too much to live for, that life was good and he had a young daughter to think about. This is the problem of what reality TV does, and I think you know, it's ALL reality TV these days: whether you're a video opinion personality eating and traveling around the world, an MMA fighter and Green Beret turned Nazi hunter, or a treasure hunter going after Aleixo Garcia's lost Treasure of the Trinity. The question is when will reality TV get real, and away from the scripted for drama that has taken the globe, content fraudulently advertised by networks that would rather hoodwink an audience?

I had hoped that there was some sanctuary for those looking to do real reality TV and true documentaries at the "Dirty Half-Dozen" (that's the name for A&E and her networks for those working at Discovery), but after seeing those scenes on HUNTING HITLER, I've lost hope for the whole reality TV, until the FCC steps in and does a proper reset, and not allowing what the corporations like Discovery Communications are doing: covering up their tracks through post-production editing and re-releasing episodes as they'd done with the BRAVING BOLIVIA episode of Dual Survival, by using a frame from Season 3, Episode 1, in the Atacama Desert of Chile, titled MARS ON EARTH, to close the end of Season 6, Episode 4, the last time Joseph Teti was on DUAL SURVIVAL. It's the scene of a llama herder wearing a hat and a blue sweater. In Chile, it's Teti and Lundin calling out, "Hola!" to her. In Bolivia, it's Matt Graham and Teti, and a cutaway the same scene.

How bad does it have to get before audiences finally turn the channel to deprive Discovery Communications, and all these reality TV producers the revenues they so hungrily lunge for, like wolves fighting over a half-eaten moose carcass?

Figure 43. Close-up of Joseph Teti and Cody Lundin in Chile of Dual Survival.

Figure 44. Joseph Teti and Matt Graham closing scene in Bolivia—amazing isn't it?

Figure 45. When I returned to Argentina a couple months after our TQ:SI Season 2 wrap, in order to check on a security consulting gig for the Prefectura Naval Argentina (Argentine Coast Guard), who have been dealing with major drugs and contraband smuggling from Paraguay—Hezbollah launders money, and a variety of other terrorist organizations get funds from the black market in Ciudad Del Este (Los Tres Fronteras). Our two magic bus drivers, Rolando on the left, and Leo Ayala, who had previously been acting as the Misiones local drinking mate, his face blurred, while Armoa did the talking on HUNTING HITLER, Season 2, Episode 2, THE COMPOUND.

10 TWEEDLEDEE & TWEEDLEDUM

Figure 46. Midshipman Graham, backrow, under the "XIN" in USS Lexington, at NAS Pensecola, 1982.

Don't screw the pooch, is a term we were well acquainted with during our orientation at NAS Pensecola. As we, in my squadron of officer candidates in 1982, were all excited about graduating university and going off to fly the then new F18 Hornet, to be told that screwing the pooch was used as a warning to not plaster your jet on the deck of an aircraft, we did our best to not screw up. Evidently, CEO David Zaslav and others at Discovery

Communications weren't taught this warning or were just so arrogant as to think they're untouchables. More importantly, that when you play with dangerous animals, you can get hurt. In the case of reality TV, it's what seems to be a common pattern of hiring psychopaths, predators.

Going back through the years, and looking at such programs as SONS OF GUNS, AMERICAN GUNS, BERING SEA GOLD, DUAL SURVIVAL, GOLD RUSH, and the never released production of LONE OPERATOR, and the as yet to be released third season of TREASURE QUEST: SNAKE ISLAND (shot in Bolivia in fall of 2017), reminds us that that it's all about drama; and what better way to build drama than to hire a crew of actors, and throw a wild card, an easily certified psychopath, into the mix? Think about it, what better way to make people scatter and run for their lives than to throw a grenade into the room like this—can you see the emotional high points?

Talk to a variety of criminal investigators and they'll easily tell you that you can profile for a psychopath. Former FBI profiler and body language expert Joe Navarro wrote an excellent book on the subject, titled DANGEROUS PERSONALITIES: AN FBI PROFILER SHOWS YOU HOW TO IDENTIFY AND PROTECT YOURSELF FROM HARMFUL PEOPLE, and did just that professionally for years as a counter-terrorist. Normally, any healthy work environment HR administrator would profile such people in order to screen them out. Navarro did so when he interviewed a potential new hire for the FBI and recommended that the individual not become a new agent. What if, instead, a company profiled for psychopaths to do the opposite?

What if Discovery Communications is actively hiring talent to build drama in their shows? What if Discovery Communications were not only using a psychological profile in order to build a cast of characters for their emotion-stirring broadcasts on such shows as DEADLIEST CATCH, BERING SEA GOLD, DUAL SURVIVAL, and TREASURE QUEST: SNAKE ISLAND, but adding to the mix sex, drugs and anything that might jack up the tension on set?

According to Steve Riedel, formerly of BERING SEA GOLD, for drama's sake was exactly why a female producer was plying fellow cast member Zeke Tenhoff with: sex and drugs all hours of the night. Now, if you've been on a production, reality TV, or bonafide film, you know that's kind of normal. Drugs and sex are rampant on sets. What's not normal is plying a cast member with various stimulants in order to have talent so beat, and frankly bonkers, that when productions puts them in front of the camera, they're exactly the loose cannon, show monkey, that brings in the viewer looking for a train wreck to get off on. Documentary? No. Reality? No. Pile up on I-5 drawing the attention of rubberneckers? Absolutely!

The big joke in Alaska is that most all of us know what is happening on the shows shot here. And, of course there are those who come to Alaska drawn by what they have romanticized in their minds after looking at Alaska through the lens of a reality TV show.

The Kilchers don't live in the wilds of Alaska—they live within ten minutes of downtown Homer: they just frame the drone shots so you never see further down the shore of Kachemak Bay, just like you don't see the waterski club on the Parana River on TQ:SI and HUNTING HITLER. To even come close to what Yule Kilcher experienced in 1939, when he first came to Alaska to check out possible homesteading sites, nowadays you'd have to venture deep into the wilderness of the Alaska Interior, miles north and west of Fairbanks, and miles east and south of Barrow, which puts you in some of the most inhospitable wilderness of Alaska.

If you think any part of Alaska is holding a plethora of homesteading areas like ALASKA: THE LAST FRONTIER tries to create from what was an illusion in the first place, think again. Eivin and Eve Kilcher will not starve in winter if he doesn't get a black bear—he'll just make the gorgeous, ten-minute drive from the Kilcher homestead down to Safeway, or McDonald's in Homer. Your greatest dangers in the Homer area aren't the bears; it's the methamphetamine addicts trying to steal your stuff, and the Trustafarians, trust fund babies who come to Alaska to lose more old family money than the average middle-class breadwinner will ever earn in three lifetimes, while playing at homesteading—if it doesn't work out they can always go back to their old family mansion in the Lower Forty-Eight.

There's a reason that Yule Kilcher decided to found his almost hippie, beatnik community for German and Swiss artists here at the End of the Road. Yes, it's the same End of the Road that Tom Bodett learned to leave the light on for Motel 6. His house was just across the way from the A-frame I lived in when I first arrived in the area in 1990 to come to grips with my memories of the war in Central America and write the first draft of THE BAMBOO CHEST. What better place for Kilcher to found a commune of Swiss and German artists, than an area that seems so like Northern California, except spruce instead of California redwoods and where the hippies carry guns, too, to put a moose on the table?

There's also an anger in Alaskans at how Discovery Communications depicts Alaskans by using these actors. As depicted by ALASKAN BUSH PEOPLE, it's clear they don't even want to use real Alaskans in their shows, evidenced by the legal action the state of Alaska took against the Brown family for drawing their PFD , or permanent fund, for which in order to receive you have to reside in Alaska for a set amount of time each year to draw. Many who reside in The Bush rely on this annual infusion of cash from oil taken out of our beautiful state to augment their income from trapping, fishing, art, farming, logging, and mining. It's an insult when someone as affluent as the Brown family, who descend from a wealthy

Texas oil family would not only not reside in the state to fulfill the, frankly very easy to fulfill, requirements of residency, but to draw it considering how much they must be making off the show and the speaking circuit.

But, that's the way it is with Discovery, façade before facts. Drama before reality, even going so far as to break international laws, criminally endangering Discovery cast and crew, to bring that drama to the viewer's living rooms. In the process they bring some very unsavory types into your living room, too.

In the DIAGNOSTIC AND STATISTICAL MANUAL OF MENTAL DISORDERS (DSM), *antisocial dissociative disorder* is the term used for *psychopath* and *sociopath*. Many play with the terminology, but outside the medical community, a person who is hot-headed and self-absorbed would be labelled a sociopath. They just don't get along with society. A psychopath on the other hand, according to WebMD, is "cold-hearted" and calculating. They carefully plot their moves and use aggression in a planned-out way to get what they want. If they're after more money or status in the office, for example, they'll make a plan to take out any barriers that stand in the way, even if it's another person's job or reputation."

What better way to describe my co-star, Jeremy Thomas Whalen, and his younger brother James Kendall Whalen (otherwise known as Kendall D. Mckibben), of Washington State? I would not learn until I was sucker punched by my co-star on set in Argentina, that he and his brother had been secretly attacking me online for more than a year, trying to smear me in a major defamation campaign that started all the way back at the beginning of production of first season of TQ:SI in Brazil. What a pair of deviants these two make, and from what I've sadly had to find out about their family history, it's clear that they don't fall far from the family tree: environment over genetics, creates psychopaths.

Wikipedia, Amazon and variety of Internet outlets had been their modus operandi, finally resorting to a desperate act of cyberstalking and harassing me directly through emails and sending me photos taken at SEATAC airport, as if to threaten, they knew where I lived and where I went…Stupidly, these morons sent it to my private email address: only MAK Pictures, Discovery and members of the cast and crew would have known that email address.

Cyberstalking is a modern criminal activity that appears to surpass the psychologically damaging crime of stalking and harassment. As FBI profiler Joe Navarro has stated, the best thing that a victim of a psychopath, a predator, can do is to just put distance between you and them. In the old days, it was a lot easier to do that. You could get a restraining order, and depending on the country and state, or province, you could physically defend yourself with whatever means were legal, should they go past stalking into the realm of causing, or threatening to cause, bodily harm.

What the technology the Internet brings into the world of stalking and harassment is that recognizing and identifying the perpetrator is made that much more difficult, because an attack can be launched not just from next door, but from anywhere in the world that the predator has an Internet connection. Law enforcement, even with the new and seemingly ineffective laws, is still pretty much powerless to stop this new scourge on society that thrives through enabling predators to do better what they'd been doing well all along—cause emotional distress. It has led to a new population of people who though never having been in combat or been in law enforcement or emergency medicine are dealing with the effects of various forms of resulting psychological duress, such as post-traumatic stress.

Because of how I'd already learned from a friends' experiences about how nutjobs come out of the woodwork when you appear on TV, I've made descriptions about me on the internet as vague as possible: When there are inaccuracies, such as those on the page that Discovery Communications put up on me, where they said I went through sniper training at Salvadoran Navy SEAL course during the war, I didn't correct the writer at Discovery: After I completed the Salvadoran Navy's Special Forces course I went through sniper training at El Salvador's *Centro de Entrenamiento Militar de la Fuerza Armada* (CEMFA), Military Training Center of the Armed Forces, which most people haven't even heard of, unless you were with the Salvadoran military, US State Department, CIA, or MILGROUP; or you were with the FMLN trying to target it, during the civil war in El Salvador.

It was just down the road from La Union, where the Salvadoran Navy SEAL base was at Punta Ruca. I'd received other training over those years, of course, but I'm still most proud of the diploma I received from the Salvadoran Navy, because there are only two Americans who received it, and the other one is Steve Salisbury of SOLDIER OF FORTUNE MAGAZINE, one of the best sources of unadulterated reporting during that time—no wonder you would always find the latest issue in someone's office at Langley or the Pentagon, and sometimes at State.

Figure 47. The author trying to survive one more day to get his diploma in 1986 at Salvadoran Navy Special Forces.

In August of 2016, I would notify our "talent manager" at Discovery Communications of something very disturbing. *Discovery talent manager* was in of itself something very disturbing, but that's another matter—most talent has their own managers and agents; they aren't normally conferred upon cast by a network, especially a network that tries to distance itself from its employees by trying to call them contractors. But, we, the cast, had one, and his name was Dan Jolly. Unlike real talent managers, who are intended to drum up more acting jobs for their clients, Discovery Communications talent manager are there to control the talent, making sure they keep to the employee contract and don't appear on a competing TV show, or come out with a book, unless it's okayed by management.

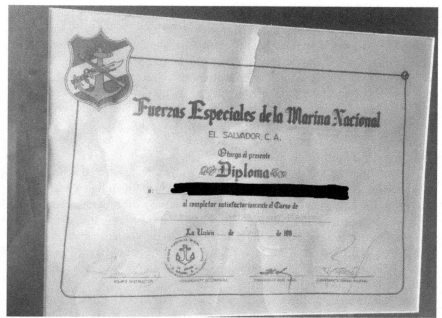

Figure 48. The author's diploma received after graduating from the Salvadoran Navy Special Forces Course during the war—One of only two received by non-Salvadorans.

Mine was there to make sure any new books I wrote would become property of Discovery Communications, and since I'd been in the book business for 20 years by then, there was no way I was going to sign a contract with them about a memoir or anything of the like: I was amazed at how they had tried to sucker me into a contract more mind-blowing than the one I had initially signed for TQ:SI. What writer, except a hungry one, would sign a contract with any company, where they actually have to split their book advance with the company, after the agent is paid their rightful share, too?! Evidently, Discovery legal thinks this is a good deal—for suckers.

I've held the position of senior editor, and editor in chief at magazines. I've edited books. I've ghost-written books for much more famous personalities, even writing in their own voice. So, here's the purpose of an advance. It's two-fold. One is to give you a percentage, often about 5-percent of what they think they'll gross in sales. The second is to make sure your bills are paid while you work on the book, so that you're not doing odd-jobs to make sure you're housed, clothed, and fed, which could possibly affect your deadline. A book advance is a tradition that goes back to the patronage of the wealthy and influential, who, for centuries before modern publishing houses, brought the works of many famous authors, musicians, painters to the public.

When an entity, such as Discovery, which acts like the old film houses (notoriously like Metro-Goldwyn Mayer in the 1930s, when they kept their actors like starved and amphetamine-pumped racehorses in the stables, taking them out for only a run or race), turn and look elsewhere. You can do better. If you don't think you can, then you should really investigate the reason of what and why for your looking at such corporate beasts. As you'll soon see, much like the cast of Mark Burnett's SURVIVOR, reality TV came to be a great way to make millions off the low-overhead of poorly paid actors, who will never go onto any other production of worth that they think this media will bring them.

About the time I was becoming more and more frustrated with the get everything for nothing attitude from Discovery's publishing department, I was getting an influx of new emails from a variety of cyberstalkers. If not for Keith Plaskett, finally admitting to me that they were coming from one person, Jeremy Whalen's brother, James Kendall Whalen, aka Kendall D. McKibben, who ran his IP address under his shell company, Timbuktwo, LLC. of Enumclaw, WA, I would have never been able to put together such a solid case of what they'd been up to.

As mentioned earlier, the psychology industry prefers to label psychopaths as antisocial dissociative disorder, but that includes a lot of other personalities and qualities. In the world of criminal investigation, and hunting down really screwed up people that can, and will, do major harm to others, physically, emotionally, socially, and financially, they are called psychopaths, and they can be so much more dangerous than any viper or landmine you might encounter in the jungle.

When Plaskett informed me, it was our co-star Jeremy Whalen who had been rewriting my Wikipedia page with his brother James, or Jaime, or Kendall, as he also likes to be called, I was frankly more than a little perturbed. When I first went to Wikipedia to read it in 2017, I found the rewrite hilarious and entertaining. The Whalen brothers had rewritten the story of my imprisonment by the Socialist Republic of Vietnam in 1983 to 1984 as the result of being newbie photojournalist covering a British comedy-actor going after Captain Kidd's treasure on an island off the coast of Vietnam as me having gone on an "oyster hunt."

Curious, and knowing which IP address to track, I followed back through the months and years. That's when I became furious. The attempts at trying to defame and libel me through the Internet, just to get me knocked off TQ:SI, in order to make James Whalen's brother Jeremy the team leader on the show, went all the way back to 2015—I was livid! Even more so, I realized that all those years Jeremy had been using the pretense of being all friendly with me, he had been doing a good job of slandering me amongst our coworkers.

During all those times that Jeremy Whalen was being all friendly, and trying to build rapport with me, he was working behind the veil of his psychosis with his brother, to do some very dark, sick and twisted deeds. As you can see in appendix exhibits, Jeremy and his brother had the audacity and lack of healthy societal upbringing to write. Who but a couple of psychopaths would rewrite a very public page to state the following?

ABOUT JAIL TIME IN VIETNAM|last=VO|first=KIM|date=March 26, 2005|publisher=Mercury News|pages=1B}} </ref> is an American author of [[political thriller]] novels and adventure [[memoir]]s. He is a former [[War photography|combat photographer]], who was imprisoned in [[Vietnam]] for [[illegal entry|illegally entering the country]] while supposedly looking for [[buried treasure|treasure buried]] by [[Captain Kidd]].	ABOUT JAIL TIME IN VIETNAM|last=VO|first=KIM|date=March 26, 2005|publisher=Mercury News|pages=1B}} </ref> is an American author of [[political thriller]] novels and adventure [[memoir]]s. He is a former [[Child photography|animal photographer]], who was imprisoned in [[Vietnam]] for [[illegal photograph|illegally photographing children]] while supposedly looking for [[buried treasure|treasure buried]] by [[Captain Kidd]].

Figure 49. Wikipedia libelous statements by James and Jeremy Whalen.

9/11 was a striking example of what happens when an intelligence service relies too much on signal intelligence, anything related to the gathering of intelligence through technological means such as spy satellites, the Internet, etc. Human intelligence, of which we seemed to have been lacking, or likely more importantly, ignoring at the time, is that intelligence collected by real people with real boots on the ground, interviewing and talking to people. If not for Keith's admission that all the attacks were coming from Jeremy and his brother, I'd not have been able to get such a solid grasp of what was happening. Without human intelligence, or what we called HUMINT (versus signal intelligence [SIGINT]), I probably wouldn't had learned about the Jeremy and James Whalen dark family history, and the *hows* and *whys* of their attempts at character assassination for Jeremy's personal financial gain.

Jeremy did mention on the magic bus that he lived in Hoonah, Alaska with extended family when he was a teen. I thought he had just come to Alaska to do a bit of adventuring, making some extra summer cash working for his family on a logging operation. What I couldn't have imagined was that it was a result of his father's arrest as a pedophile. In consequence, according to Keith Plaskett, the mother had to heal in a sanitarium, while the father was in prison, and the children were farmed out by child protective services. According to Keith, that's one of the reasons that James Whalen had his name legally changed.

When Keith went further in giving me the full skinny on Jeremy Whalen, after I think Keith finally, fully, realized Jeremy had been his friend only to see what he could get out of him (per form for a predatory psychopath, especially riding on his shirttails to get on TQ:SI), it was like a faucet had been turned on. He was more than forthcoming with information.

At first, I thought Keith had said Jeremy and James' father had sex with an underage sister, Myron Whalen's sister, but when I received the arrest report from the King County, Washington clerk it wasn't the father's sister at all, but Jeremy and James' sister! That was creepy and sick enough already, but it was as I was reading the arrest report that I got a really bad raising of the hackles on the back of my neck. I had a similar feeling when I met Jeremy for the first time, but I stupidly ignored it, like most of us who do who have a healthy upbringing in a good family—like most of us did in the pre-1980s, and before the carefreeness-destroying major coverage of predators in the news, and society telling us to rightfully be that much warier of strangers. I realized what was making the hair on the back of my next stand on end was a part of the report I was reading:

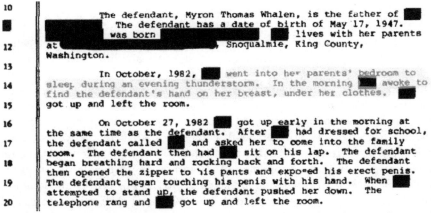

Figure 50. If this section of Myron Whalen's arrest record doesn't make your skin crawl after reading what Keith Plaskett told me about Jeremy's daughter's sleeping arrangements with her father...Full copy in the exhibits in the appendix.

"...went into her parent's bedroom to sleep during an evening thunderstorm." made my skin crawl as I recalled what Keith Plaskett had told me about this little bit of family history, and then mentioned that he found it disturbing that Jeremy's daughter still slept in Jeremy and his wife's bed. Keith raised his own daughters under some major trials and he considered it very inappropriate that Jeremy had his daughter still sleeping in their bed at her age.

I met Jeremy's daughter, when he brought his Peruvian wife and daughter to the set just before we left Brazil. The daughter seemed around eleven years old. She was definitely a bit too old to be sleeping in bed with her father.

Jeremy said that he lives in the South America because he can't deal with living in the US. I've found these kinds of expats to be of two kinds. There was my father who went overseas to find adventure, and in the process did some good as a member of USAID, and later as Director of Asia/Pacific Rim for Kohler Company, out of Wisconsin, and I think, even though he despised the Agency after our time in Vietnam, he did good even working for the CIA. Then there are those others who are overseas because they're hiding out from the law, society in their homeland, and think they can more easily get away with despicable acts that would never be allowed in the US, the UK, Canada, or Western Europe.

Considering how long he'd lived in South America, and how many women he'd married from Peru, I asked Jeremy one day while we were filming in Argentina, if he ever got a Peruvian passport, since having a passport from a country other than the US, during these days of terrorists easily recruited, educated and deployed through the Internet, can be helpful for personal safety while travelling. He said he investigated it but didn't think it was worth it. Imagine the smile that overtook me when I surprised him the last day I saw him in the lobby of our hotel in Argentina, and low and behold he had an easily recognized Peruvian passport.

When I say I surprised him, it was enough for him to attempt nonchalantly hiding the passport with his hand, though I could see its color and recognize it being from Peru—it surely wasn't his wife's as she'd have needed it to stay in Salinas, Ecuador. This guy lives through deception and diversion: the day he assaulted me, it was out of character for someone who calculates and tries to keep two to three steps ahead of everyone, and I mean everyone. Verifiable psychopath—manipulator of the most cunning, almost.

Taking into account the Whalen family history (and a present situation in which a diligent investigator from Washington State child protective services (CPS) might look into the activities and track of Jeremy Whalen, and possibly James Kendal Whalen [as said before, psychopaths, of which all pedophiles are clearly are, come to being through environment], the same entity that took action in the Myron Thomas Whalen case); the William Hayden case, where the patriarch of the SONS OF GUNS family was found guilty of sexual liberties with his daughters, which put him in prison for life; and the Honey Boo Boo pedophilia story at TLC, there seems to be a pattern at Discovery Communications. This is an underlying theme that even goes into a show that's supposed to be all good family, Alaska homestead fun, in the form of ALASKA: THE LAST FRONTIER. Just ask Sunrise Kilcher, or just get into a conversation with her about Yule and you get the whole story, of what kind of relationship she was thrust into with her father, when her mother left Alaska with another man. It's a very un-Disney Swiss Family Robinson story.

Pedophilia and rewriting and whitewashing old family wrongs through the illusion of TV and film are not new to Hollywood. Read the biographies of some very famous film and TV actors through history, and it's clear many came from abusive and broken homes. They escaped their pasts by taking on the life of another person, if for just the time of that moment on set, through another person's character. What's different in reality TV, is that it's still acting, it's still make believe; but this time you're playing yourself, just a different version of yourself: the one created by the scriptwriter—many times contrary to the real you. It's a whole new world of documentary. It's the land of fakeumentary, where Hollywood has taken its creative license and built Frankenstein's monster.

Interestingly, and this is typical of those who have been a victim of a psychopath, is that Keith was still defending Jeremy, by saying that if Jeremy didn't get hooked up romantically with Mehgan, she wouldn't have manipulated him toward joining forces against Keith, in their bid to take over and make the show all about them. I smiled when he told me that. I'd already been assaulted on set by Jeremy and Brett, and I had no rosy views of either, especially since I'd already been doing my own investigations, greatly aided by Keith's filling in of the blanks that made my case so much stronger.

I will admit that even though I was collecting such damning evidence against Jeremy Whalen and his brother James, I just couldn't believe that anyone who wasn't already killing and raping, as is the more common interpretation of the term "psychopath," was doing what they were doing. Who would slander and libel another that they didn't even know with such terminology as would have gotten me thrown in jail if anyone actually believed such libel. But, then going back through the family history of Jeremy and his brother and understanding that psychopaths might be the result of genetics, it also takes environment to really develop a psychopath.

Joe Navarro has an excellent list of signs his book, HOW TO SPOT A PSYCHOPATH. There are many more, but these were the ones standing out as I thought of my cyberstalkers, the Whalen brothers, and checked out this quick read:

1. *Disregards the rights of others by abusing them and taking advantage of them.*
2. *Is manipulative, gets people to do things for him.*
3. *Was a juvenile delinquent.*
4. *Has narcissistic qualities: is self-absorbed, self-promoting.*
5. *Has a sense of entitlement and things he's above others.*
6. *Proudly flaunts violations of law and rules.*

7. *Is deceitful, enjoys lying; lies when doesn't have to.*

8. *Feels that rules or laws are for others to obey, not for him.*

9. *Repeatedly violates laws, breaks rules of custom or decency.*

10. *Recognizes weaknesses in others quickly and seeks to exploit their weaknesses.*

11. *Proudly flaunts violations of law or rules.*

12. *Recognizes weaknesses in others quickly and seeks to exploit their weaknesses.*

13. *Blames life, circumstances, parents, others, even victims, for his actions.*

14. *Control and dominance play a big part in his life. Tries to dominate others.*

15. *Takes delight in duping others.*

16. *Doesn't take criticism well.*

17. *Skilled at gaining trust of others for the sake of taking advantage of them.*

18. *Committing crimes come easy to him, very agile at it.*

19. *Plays psychological "head games" to keep others down or harass them.*

20. *Being respected and having power are big issues for him.*

21. *He overvalues himself and his abilities, devalues others easily.*

There are one-hundred and forty more indicators in Navarro's list of which Jeremy and his brother easily fulfill, by their actions, and what I've personally observed in their character and demeanor. As indicators of a psychopath, these are indicators that could have easily been turned into casting questions asked by Discovery Communications: Meisterheim, Teti, Whalen...BERING SEA GOLD, DUAL SURVIVAL, TQ:SI. As I thought about that list that many take years to gather in their own minds, but Navarro so succinctly put together, I thought back on those days back in Los Angeles, when we were all on our chemistry test. Anyone trained in profiling—profiling is exactly what a casting agent and a producer do before and on a chemistry test—could have easily seen that Jeremy's actions not only on set, and how desperately had he had tried to get on TQ:SI before that, were indicators of a narcissistic psychopath.

Considering the number of psychopaths on other Discovery Communication's shows, many might think that it goes beyond this type of media accidently drawing this type of talent. It's more than just those going for casting, thinking the role will lead to anything else other than a big money day for Discovery Communications, and through major stock holdings, big money to CEO David Zaslav. Tracking all the castings and casting, there's strong case for Discovery Communications having a template targeting psychopaths as talent, and specifically casting one or two, to throw in amongst the rest.

Having the Whalen brothers after me as a two-pronged, cyberstalking and harassment team was becoming tiring after a while. Jeremy would be all friendly and charming, while his brother worked behind the curtain, like many psychopaths and just plain, below-average, common criminals, like to imagine of themselves in images of grandeur—all that power that's so lacking in their real lives. It's clear from the progression of corrupting the Wikipedia page on me, to sending threatening emails from various IP addresses resolving from Enumclaw, such 204.106.232.135, 204.106.238.41, 204.106.233.153, 204.106.238.248, and when James, (or Jaime as he likes to be called in South America along his drug running route) got the idea that leaving your IP address all over the place might not be a good idea, he went with the Yohimbinihydrochloride nickname: criminals like to take credit for the crimes as an ego stroke—Jaime, James, Kendall, whatever he likes to call himself, must be into freebasing.

Freebasing is the act of drawing cocaine alkaloids out of the cocaine hydrochloride—Remember when Hollywood brought fame to freebasing with Richard Pryor turning himself into the human torch? Clear to me what he and his brother, Jeremy (especially after Jeremy said he couldn't get out of the bathtub one morning to go to production, a few days after he physically attacked me), liked to smuggle up from the Andes of Peru and freebase, was cocaine hydrochloride. Remember my comment about language? Like the libelous statements about sodomy in prison on my Wikipedia page, they continued to use a vocabulary native to themselves and their culture, with the references to cocaine. Too bad they used the handle to send me a harassing email. Stupid, arrogant criminals should be everyone's favorite psychopath to hunt down: They make it so easy to find them.

Tracking all these criminal attacks by Jeremy and his brother were so mind-blowing in how they went contrary to how Jeremy tried to present himself as the friendly, conscientious and charismatic person he comes off as on initial meeting. As Scottie Mckibben commented when I grabbed lunch with him in New Orleans, on my way back from Argentina, he said, "I had so much respect for him until he did that"—referring to the assault and battery. That's a very prominent quality of a predatory psychopath, being two-faced, and very charismatic. When I left Brazil in 2015 I gave Jeremy my Blackhawk pack I carried on camera during the first season, along with a rock hammer. A hobby geologist, I brought it along to see what I could find while in Brazil. Jeremy said when we reconnected in Argentina for second season, that his daughter loved it. All this while, he was colluding and conspiring with his brother to take me out of the production equation through an Internet character assassination campaign.

The Whalen brother's campaign started with editing of the Wikipedia page, and then libelous statements on review sections of my books at Amazon. When that didn't work, they jacked it up by trying to get Don Shipley, former US Navy SEAL to go after me for stolen valor. When that didn't work as they had hoped, James Whalen created a page on Facebook and on Amazon to impersonate Don Shipley. When that failed, they started resorting to impersonating Shipley by sending me emails directly through my official website contact form. This of course grabs their IP address, and low and behold, those address resolved to the same physical addresses in Enumclaw, Republic, and Roslyn, Washington locations in King and Ferry County, Washington. Interesting that James Whalen still resides, and commits crimes, in the same county in which his father committed his crimes against his own family.

Cork Graham

From:	Donshilpey@hotmail.com
Sent:	Tuesday, March 14, 2017 9:14 AM
To:	███████████████
Subject:	Form Mail from corkgraham.com
Follow Up Flag:	Follow up
Flag Status:	Flagged

The form below was submited by Donshilpey@hotmail.com form Ip address: 204.106.238.248 on March 14, 2017 at 1:13 PM

----

firstname: Don

lastname: Shipley

phone: Don't bother

email: Donshilpey@hotmail.com

message: Congratulations! You just graduated!

Figure 51. Whalen can't even spell Shipley's name--and that's not Shipley's email address: perpetrators have traits—James Whalen's consistently misspelled words in harassing emails and libelous Internet postings from his IP addresses.

Figure 52. James "Jaime" Kendall Whalen, Sgt. Mac, aka SGT Kendall D. McKibben, of Roslyn and Republic, Washington, even thought it a good idea to attack me on Amazon by impersonating former US Navy SEAL Don Shipley, and using my picture from Discovery Communications as his photo. For someone with a questionable 100-percent disability from the VA, according to older brother, Jeremy (who seemed proud of it), he's got a lot of time on his hands—aside from travelling to Asia for sexual adventures with prostitutes, and teaching English, again, according to Jeremy Whalen on the Magic Bus.

Then, one evening, when I flew into Seattle to visit an old friend, as luck would have it, James Whalen was also at SEATAC. I think he was probably picking up his brother Jeremy who often flew back home to see family after a new infusion of money from acting on a new season of Treasure Quest: Snake Island. Predators go for targets of opportunity, like a coyote that happens across a defenseless cottontail or pheasant. They don't think; they just lunge. James "Jaime" Whalen, aka Kendall McKibben, or whatever, lunged without thinking by taking photos of me as I waited for my buddy to pick me up.

Remember, psychopaths are powerless, weak, scum of the earth, who prey off fear, but heaven forbid they get into a confrontation, like a moose that beats the living daylights out of a wolf. Still hiding behind this charade that they had built on the Internet, still thinking I didn't know who they were, they stupidly sent me these three photos:

Figure 53. My lawyer who is going after Brett Tutor in Austin, TX, as the second tortfeasor in the assault and battery initiated by Jeremy Whalen on the set in Argentina, says any self-respecting judge would give me a lifetime restraining order against James "Jaime" & Jeremy, like Mykel and Ruth Hawke have against Teti—what do you think?

This was about the time that Discovery Communications was finishing up third season in Bolivia, that no one was supposed to know about. They finished filming in November 2017. But, considering they're dealing with a hot potato of stolen artifacts, salted archeological sites, and the only one still on the show from the original season being the artifact-smuggling tortfeasor, Jeremy Whalen, they've put a hold on releasing it.

But, I can tell how it was written, as I've been on enough of these fakeumentary episodes to know. Pretty funny when you consider they're fully scripting reality TV shows, but to write such crappy scripts is what's so hilarious. One of the ways a writer keeps him, or herself busy is to not only ghostwrite books, but to also edit and rewrite more famous scriptwriter's scripts: I'd never turn out what I was receiving every day on set, and especially the dialogue I was being told to record as wild lines, from the comfort and safety of my Alaska home, so far from the heat and dangers of the jungle, like "I'm stuck! Look out snake!"

Perhaps I shouldn't have made a comment on one of my recordings, as to the quality of writing. The one who would listen and rewrite, based on directives coming through Discovery Channel executive producer Joseph Boyle from Discovery Channel president Rich Ross. When fans made comments on the show's Facebook page, it was a hard fight against me to not comment when people either said how exciting it was to follow on such an amazing adventure, or when others commented on how scripted the show seemed. I would have asked those of the former group to look critically at the bilge coming from TV these days, and then applauded the latter for seeing through Discovery's scam. The worst day was when a fan of the show said, that TREASURE QUEST: SNAKE ISLAND was proof that you don't need to read books anymore, and that you can get all your history from watching TV—OH, MY GOD! I was floored, then I almost cried in response to how effective networks like Discovery Communications have been in destroying our society by dumbing down the world.

When I started out as a journalist in 1983, I was told that the press was writing for a high school sophomore-level readership. It has been the saying in journalism for the last fifty years. The problem is that sophomore-level now, means something totally different from what it meant in 1948 when my father graduated John Rogers High School in Spokane, Washington. Back then men and women were expected to become contributing, and prepared voters and citizens by the time they graduated high school. Instead of university, many likely were going to become housewives, or go to a trade school, join the military, or enter an apprenticeship when they graduated high school. I've still got my father's history book he was given on graduation as an award from the publisher of THE SPOKESMAN REVIEW, W. N. Cowles, with the inscription, "in recognition of your graduation from John R. Rogers High School" on January 7th, 1948. That book, THE CONSTITUTION OF THE UNITED STATES ITS SOURCES AND APPLICATION, is of the level of what would be taught in a master's program history course nowadays.

Remember, this was a gift given all graduating students, by a publisher who saw the need of every graduating high school to know and understand the very document, through whose following and protection of the United States and its citizens lay with those graduating high school students. Now, reality TV producers, the new publishers of the world, sendoff high school children to determine the world with fake history and education from naturalists trying to get publicity by attempting being swallowed by anacondas. It brings much meaning and understanding of the impact, and potential disaster, of one of Discovery Communications biggest moneymakers: Discovery Education.

Is it any wonder we now have generations of kids that would try to lead the country without any real life experience, like such "useful idiots" as David Hogg, or those of Jeremy and James Whalen's ilk who have such lack of scruples as to think it's totally fine to send photos of a person at the airport, with the intent of creating emotional and psychological duress, as predators are want to do?

Figure 54. At least I didn't let Jeremy and James Whalen's last attack ruin a grand week of travel to see old and new friends, like Frank Stallone and Patrick Kilpatrick at celebrity Grand National Quail Hunt in Enid, OK; and American patriot Admiral James "Ace" Lyons in Washington D.C., whose pre-US Navy days in the Merchant Marines qualifies him as "mustang" in my book—the best officers in the US Marines and Navy.

When I saw the photos of me waiting for my friend to pick me up at SEATAC in my email the next morning, I made note of two things: the hood of the vehicle that was in the bottom of the photo, and the email it was sent to. Jeremy and his brother James were so excited to see me and thought that finally, they'd get a rise out of me by sending me photos, as if they were tracking me, and were able to show up where I was, whenever they wanted, that they forgot to think about which email to send from: the one that's an autoresponder, or the private one that only MAK Pictures, Discovery Communications, or cast would have?

Stupid monkeys make stupid criminals, which is why psychopaths can make easy marks, when we, as a society, look up from our smartphones and really pay attention. As mentioned earlier, there's a list of indicators that you can use to save yourself from a mountain of grief from these types of individuals. They come in many forms, but man, woman, teen, they all have these similarities, and they can be broken into four different types of psychopaths: narcissist, emotionally unstable, paranoid and predator personalities. Jeremy and James, and their father are predators, as evidenced by his actions towards his own daughter, so is James based on his total disregard for societal conventions, his defrauding the US government through his abuse of the VA system, and his use of the Internet in an attempt create mental stress through cyberstalking and other forms of harassment. Jeremy Whalen, on the other hand, is not only a predator, but also a narcissist, as evidenced by his suicidal attempts of staying on TV: Predators thrive by hiding in the shadows, like James (hence a need for a legally changed alias Kendall D Mckibben) and their father Myron, who I find is not listed as a sex offender in the state of Washington, though that's where he resides, and yet continues to exhibit signs of a psychopath, according to his son, Jeremy—interestingly, Jeremy didn't recognize them when he told me about an incident.

Fame and notoriety are so addictive to those narcissists from broken homes, narcissists who are also predators, will do anything to stay on camera. This has been proven again with Mykel Hawke's stalker Joseph Teti of Dual Survival, who harassed him in a weird, almost twisted mentality like a Buffalo Bill predator in the movie SILENCE OF THE LAMBS (taking on the skin of his victims), where Teti was creating websites to say they were created to attack Teti, and then telling his own web masters to make a personal business website like Hawke's. This mentality is like that which Keith Plaskett had commented on with regards to Jeremy and James Whalen, "I don't know why they hate you, but they REALLY FUCKING HATE you!" It's a form of transference: a third party through which to get their anger out at their self-loathing and hatred of their father, whom they can't attack outright, because of a restraint resulting from family dynamics.

Like we, meaning my combat buddies back in Central America, used to say when talking about our next target, someone who was often the more narcissistic type of predator, the kind that liked using car bombs, and indiscriminately killed innocent women and children, criminals who would have been nothing more than murderers, had they not had a global communist insurgency on which to piggyback and pay for their tools, "That's some really crazy shit!"

I experienced a bit of that rage at their father from James, even though I had met him for the very first time, when he came out to production in Argentina, smuggling cocaine and the stolen Incan artifacts to salt the production in the form of a couple copper *tumis* (Incan surgical and sacrificial knives) and the Incan fetishes turned green through ages of oxidization. It was a weird feeling, and frankly just weird meeting him—somehow, I had forgotten all my training from my twenties on how psychopaths are easy to recognize, partly because of how our subconscious warns us with the hair on the backs of your necks or an unexplainable feeling of uneasiness.

When a family member comes to a production, the family member on the set is most often all excited about introducing the family to the rest of the cast and crew. When James, or Jaime, as he preferred being called, wasn't introduced to me until nearly a day and a half after he arrived, even though I'd seen him moving about the hostel. It was as if only when he was in the lobby seated next to me that Jeremy felt compelled to introduce him.

Looking back on all of it now, after a year of investigating and reviewing evidence, with some major insight, after all that I've learned about Jeremy Whalen's criminal activities, his brother's bilking the US government on his medical disability, the psychopathic father who sexually abused their sister, it's clear how this dynamic had all transpired. From what I'd researched of Jeremy's father and remembered how Jeremy operated, Jeremy was an all or nothing guy. That's why he acted in such a self-destructive manner with regards to relationships and especially business, and potential business relationships, that could have been of some great benefit to all involved. The problem with people like Jeremy is that they look askance and talk badly at beneficent actions, favors by people like Steve Quirola, governor of Ecuador's Oro Province, out of a need to control.

Remember what I told you about drug dealers? They don't deal drugs for the drugs, they deal drugs for the power and the sense of control. When you do something out of their control, like me not handing some media demo request template over to him, or offering something like Quirola, both that he wasn't able to dictate, to control, it sends the mind of a psychopath, a narcissistic/predator type, into a tizzy. They also have a propensity to not leave people's interpretations of them, and those around them, to chance.

This need to control opinions and perceptions of them and others around is what drives most psychopaths.

In Brazil, Keith came up to me and told me that Jeremy had told him about an unflattering article about me in a socialist rag I knew well during the war in Central America, because fakeumentary patriarch Michael Moore was the editor of MOTHER JONES, and publicly stated he didn't care about the atrocities committed by the Sandinistas, just as long as they stayed power. It was part of Eric Holder and Obama's attempts to discredit and shut me up in 2011, for coming out of the cold and speaking out publicly about my time as a paramilitary officer for the CIA, when I was in Central America, in response to Obama trying to railroad fellow PMO Steve Stormoen on trumped up charges by the administration to make good on their promise to distance themselves from the previous administration.

My article was published in HUMAN EVENTS, one of the oldest conservative publications in the country, and delivered to the office of every congressman, and reviled by President Clinton during his term, was titled MR. PRESIDENT, PLEASE STOP FEEDING YOUR OWN TO THE WOLVES. It was a total sham by the Obama Administration. But, instead of referring to three-piece rebuttal where I really laid it all out, especially my simmering rage that we were basically left to fend for ourselves after we won the war in Central America—on the military side, they're still waiting for full recognition, as evidenced by former Green Beret Greg Walker's noble efforts.

Needless to say, Obama was pissed that I not only came out and spoke about something publicly I'd kept quiet about for 21 years, but that I did so with facts collected from the special operations community in defense of Stormoen. Perhaps I was also a more than a little furious that earlier that year, Obama had gone to El Salvador to apologize for our actions to the very communists that had been trying to take over the country and led to the one of the most horrific and bloodiest wars in Latin America since the conquest of the Americas by Spain. I was more than angry that Obama was spitting on the blood spilled by Americans from the United States all the way to Argentina, who had died fighting in Central and South America from 1978 to 1991, some of them close combat buddies of mine.

What I keyed in on with Jeremy, was that he made no mention of rebuttals to the attacks by such Obama lackeys and hacks as the one for MOTHER JONES. Until that point, I had thought of Jeremy Whalen as just a gopher. Every production or operation needs good gophers. They can get supply like no one else. But, seeing that Jeremy was always being friendly and charismatic in front of me, but talking badly about me behind my back, I realized he was a weasel, but I couldn't have imagined that he would turn out to be such a "super weasel." Gophers and weasels are two different species. One is benign and helpful, the other is dangerous. One is an herbivore, the other is predator. Jeremy is a super predator. Bears are predators, but they're also herbivores. Coyotes are predators, and all they do is slink around, use the canopy to hide, but are always calculating on the next move. There's a major dynamic when two psychopaths get together. They try to outdo each other: remember Leonard Lake and Charles Ng?

As I had said, psychopaths are bred based on environment. The predator type of psychopath is created through the childhood they experienced, and it all revolves around control, like it is for all predators. Read the reports and news articles on such famous predators as Ted Bundy, Jimmy Savile, Israel Keyes, Charles Ng, and it's totally about power and control. When Jeremy Whalen shared that he had asked his father, why hadn't he ever come down to South America to visit him, his father responded with the question of why hadn't Jeremy bought him a ticket?

It brought me back to my eight years working as a drug and alcohol rehabilitation for Friendship House Association of American Indians in San Francisco, CA, right after I came back from my year of healing from Central America, in Alaska. Many ask, "Is Cork, your real name?" No. Unlike James, or Kendall, or Jaime, I didn't pick Cork, to hide my identity and run from my family history. The name picked me. My birthname is Frederick, after my German and German-Swiss great uncle Fred Aebischer of Chicago, Illinois, after who my father was also named. Cork, or Corky, was the name of a little boy who died of spinal meningitis in 1940 on the Pine Ridge Lakota Reservation.

According to my extended Ogalala Sioux family, I'm their little brother who died, Albert Claymore, or "Corky". Take it as you will on your beliefs of reincarnation, but I've seen too many wild and bizarre events to say there's no such things, especially when you have a memory of your own funeral, without anyone having previously told you about it—in fact, you tell them about it. It put the Tibetan Buddhist BOOK OF THE DEAD, the BAROD THODOL, in a whole new light for me, considering the Buddhists believe the spirit hangs around the body for three days after death. The book is supposed to be read into the ear of the corpse, to lead the soul to rebirth on a higher plane.

I will say, it's always nice to be loved, and to share back that love is even better, especially out of care and respect. I took the name as respect to my extended family in South Dakota. Then, as I started doing more writing, I noticed it's actually a pretty good *nom de plume*, and for my extended family, a reminder that I still think of them—at first many think it's Cort, or something phonetically similar, but then they learn it, they remember it.

While working as a counselor, I specialized in helping those confronted by post-traumatic stress, of which many drug abusers do. The issue is that instead of dealing with the problem, they deal with the symptoms through the abuse of drugs—don't even get me started with the VA and military doctors throwing drug prescriptions at a psychological dilemma. As many of our clients were tribal members who were at the in-house, 90-day rebab clinic as the result of a court order, we had to deal with many who abused the system and the opportunity to use a get out of jail card by becoming sober. It would infuriate me when I thought about how many others could have benefitted had they been given the slot instead taken and abused by someone who was playing the system, as a substitute for doing some major internal work to change and improve their life.

Figure 55. One of the certificates awarded me by Friendship House, this one by TV/film actor Benjamin Bratt, Quechua from Peru on his mother's side, and one of the organization's board members. Told him I found CLEAR AND PRESENT DANGER, in which he had appeared earlier that year, an interesting interpretation of covert war in Latin America.

This knowledge and experience put me on alert for such types of behavior, to the point that my co-workers, and especially my boss, started calling me "The Hammer" because I'd catch these system abusers and recommend sending them back to prison—everything I learned about confronting PTS and the need to feel like a victim, I learned through experience in my solitary confinement in Vietnam in 1983-1984, and when I sought a similar, but not as stressful experience in the wilds of Alaska, in 1990.

Remembering what Jeremy said about his father just lit into me as I investigated their criminal family history, that runs through the father and into the sons. It's clear Myron T. Whalen simply skated through the system back in the 1980s, like predators can easily do, not learning anything other than how to manipulate a probation officer into signing off.

To clarify with an example, here's what someone who has truly done work would have done, had they been confronted by a son asking why he'd not come and visited him in Peru. They would have said, "Son, I'm sorry, but as you know, I made some poor choices in my life. I'd love to come down and visit you in South America, but I just don't have the money."

It's that simple, but a predator can't see that, as they're always working from a state of keeping in control of self, and others. Predator and psychopathic behavior starts with the parent, and is taught consciously, subconsciously to the child.

At first, Keith wasn't too forth coming with information about Jeremy and James. He was more into hinting, such as when I shared a copy of the text from a cyberstalker and harasser I hadn't yet pegged:

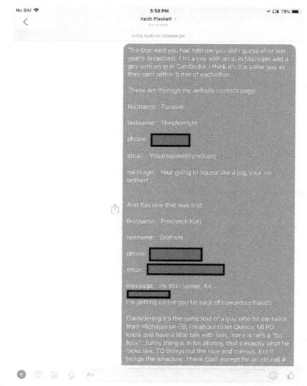

Figure 56. DELIVERANCE, the movie, threats of physical harm through lynching with regards to pigs squealing, and stifled, self-loathing anger at their father's overweightness and more importantly the cowardly crime against the family? Interesting constant trait of misspelling on the author's part in every cyber-attack.

Figure 57. When I saw this photo of James "Jaime" Whalen, aka Kendall D. Mckibben, after reading Jaime's harassing email with the "lynch.org" and "Your going to squeal like a pig, your no bother!" I immediately thought back to the banjo playing character that the DELIVERANCE director John Boorman described as, "inbred from the back woods." Probably where they really fine-tuned their taste for cocaine and speed like so many commercial fisherman—helps keep them up those long hours.

Keith responded with this, saying but not saying:

> No Cork I have not had any problems recently last 5 years.
> I am on Al-Qaida's hit list is all thats what he the was probably referring to...
> This sounds to me like someone close to you by the wording used like maybe someone on the show??
> Fuckin assholes...

At the beginning, before Keith finally had had enough of Jeremy's manipulations, he hinted with "sounds to me like someone close to you by the wording used like maybe someone on the show??"

Keith didn't want to come out and say that it was James and Jeremy Whalen, even though he already knew, and would confess later that it was those two: basically, he was hedging his bets. That was until he realized how sick and twisted Jeremy is, and how it wouldn't be me being the only one paying the price. Keith kept commenting on how the captain's license Jeremy had just passed the test for in Seattle, could easily be pulled:

All they have to do is give Jeremy an unannounced piss test while on the show when he's smoking pot with the rest of them..

I hope they don't kill the show. I need the money to get my Moringa business going in Brazil..

 After this season I don't care if they kill it!!

Just got off the phone with my buddy. Says all can be done to yank his license is to contact the USCG captain where he was issued it and they'll keep tabs as he convicted of drug and artifact smuggling.

I was far beyond wanting the show surviving. Did he forget that we were invited on the show with a manipulative lie from MAK/Discovery Channel: "Would you like to go on a treasure hunt?" That they then tried to keep us quiet about their fraud by having us sign NDAs? Regarding needing the money, Hollywood is littered with hearts and bodies, literally, of those who thought they'd come to that city of illusion and make it big. Best financial security I heard of in Hollywood, during both productions was showrunner David Carr talking about his building in los Angeles that was a financial investment.

Like the guys who brought shovels and gold pans, making a killing selling them to miners during the California Gold Rush, better to be into real estate business in Southern California: that's where many productions get funding, that an drug dealers wanting to launder cash. Everyone needs a place to live, but not everyone's going to make it big, especially where Hollywood agents and managers wait for a call from a prospective client, like pimps prowling the bus stations for fresh meat.

Ironically, like most people who deal with a predator for a while, Keith was still hoping that Jeremy was going to come around, that evil deeds, especially ganging up with Mehgan wasn't in his true nature. How Jeremy could turn on a buddy, one who had become a father figure, even having been in the US Navy like his dad, according to Jeremy? That's why Keith hedged his bets by giving me enough information that if I ran with it, I'd succeed, and if I didn't he wouldn't have burned his bridges too far with Jeremy. More I dealt with Keith, I would even begin to question his PTS abreaction that happened after he'd been drinking two bottles of the rum the night before it happened on set, and which was heavily dramatized in post-production for Season 2, Episode 5, JAGUARS GOLD.

Predator's thrive off the premise that people will give them the benefit of a doubt. It's based on those of us in society who are brought up to be basically good people, to not jump to certain conclusions based on those people we'd normally deal with, such as "He didn't do, what he just did…did he?"

But, Jeremy did screw Keith. He had no remorse in screwing anyone who stood in his way to success: in that he was in good company with those at Discovery who had proven themselves to sell their first born with the illegal, and frankly morally reprehensible, acts they committed in protecting Joe Teti, until Teti's actions became too outlandish and no one could protect him. When these kinds of psychopaths get going, and get a sense of invincibility, as shown by years of successful drug and artifact smuggling Jeremy Whalen had been into, starting in high school and going on through adulthood to support himself when he went back to South America as an adult, they really get going. According to Keith, Jeremy got into the stolen artifact business when he returned to Peru, after his initial entry to South America as an exchange student when he was sixteen years old. When he brokered the artifact smuggling deal with Discovery Channel, he was setting it up with his old smuggling contacts back in Peru.

Jeremy Whalen…Will Hayden…Joseph Teti. Are you seeing a common theme? Let me send up another flare then: Discovery Communications is actively profiling and hiring psychopaths to throw in the mix in order to jack up the drama on their reality TV shows.

Normally, security consultants hired by corporations are tasked with screening certain individuals with psychopathic tendencies in order to keep them out. Since it's clear that Discovery Communications is all about drama and building drama in their productions these days, because that's what ignites the mind of the female audience they so desire, doesn't it make sense that they'd target psychopaths to throw on production, like you're throwing a viper in a room full of people. Talk about drama.

When CEO David Zaslav went to Hollywood to get productions developed and in the can, he basically threw a fox in the henhouse. Journalism, documentaries, these are the jobs of those educated, trained and experience in the process of observation and recording history. This is the picture that comes to mind in most people, when using the term "true-life," "documentary," and even "reality" TV. When people think of Hollywood, we think movie scripts, glitter, drama, illusion, and fake, terms totally contrary to journalism and documentary-making. But, bonafide TV and film actors, directors and producers, are not cheap.

In comes "reality TV," and David Zaslav priding himself in interviews that while it takes millions to produce scripted shows in Hollywood, he's getting pennies on the dollar. What the public doesn't know, is that the scripts are cheap, and the talent where the big money is spent on normal, Hollywood dramas, price slashed by bringing in personalities and employing them as actors, most often unknowingly until it's too late. What Zaslav has done is to get cheap talent, produce majorly scripted shows, and

FRAUDULENTLY release them as "true-life" documentaries—this is horrifying on a sociological level when you remember Discovery Education revolves around Discovery Communication's "true-life" documentary content. But in every drama, going all the way back to Shakespeare and Homer, there's the need for the anti-hero.

Here's the crux, it's too expensive to hire the Robert de Niro of CAPE FEAR, or the Anthony Hopkins of SILENCE OF THE LAMBS, it's so much cheaper to hire a Teti, Hayden, and Whalen to see how they prowl the set. It's no different than someone who takes delight in taking a mature gourami and dropping it into a goldfish bowl to see how many feeder gold fish the gourami can swallow in a couple seconds—the drama of it all…

I was taken by three thoughts: Jeremy and James Whalen's need to confront their dad, for his transgressions during their youth, instead of continuing this sick and twisted transference of anger at him to anyone unlucky enough to be a psychological catalyst, a mental anchor, for that transference; the office for the district attorneys of King and Ferry Countys, and Attorney General of Washington State should visit and revisit the case of the Whalen Clan; and finally, the Inspector Generals of the US Federal Communications Commission, and Federal Trade Commission should have a conversation with the CEO of Discovery Communications, David Zaslav on the inappropriate business practices of a mega, media corporation that calls itself the last "true-life" documentary network out there.

Figure 58. Such smiles at this father-sons get together of predators

11 FOOL'S GOLD

My introduction to gold mining in Alaska, was a month of hell deep in the Interior of Alaska. Lots of times you get that uneasy feeling that puts the hairs on the back of the neck on edge, where you know you don't want to go there, because it's an ambush waiting to happen. Still, you go, whether it's because you have a job to do, as when you're in war, or you go because you have to bring in the bacon to feed the wife and kids, or you go because, well, you'd never done it, and you've always wanted to see gold in its original state.

So, you get in the truck with the project manager and take the 18-hour drive north to Pump Station Number 5, on the Haul Road (known by non-Alaskans as the Denali Highway), and as you ride along, you wonder if the guy you're sitting next to is going to turn out be the bossman that you'd follow to the end of the earth, or one major nutcase you'll run naked away from and into the mosquito-infested forests of Alaska in July.

He seems to be religious and pious, but then you see the two coins of God in man, that expresses itself as someone truly spiritual, but turns out to a born-again, holier-than-thou-Bible-thumping nutcase, who's just running away from the alcohol and drug demons he thinks in his mind are chasing him down. This turns out to be one tense cat, that you'd not want to spend that much time on a long drive, much less a month in the Bush.

Figure 59. The summer before the TQ:SI production in Brazil, the author deep in the Alaska Interior, .45/70 and .44 Rem. Mag. loaded for bear, and learning along with his buddies, Joel Holder and "Jeremiah Johnson", how gold mining would be a precursor to shady world of reality TV.

A Cessna 206 lands at the runway that supplies this oilfield relay on the Alaskan Pipeline and takes you to Bettles. In Bettles you hang around at the airport for a few hours while they gas up the DeHavilland Beaver on the lake, and then you take a short flight to a lake just up the Wild River.

You then make a five mile walk across the tundra of ankle-twisting hummocks, basketball-sized balls of grass that roll as you walk on them to camp. For the first week of your next thirty days, you build your hooch out of spruce poles and Visqueen. It's Interior Alaska in summer, so it's unbearably hot and humid. You thought you knew mosquitoes having been raised in Southeast Asia and having fought a war in the tropics, but they have nothing on Alaska's state bird—the Alaska skeeter. Mosquitoes, after all the bullets and shrapnel that were flying through those times in Latin America, were what actually almost killed you—there are times still, when you feel fatigued and your eyes go jaundice from the effects of that malaria.

You're up at the crack of dawn because once that sun peaks over the spruce, you're roasting in your clear-walled mining camp home. It's your duty to cook breakfast, as you were hired as camp medic, cook and newbie miner. Based on what you're told on the original USGS sample, you're going to bring in about $60,000 for a month's amount of work. You're excited!

It's a different kind of excitement than the night when a giant black bear sow shows up at camp. You see her first, through the Visqueen of your hooch, and ask yourself as you're still in half-sleep, is that a bear? She's so big, her head reminds you of a young, 600-pound grizzly. You pull your JP Sauer and Sohn Western Marshall .44 Remington Magnum from its holster because it's the easiest to maneuver without making too much movement. The bears only eight feet away. At first you aim for her chest, but then you remember you don't want to kill her even in self-defense. If you do, every bear within 10 miles of the camp will be following that scent of dead bear to fulfill its cannibalistic cravings. It'll be a mess. You send a round into the tundra on your side of the wall and she's gone.

Figure 60. Camp home for thirty days.

But, then someone yells. There's a bear by the kitchen. You growl a few profanities and switch the .44 for the .45-70. This time you see a much smaller bear. It's so small that its ears make it look it look like Mickey Mouse. You laugh as it sticks its head out from the corner of the tent. You yell, "Get outta here bear!" That doesn't work, so you bring up the rifle and fire a round into the ground near the bear. Mickey disappears into the twilight of the midnight sun.

The days turn to weeks and the excitement wanes. You're losing weight like crazy, but that's fine. You've been overweight for much too long since having entered a sedentary lifestyle in the corporate world. You cut logs and carry them on your shoulder to build just about anything: miner's cabin, storage shed, sled for dragging the parts of the monster 8-inch dredge that was more designed for ocean mining off Nome, than suctioning up material in a small, shallow trout stream.

If not for an excavator that dredge would never had been able to move, as it had to displace material in front of it, to behind it, in order to create enough depth to move upstream. Filming of THE AFRICAN QUEEN, John Huston's cinematic nightmare, and transporting opera up the Amazon in FITZCARRALDO was easier to complete than this endeavor.

Then it all becomes clear to you and your fellow newbie miners, one of whom had actually put money into a few claims the flim-flam project manager sold him. This was no mining operation and the mine manager was getting pretty much free work out of three guys who built the camp, and was prospecting the area for himself to try and sell later.

In the end it's a bust. Over $200,000 paid for a large dredge that had to no business in the Interior, when one or two smaller 4 or 5-inch Keene suction dredge would have been so efficient, and so much less expensive, than that custom order beast. You wait at the same lake you were dropped off at during the start of this adventure, and then have to deal with a bush pilot who's afraid to come in because he thinks the lakes too small for the same Beaver you landed in a month early.

You wonder what happened to the bush pilot who dropped you off in the first place. He was cool. He'd just taken this new bush contract after completing a flying contract for the CIA in Afghanistan. That guy would fly anywhere. Not this guy. Instead of beaching the plane for ease of loading, he hangs out so you have to put your waders on and walk out to him with gear. Thankfully the bottom of the lake is still frozen below an inch of debris, else you'd be fighting that suck, too.

As the swindler project manager is all about himself, he'll be on the plane first out with one of the other guys. You're more than too happy to be able to spend time away from this holy-roller, flim-flam man—it's clear now, after a month in the bush with this guy that he got investors to put the over $200,000 into the operation by strumming their born-again religious strings, easy marks for this kind of guy in Alaska. Who would be suspicious of a man who recites the Bible at the drop of a hat, right? You've got your .45-70 lever-action Marlin 1895S incase grizzlies come. You wait with your fellow newbie, now veteran, gold miner, for the second flight out of there, and share elations about how you'll never have to see the nutjob again.

The loading and boarding goes a lot better this time, without the numb-nuts, micromanager. As the DeHavilland Beaver pulls away from the tension of the water, you give an elated thumbs-up as you promise to yourself to never, ever go on a gold mining operation with someone who clearly doesn't know what he's talking about, but gives a pretty good sales speech...

Figure 61. The author on his way home after a lesson in how NOT to mine gold.

Showrunner David Carr looked at me, trying not to laugh, "Discovery wants you to jump in the pool and take a shower under the waterfall."

"Yeah?"

"...Will you do it nude? They want to make it look like you're feeling grimy and just want to get clean."

"What?" I chuckled. I wanted to get clean alright...I wanted to get clean of this joke production that even more clearly than in Brazil, was trying to come off as real and using our real personal histories to create their fraud.

"They want a humorous moment."

I rolled my eyes. "Tell you what I'll do, I'll strip down to my skivvies and then take a shower in the waterfall. Will that work? There's no way I'm going to hang out in that pool of water, with who knows what's growing in it—less likely of me to get some weird staph infection in the waterfall."

I should have been more scrutinizing of their request. Amazing what you can do in post-production, to make it look like the actor is naked, by blurring his buttocks and having the rest of the cast make derogatory remarks to continue building character assassination in order to put Jeremy Whalen in as team leader. How many viewers asked the question of why

Jeremy was made a team leader in Argentina, instead of Keith Plaskett? Even though Plaskett lives on Ilhabela now, he still teaches archeology at a university in Peru. Jeremy's a boat mechanic, welder, and boat yard manager hiding out in Salinas, Ecuador.

Too bad Plaskett wasn't the devil that Discovery Communications had made a deal with. When they took Whalen's offer to have his brother James purchase the graverobbed Incan artifacts and smuggle them across the traditional drug smuggling routes from Peru to Argentina, he had them by the balls. If Whalen went down, or spoke out, Discovery would go down, too. Just like in Joe Navarro's description of a predator, or psychopath, especially a narcissistic type, it's all about their goals and objectives—they will burn anyone and everyone to get there and won't even bat an eye about the damage to others.

It's amazing that once Plaskett knew of the deal with the devil and the potential fallout resulting from the public learning of the stolen artifact smuggling, that he didn't take his earnings up until then and boarded a plane the hell out of there—I guarantee I would have, had I known. Personally, having to look over my shoulder the way Whalen will, until he's arrested, is not worth it. But, that's the thing about psychopaths, they don't have that healthy fear switch, that says, wait, stop, think. Theirs goes like this: slow down, calculate, adjust, move quickly toward the prey.

"We'll have a fire ready for you when you get out," Jeremy said, motioning to Brett and himself.

"Yeah, ok," I said, begrudgingly. Mehgan was the mermaid. She had just been swimming in a pond at a caiman farm, and been in the river for weeks—the bacteria and parasites in the water were more dangerous than the caiman. Even the caiman that appeared in the fake caiman attack scene, was resting and minding its own business until Jeremy teased it with an oar to get it to attack. I had happily avoided getting into that murky, polluted water that we'd been videoing in for the last two months. A childhood growing up in Southeast Asia, gave me a healthy respect for the types of bugs that can ruin your day, or even the rest of your life.

Figure 62. Poor little caiman, all by himself at the caiman farm, just minding his own business, until Jeremy jabbed agitated it with a boat oar for the scene.

At first, they had me stand in only my skivvies and boots, in a pool downstream of the jungle waterfall. Then, when Carr realized how stupid I looked trying to bath in a pool only six inches deep, he and Dorman called me over to the waterfall at which we had been shooting all our waterfall rappelling scenes for the last two weeks.

It was cold, which of course appeared in that episode. I was really looking forward to a warm fire when I was done. A couple takes of stepping into the waterfall and whooping and hollering and Carr called cut. Someone tossed me a towel, I dried off and headed for what I thought would be a raging campfire.

Huddled together around a tiny pyramid of half-inch diameter twigs, about ten inches long, were Brett Tutor and Jeremy Whalen. They went back and forth, each trying to use a cigarette light ignite the fire. Based on the soot and scorch marks on the twigs, they'd been at it for as long as I'd been in the waterfall and pond. Anyone who has started a fire would easily have seen neither knew what they were doing.

Here was Jeremy Whalen, someone who had lived in South America for almost two decades, supposedly travelling into the jungle. There was Brett Tutor, who supposed had tried out for the coveted titled of US Air Force PJ. Para-Jumper. USAF Combat Rescue. From Austin, Texas, he said he had hunted elk in Colorado. I also knew from our meeting that he had said he had washed out trying to get into the PJs by tearing his Achilles heel, though later I'd learn his DD214 indicated a reason much different. Still, there must been some kind of daring do that appealed to the Mark Kadin and Will Ehbrecht to have hired him as the "survival/security expert."

As I stared at them crowded around the fire, I was warming rapidly inside, not from having dried myself off and putting my clothes back on. No. I was warming quickly by doing my best not to laugh. Anyone, I mean anyone who went through Cub Scout, no need to even do Boy Scouts, I literally mean Cub Scouts, would have learned how to start a fire with those pieces of wood, with a bow drill or even rubbing two sticks together no less. Here were these accomplished adventurers, and they couldn't even light a simple fire with a lighter.

I never did Boy Scouts when I was a little kid in Singapore. I only went through Cub Scouts and enjoyed myself immensely, knowing even back then how important being taught lifesaving skills for the wilds would be. We learned quickly that flame is all about oxygen, heat and fuel. By age ten, I knew how to properly place wood and ignite a fire, so that I could confidently start a fire with wet wood in the jungle, in the arctic and or high atop an alpine mountain. Like every military officer should be required to complete a sniper course, so too every boy and girl should go through Scouts, for the information so important.

Clearly, Jeremy and Brett didn't get that memo. All they would have had to have done was grab a knife, or machete, of which there were many on set, and whittle the twigs to look more like pine cones, or little Christmas trees. The little featherings of shaved tinder would have burst into flames, had they done so. Instead, they waited for someone to bring gasoline up from the boat that part of the production team had travelled up the river in. There was a blazing fire later that night, but long after I needed it to warm up.

Thankfully, I live in Alaska, and if you don't know how to start a fire, or at least know how the body regulate heat, you die. These two clearly would have been dead long ago had they needed survive on their own. That bit about not being able to start a fire never got onto camera. This may be extremely funny to you in the way it sure is to me: considering how many campfires we shared on camera, not one was ever lit by the cast. That's what fixers and grips are for, just like in Hollywood.

It does bring questions. The biggest question I later had, especially as Brett Tutor was being groomed for a role as Ty Pennington's replacement TLC's TRADING SPACES, was with all those many times that Tutor looked like he didn't know what he was doing, so lacking in many skills and understandings related to survival and security: what was Tutor's purpose? Some might say after the initial broadcast of TRADING SPACES, the grooming for TRADING SPACES was a reward for keeping his actions and keeping his mouth shut about the various illegal activities occurring in Argentina.

The biggest question about Tutor is how far will an actor go to keep working as an actor in Hollywood? Tutor just hasn't been truthful about his reason for leaving the US Air Force. According to his DD214, Tutor completed basic, but then it stops there. He said he washed out of training for PJs, but that would at least have been having gotten to what the PJs call Indoc.

The question now is, was Tutor busted for drugs, or did he assault someone—why else would such redactions be included in a DD214? If he did wash out from the PJs on a medical, the Armed Services would at least keep him for another 90 days to see if he'd heal up enough to try again or do something else in the military. Wasn't it always that when you signed up for the military, if you were physically fit, they kept you until you completed service?

Most people who have had that type of discharge wouldn't have even mentioned they were in the military. It's like saying, you went to college when you're applying of a job, but you didn't graduate. No hiring manager likes to hear that a potential employee doesn't have a stick-to-itiveness—no one likes a quitter. If he did, he would have just finished out his service in a less romantic MOS.

Stardom's attraction for actors is addictive. It causes many to make claims such as those by film and TV actor Brian Dennehy (who starred in a film based on former Marine officer Philip Caputo's A RUMOR OF WAR), a former Marine, who never went to Vietnam, but said he did. There was also Grady Powell, who was in the US Army Special Forces, and was advertised by Discovery and then Fox as a combat veteran, but his DD214 doesn't seem to have a CIB (Combat Infantry Badge), or have any mention of combat, which it definitely should if he was in combat in Mali or Iraq—It's not El Salvador and Nicaragua in the 1970s and 1980s after, all.

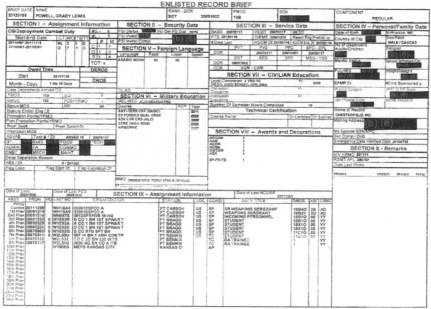

Figure 63. Figure 65. Grady Powell of AMERICAN GRIT and DUAL SURVIVAL claimed to be combat veteran of two campaigns, but his records here show zero combat awards, one deployment, (NO company medal, NO combat action badges [CIB]) and one deployment to Mali, (NOT a combat zone). Green Beret is a great achievement: why the combat lie?

Discovery Communications has done a good job of attracting people who can initially say they're military or they're combat veterans. But, no one ever checks their records, or at least some type of evidence—guys in combat love to take pictures. Let me tell you, even when you're told not to.

Mykel Hawke, who was host and a producer on ELITE TACTICAL UNIT, had this to say of Powell, who had played a drug kingpin on ETU, "he demonstrated gross misconduct, and he worked on NatGeo Extreme Alaska where he conducted misdeeds against Rudy Reyes and finally, he was caught being a fraud and drinking too much on set of DUAL SURVIVAL."

Once Brett Tutor was on TRADING SPACES, he must have felt invincible, at least for little while, as he had already been served by my lawyers in Austin, Texas for jumping me as I was defending myself from Jeremy Whalen's cocaine-pumped sucker punch. Most of production was done on TRADING SPACES by the time he was served. It was no easy task by the server by the way. Discovery Communications must have told Tutor to hide out long enough to keep from being served before TRADING SPACES released to the public. The server found him hiding out in a house that his mother was representing as a real estate agent.

Seems the house in which he was found was one of the houses that he had posted on his Instagram page. Tutor loves Instagram. It's very telling. It's more of the "look at me," as compared to the "let's connect" of his Facebook page. What was important to know was that he went a little too far, and in the process launched a request by those going after stolen valor perpetrators, such as at THIS AIN'T HELL: http://thisainthell.us/blog/?p=79931

What drew the roving eyes of those looking for people pretending to be US military veterans was his page, that goes further than just talking about a USAF record of non-record. The part of being picked to lead a 60 man team during basic drew the ridicule of many who have actually gone through basic: it was likely because he was so old for someone going into boot camp, especially someone who had never really held down a job other than the home building and an inspection business he got from his grandfather. That hand me down business from his grandfather was his major lament on set in Argentina—all Tutor could talk about on set was how much he hated it and that TQ:SI had to make the break for him. Truly ironic when looking at how he's now on a show about home building and remodeling.

But that's the gift of gab that Tutor has, or as many who have seen past the veil at Discovery: the gift of BS. Not only was he selling himself as a PJ who washed out after he just got through basic, or what the Air Force calls Basic Military Training (BMT), and then stated he went out for SWAT, and even had some "unconventional emergency medical training," on his website bio.

So many posers working for Discovery it just gets so confusing in this unreal world of reality TV. On set, every moment together for Brett and Jeremy seemed like a penis size comparison test. In his self-description which made him look more like a professional student than an expert in anything, Brett told Jeremy that he had gone to Hawaii to train in mixed martial arts to become an MMA fighter. Jeremy's response was that the biggest drug lord in the area of Peru that he lived in jumped him and tried to kill him but he fought his way out of it.

It was constant on the bus like this, and such a relief to either put my earphones on and turn up the volume on my MP3 player, or turn down the volume, and listen whenever I thought Jeremy was plying others with negative talk about me, or anyone else that Jeremy had targeted in his twisted little predatory campaign to control opinions on production.

Keith was already on edge, having told me that he was absolutely sure that Mehgan and Jeremy's conspiracy to get rid of him and I and was in full swing. Keith was adamant that Jeremy was manipulating the MAK office by getting them maps and information from a history professor in Ecuador.

He was totally convinced, and he was angry. He was furious at the plot that formed with Jeremy, Brett and Mehgan.

Looking back on it all, I sure would have enjoyed more warning from Keith, than what little he gave me in those days before Jeremy had become so coked up and couldn't restrain himself. It would have explained why Jeremy's brother had come all the way from King County, Washington, in order to smuggle some cocaine from Peru to his brother, along with stolen artifacts for Discovery Channel to salt the site, in Argentina.

Figure 64. The drug and artifact smuggling brother of soon to be tortfeasor Jeremy Whalen, cooking with the soon to be second tortfeasor Brett Tutor—March 29, 2016.

"Do you think you can put your backpack on a rock and have it fall in the river, as though it were an accident?" David Carr asked me as we stood just below the majestic Nacunday Falls, just up the Nacunday River from where it flows into the Parana River, which makes the border between Paraguay and Argentina.

With my hand up to my face to shade my eyes from the sun that so beautifully cut through the mist lifting high above the torrent of the river just below falls, forming a large rainbow in the mist, I checked out the rock. "Sure, no problem," I said. "I can easily make it look real."

"Can you empty it first?" Tom Dorman said.

Figure 65. The backpack placement rivals my "don't cry scene" for acting. If my pack were actually filled with gear, instead of inflated garbage bags, that pack would have sank to the bottom immediately, instead of floating.

I found a small nook in the rock, out of frame, opened the pack, and dumped its contents out. A chuckle hit me as I looked at the meager belongings I was now carrying in my pack. Back in Brazil, when I thought we were really going into the jungle after treasure, I carried just about everything I needed to survive if it hit the fan, or just to make it comfortable in the jungle. Doesn't take much: lighter, water, hammock, mosquito net and some snacks. That was before I realized that this was a Hollywood production and not a reality TV documentary. On real documentary production, you're like a real journalist. You carry gear to survive and augment your reporter's video's camera.

On a Hollywood production, even if it's as cheap and chintzy as it was on this Discovery Hollywood production, you have a producer's assistant and local fixers. These folks make sure everything runs perfectly off camera, so that the crew and cast can focus on their acting and film, or in this case, video and audio recording of the scripted action. The PA and the local fixers always have food and water at the ready. A bit cold, no problem. A poncho or sweater will be on set to make you more comfortable.

While Carr and the rest of the crew talked amongst themselves, and began blowing air into garbage bags to stuff in my empty pack, one of the local fixers, Franco Barrios, brought us bottled water. While Keith and I were enjoying a bottle of water after a scene in the humid heat, he said. "Look at her."

Downriver she and Jeremy were talking while she accepted a bottle from Franco who then moved among the rocky shore with great deftness to the rest of the crew.

"Isn't it funny?" Keith said, "She's always talking about not using plastic, is always picking up plastic trash wherever we go, but she's always filling that metal thermos with water from a ton of plastic water bottles."

Figure 66. Still amazed no one has ever made a comment about that pack still floating...

Mehgan was a true believer in keeping hydrated, and rightfully so—I had passed out in Central America once due to forgetting to take my salt tablets and not drinking enough water. Swore I'd never let that happen again. You can imagine how many bottles she used to fill that metal thermos on the set alone. Now, it's known how much a scam the recycling business has become, with China no longer willing to take the US plastic refuse for recycling, and how much of a sham it was in the first place with all the labelling and separation of various materials, that were, in the end, just dumped into the same container at the garbage company lot.

"She's a Hollywood environmentalist," I quipped at the hypocrisy, and grinned. "All show, but no substance...it's like those new age, vegetarian medicine men in Hollywood—PC marketing."

Keith chuckled. "She's an Instagram Girl!" he said, making reference to her inclusion in what the Huffington Post termed, "Instagram's #MyStory initiative will launch with a photo exhibit featuring 28 women shattering stereotypes and using their voices on the platform in a positive way."

Remembering Rich Ross's comments, I paraphrased the title of the article that so excited Mehgan that week neared a wrap of production in Brazil, "DISCOVERY CHANNEL WANTS MORE WOMEN, MORE FAKES."

Keith got a good laugh.

Figure 67. The author and Mehgan Heaney-Grier, and her infamous thermos, just arrived in Brazil.

As if on cue, Brett Tutor said he was ready. Carr called me over to join Tutor down by the river's edge. He was getting pumped up to jump in the river by talking himself through the plan.

"You sure you want to do this?" I asked, as I held back ten feet from him, thinking this was going to be the stupidest thing I'd ever seen anyone do for such little money. Broken legs, concussion, drowning what a menu lay before him of what could happen. I've seen very brave men in very trying situations. This was not an act of bravery—it was an act of desperation. As he said many times, he had to make this role work, because he dreaded having to go back to his life as a building inspector in Austin.

Tutor nodded to Carr. "I'm ready!"

Carr cued the cameras and then said, "Action!"

Figure 68. Our fake "survival/security specialist," does his scripted jump for the drama.

Taking a step, I moved toward the large rock and removed my backpack, that I had to slow myself in order to make it look as if there was still kit in it—It felt as if I was slipping a balloon off my back and putting it on the rock, it was so light. I did it in one take.

Figure 69. Mehgan saves Brett in another scripted for drama scene, to have a female empowerment moment that would hopefully draw more of the female viewers CEO David Zaslav desires—pack still floating.

Adding the emotional excitement of screaming on my part, that all my most important data was in the pack, it was all completely scripted to be Brett Tutor's Superman moment. He jumped in the water, and was pulled out three times. The first two attempts, he couldn't catch up to the backpack as it floated downriver. Thankfully, we had our boat crew waiting, else I would have lost a pretty darned nice backpack Blackhawk had given me during a gun writer's conference in Montana the year before.

Three times the PAs threw the pack in the water. The first time he caught it he couldn't make it to Mehgan who was placed with a stick to pull him out of the water, so she could have her "superwoman" moment for the female audience David Zaslav and Rich Ross so craved.

The impact of all this didn't make itself known, until I was back in the US, watching the show, still feeling pretty good that I had put in a good performance for story that Discovery Communications wanted. Not until I watched the progression of the scripted events on the broadcast, and remembered especially how they were shot to seem benign during production, did I realize how really maliciously shot they were. Anyone who watched season one versus season two can see how Rich Ross loved using me and my personal history to sell the story. Then, in second season, it was all a progression to make it look as though I was losing my mind, making way for Jeremy Whalen to become the team leader and Mehgan as his new co-team leader.

Watching the second season, made me livid as I realized the same thing that happened to Cody Lundin, when Joseph Teti's attacks on his psyche became too much, and he left the show. See, many don't know it, but Lundin was repeatedly threatened by his co-star Teti, who replaced Canterbury. According to Lundin, Teti was even showing him photos of what we used to call "crispy critters" back in the day. They were probably photos Teti took during BDAs (battle damage assessments) when he was a contractor for the CIA. Most guys try to get rid of those photos, but Teti seems to have kept them and used them as a harassment and intimidation tool against Lundin.

Lundin said that Teti threatened him with death if he screwed it up for him with Dual Survival. Can you imagine having to be in the field with Teti, in a foreign country, day in, day out? As if the stress of production wasn't enough. Added to that was the active character assassination on Discovery Communication's part that had led to a defamation lawsuit filed by Lundin against Discovery Communications. Matt Graham had already replaced Lundin by then.

Lundin is in the real business of teaching people how to survive as a true survival expert. I'm in the business of success coaching and teaching people, civilians, military and law enforcement, how to shoot, and win wars. I'm also in the business of writing about it, having written books and magazine articles of the subject mental focus engineering, shooting, hunting and civil defense. This is what we really do in real life: we don't teach people to do hazardous things to survive, and we don't hunt treasure.

When I saw the episode that was supposedly capturing Lundin losing his mind, the first thing that hit me was, "Why are they telling Lundin to do that? The director had Lundin throwing matches into the jungle pool in Hawaii, while Teti was becoming angry and questioning what he was doing. It looked so scripted and heavily edited in post-production.

No survival instructor would ever, and I mean, ever throw good matches into a pool. When I had my own experience of putting the backpack on the rock to perfectly fall as if by accident, and the shower in the fall scene with separately shot comments by the rest of the cast, it all became clear how Lundin was set up and I had been, too. No survival instructor would have done what Lundin was directed to do at the pool. No one who lives in Alaska, and hunts, fishes, works with firearms and other dangerous tools, would ever be so careless as I appeared in the backpack rolling into the water scene. Both Lundin's and my businesses are based on trust of our credentials and our experience.

As mentioned, unlike like a real documentary or reality show, but very much like a produced for TV drama, everything on TQ:SI is shot out of sequence. Nothing reflects the order in which it was broadcast. One day I was videoed taking a shower in a waterfall, and everyone's delighted that I had the guts to do it—Carr asked everyone on set, after it was done, to give me applause for having completed the scene. Then another day, while I'm either not there that day, as I'm not written into the shooting schedule that day, or I'm acting in a nearby location, where I either can't see or hear what's being said, the crew is shooting the rest of scene, which was a collection the cast's derogatory comments about my showering under the waterfall—Carr said they wanted it because Discovery wanted a humorous scene to break up the plot, yeah, right. Most I asked didn't find the scene funny, or that it did anything for the show, other than to set me up by looking bad, just like the other scene written and edited for such effect. What you learn on a reality TV production is that good faith that a character assassination won't happen is unfounded, no one can be trusted, either on set during production, or later when they're editing it all together.

In the end, I'm just so surprised that no one made a comment on the show's Facebook fan page about how efficiently—though supposedly full of all my important and likely heavy gear—my back floated on top of the water so that Tutor could swim and catch up to and retrieve that pack from the rapids, when it most assuredly would have immediately disappeared to the bottom if it wasn't such a fraudulently setup scene. It was no different than a flim-flam, Alaska gold miner salting his site in order to sell it to some fresh from the Lower Forty-Eight cheechako.

12 LIGHTS, CAMERA…ACTION!

Rage is a very powerful emotion, if you learn how to use it, and not be overcome and manipulated by it. It can win battle and wars, and it can also get countries into wars. When it's in control, it'll destroy you. When you're in control, and channel that energy, it can enable you to annihilate your enemy. People say hate is the opposite of love. It's not. Apathy is the true opposite of love. There's a reason for that old proverb about revenge being a dish best served cold. For the five years I carried a gun in combat, I used rage every day, especially when I was put deep in harm's way.

During the night we had leaped from one hill top to the next, in two blacked out Huey's, pilots and passengers wearing NVGs. Our pilots from the Salvadoran Air Force (FAES) flew like kids on bicycles—they were naturals. Years of war had honed the skills of these pilots who had survived the base attacks and assassinations, helicopter crashes due to being shot down, and falling out of the sky simply because of equipment malfunctions. Choppers are safe and pretty much reliable, but when these birds that had been fighting since middle of the Vietnam War gave out, they did so dramatically. You took your life into your own hands when you boarded Salvadoran military choppers during the war.

Somewhere in those airborne leapfrogs in the night, our two squads, ten commandos each, exited the choppers. Immediately setting up a rapid defensive position around the chopper in case we had the not uncommon messed up luck of having landed on a hillside that had become a campsite during the night by the Gs, we had to be ready. I'd already come into a hilltop at night to suddenly see little bright, daisy blossoms appear in the dark below, the unmistakable sound and vibration of bullets hitting the fuselage of the Huey like popcorn hitting the insides of pot as it's popping.

Yelling and screaming to get us out of there as we returned fire, our selectors on AUTO, our pilots, like all FAES pilots I'd flown with, serene Buddhas in their seats, rotating the throttle as they lifted up on the collective, deftly adjusting the tail rotor with their foot pedals, nudging forward on the cyclic. These minor adjustments were no easy matter for the excited mind when bullets were coming up through the floor and canopy, and the side doors and windows. Heaven forbid you took a full round to the foot or leg, or hands or arms. Like two parts of the body, the co-pilot calmly took over as needed.

I loved these guys. I still love these guys. Without them coming in when we really, and I mean really, needed them, I wouldn't have the opportunity to become teary-eyed as I remember these *hermanos*, some who hadn't been as lucky as the rest of us. Many like to say it's not luck to survive a war, to survive combat, that it's because of skills. I'll agree with that, but I'll also say, Lady Luck can be the decider in the end, else why would there be those dead, who you'd never have thought would've received as much as a scratch, and then those "dead men walking" you saw all the time, who came out of it with nary a bruised toe. Death can be fickle.

It has been said that war gives men, unlike women who are normally offered this opportunity through society, the opportunity to experience and publicly express emotional bonds with other men without being thought of, or accused of, as being homosexual. It's why those who've been in combat have bonded with those whom they were in battle together or had been in other battles within the same war, and then on a different level, to those who had been in other wars.

When I was still working in Central America and going back and forth between there and the United States, I met a Salvadoran who had been fighting for the FMLN before he made it initially into the US as an illegal immigrant. It was during deer season in California, and I was at the Coyote Point Rifle Range in San Mateo County. It started with overhearing the very recognizable Salvadoran accent as he talked with his friends in the shooting station next to mine. I was back in time for deer season, so I was sighting in my .280 Remington. Then I saw the long scar that covered most of his forearm. His Spanish and the wound that I so easily recognized as a war wound, a bullet wound to be specific, sent the hairs on the back of the neck on end—had he been with the Salvadoran military, instead of the guerrillas, I'm sure my "spidey senses" wouldn't have gone on alert: our senses can be amazing when we pay attention to them.

Soon we were in conversation and he told me that before he made it across the California border with Mexico, he had been shot in the arm by the Salvadoran Army and spent months in recovery in a refugee camp in Honduras. This happened all before I had first arrived in Central America in 1985. He wasn't specific, but I surmised it was around 1982. He made his home in San Francisco's Mission District, where many past and active members of the FMLN resided, either home for good, or demonstrating in the streets against US intervention in Latin America, before returning to Central America for another bout.

Figure 70. The author collected fresh, totally northern Sierra totally organic, non-farm pellet fed California Columbia blacktailed deer that year soon after meeting his first FMLN guerrilla in California: three more years of war in Central America to go...

Communists in the US's, especially the Communist Party USA (CPUSA), sole role in the 1980s was to support the communist designs on Latin America, which was actively brought about by Raoul Castro and Daniel Ortega. They demonstrated against any US support of the Salvadoran government in its efforts to keep communists from taking power as they had done in Cuba and Nicaragua. New York's Mayor Bill de Blasio and fakeumentary producer and former MOTHER JONES editor Michael Moore were examples of these kinds of people in their younger years.

What a dichotomy! In the San Francisco Bay Area, we had Nicaraguans who had escaped the Sandinista takeover of Managua. We had Salvadorans who had been represented by both the FMLN and the anti-communists in street demonstration. And then there I was interacting with members of all groups, keeping it to myself as much as possible that I was going back and forth between the Bay Area and the war. At first, when I was solely a journalist covering the war in Central America, it was to build relationships and networks.

Later, after I found I couldn't believe in that work anymore because the two bureau offices I had gone to with the story of an atrocity committed by the FMLN, and after I took a friend's offer to work for the US government, I would use those same contacts and networks to help recruit assets for information to set up operations against high value targets. These would be targets such as the one we were after specifically on this operation.

Comandante Gerardo Zelaya had special meaning to me. I had arrived in El Salvador for the first time a couple weeks after the US Marines who guarded the US Embassy were assassinated at 8:45 P.M. on June 18, 1985, in an outdoor café in what was the most famous restaurant areas of San Salvador. Everyone went there, Salvadoran military, government officials, members of the FMLN. Whether you're deciding the future of a nation as part of the government, or fighting for another version of that nation, as communist insurgent, you can't be all work and no play.

When the FMLN made such a drastic play for dramatic effect they infuriated not just the residents of the nation's capitol, but also other factions of the FMLN. That's the thing about insurgents, in this case the *Partido Revolucionario de los Trabajadores Centroamericanos* (PRTC), or the Revolutionary Party of Central American Workers, is that they all want the power, and in the case of the war in El Salvador, under the FMLN, they were no different. One of the greatest achievements for the various factions of the communist movements was when they campaigned together under the FMLN flag in their attempt to overthrow the government, instead of just working independently.

During the 1980s, when people asked me if I went to university, I'd joke that I went to UCLA. The reference, much like those Marines who fought in Vietnam and like to say they went to Khe Sanh University and specialized in counter-insurgency, was that my learned about life in war. I didn't attend the University of California at Los Angeles. UCLA was a program that had been created five years before I first set foot in Central America.

It was an unconventional warfare (UW) unit of Unilaterally Controlled Latin Assets who came from a variety of Latin American nations: El Salvador, Honduras, Argentina, Ecuador, Chile, Bolivia. They came from a variety of military units from these countries. Some were also of non-military origin. But, we all had a strong thread that created an immense bond. We were passionately anti-communist, and saw, like I did, that it was better to fight them in Central America, than fight them in their family's own neighborhoods—which those from Central America were already doing. Unilateral control came from the President of the United States, through the Central Intelligence Agency.

Pseudo Operations became our bread and butter. These were operations in which we fought alongside former-FMLN guerrillas turned to pursuing their former *compañeros*. Often in our hands as the result of military action, these former-guerrillas would be like our scouts to infiltrate back into their territories and collect or eliminate specific targets of interest. We did so by dressing and acting as if we were guerrillas. We wore a variety of fatigues and mixed it up a bit with ball caps that read "FMLN" across the front, or T-Shirts with FMLN on the front, or a red Chairman star on the front of ball cap, even wearing Che Guevara T-shirts I'd bring down from having purchased them at art fairs on Mission Street in San Francisco—I hated that psychopath Ernesto Guevara; I still do, for all the grief his martyrdom has brought to Latin America through an illusion of salvation. One of our guys took to wearing a straw cowboy hat like some of the Gs. Our armaments consisted of AK47s, Galils, G3s, FN-FALs, M79s, and M16s. For heavier bug repellent, we lugged RPGs and the like, along with LAWs and the hand-held version of the 60mm mortar.

Figure 71. Gulf of Fonseca, 1986; author assisting in arms interdiction (against arms and ammunition smuggled from Cuba, through Nicaragua's Sandinista government). The twenty-three-foot Pirañas used by the Salvadoran Navy (FNES) had earlier in the decade received notoriety with the CIA on the Caribbean side of the Central America War—1986 was a tentative time between the CIA and the FNES: FNES had lost a full squad of Salvadoran SEALs due to drowning in a beach landing during waves too high, and CIA advisors were blamed. By 1986, MILGROUP, Specifically ST4 under command of MILGROUP's CMDR Dick Flanagan, was "publicly" in complete US interactions during operations and training. If you were CIA during this time, it was hard to tell who was going to put a bullet in your back first, the FMLN, or the Salvadoran Navy...Host country; home rules.

To say it was dangerous work was an understatement. It was bad enough shooting it out with the FMLN, but it was when we encountered our own side that we'd hit the pucker factor. That's when you were most likely to get killed, not by the enemy, but by small government patrols that didn't know you were working in an area and they could just as easily, or more rapidly, have killed you deader than dead. A couple of our instructors had been Selous Scouts in Rhodesia's ill-fated war against the communists, and all the former-Rhodesians had to do was describe a major *screwing of the pooch* resulting from poorly coordinated operations: one team was totally wiped out by government forces because the government troops didn't know that team was working in the area. We paid attention. Communication was of major importance whenever we were out looking for whoever or whatever.

Originally, UCLAs were deployed over on the Caribbean side against Nicaragua, during the early leadership of Dewey Clarridge, who surrounded himself with a variety of other dirty shirts from the "across the fence" programs in Laos during the Vietnam War: MACV-SOG, Air America. DCI Bill Casey pretty much rubber stamped everything that Dewey came up with. Dewey had that bravado that appealed to Casey's younger years working for "Wild Bill" Donovan of the OSS (Casey would become my "Wild Bill"), and they both had an affinity for a good drink and a cigar. After the public relations fiasco with the mining of Sandinista ports, things quieted down, more like they were redirected. This of course happened about three years before I was involved in Latin America, about the time I was preparing to take a leave of absence (LOA) from the US Naval Reserve and head to Southeast Asia.

Don't get me wrong, I didn't think anything wrong with the mining of the Nicaragua's harbors. We were at war and the only ones who didn't know that was suburban America who hadn't seen the likes of which since WWII—we had been living in a society of luxury for the last sixty years. Thing is that when you start mining harbors, you better start thinking about just sending down the Marines and US Army, as was done in Nicaragua against Sandino. Everyone who's been raised in a Marine family knows that was when "Uncle Chesty" Puller really cut his teeth, long before Chosin.

Mining harbors, ports, rocketing urban areas, these are the stuff of post-declarations of war. Had Reagan just declared war, the cleaning out of communism in Central America would have been short and sweet—there was more than enough evidence the Americas were once again under major attack and even more so than during the Cuban Missile Crisis: people were actually being killed in a war insurrected by the communists, and fueled by Cuba. Reagan, though, like the American people, didn't want another Vietnam.

It's ironic that the very attempt to keep such a large war covert is what led to this type of war being fought for more than twelve years, much longer than it would have gone, had Reagan just sent down the Marines:

though environmentally similar, the cultural differences between Indochina and Central America are far different—many of our advisors who were disgusted with a Cambodian and Vietnamese propensity to turn and run from battle, were elated with the enthusiasm for fighting and holding ground Central American combatants exhibited a decade later. How fewer deaths of who knows how many American personnel? And how many more American personnel would have been recognized for their service? A term used for keeping secret the number of American killed in action (KIA) was called "body-washing," with many who died in combat, or even flying into a jungle mountain at night, being marked as having died in a training accident, hundreds to thousands of miles from where they perished. If for just the peace of mind of family, or recognition of valor and gallantry, these combat-related deaths both in the military and paramilitary community should be recognized.

In 2016, I reconnected with a couple FAES chopper pilot buddies, who had gone the commercial fixed wing route after the war. I was so elated for them that they were doing so well financially, flying for airlines in China: having survived what we survived, they earned it…Over a bit of drink, one buddy, let's call him by his call sign, *Apache,* said, "I can't talk with anyone about what we did in those days. My family and friends who weren't there with us, they just don't understand. They just can't believe what we were able to do—they just can't believe it!"

That was the first time I had the chance to really reconnect with someone from that time in my life, who really got it, and expressed it so clearly…

As my fellow platoon leader, a paramilitary officer recruited from the Argentine naval officer corps, ordered his team to set a perimeter, I did so with mine. He offered me a pork and cheese *pupusa* from his pack after we sat down under a tree.

"Want some fruit?" he asked, as he reached up into the branches above and plucked a couple ripe guava.

"Sure."

Normally, I'd be working with the Cuban, Enrique (we all went by *nom de guerres*, and just addressed each other by our first names). Enrique was back in Miami, greeting his new born. Tomas was his replacement on this operation and turning out to be worth his salt. We got along well and shared that quality of good teammates to almost read each other's thoughts.

Many like to think that the UCLA program was short-lived and served its purpose only until the International Court of Justice, otherwise known as The Hague, came down hard on the Reagan Administration in 1986 for its actions in 1983 and 1984 in Nicaragua. What did people think, that these men and women who had left their homes, drawn by the patriotic duty to rid the Americas of the scourge of totalitarianism hiding under the much more benign looking cloak of communism, would just go home and wait for communism to take over in their homelands?

These were well-trained specialists in counter-insurgency and unconventional warfare who received their training from US Navy SEALs, CIA PMOOs(Paramilitary Operations Officers) and contractors, the USMC, and US Army Special Forces, not to mention all the training they might have had from their nations of birth. They were not to be wasted being sent home to twiddle thumbs and hope for a better world. We, the Free World, had them in Central America being put to good use.

After a bit of conversation about the hijinks of unwinding during the previous week's quick R&R on the beaches of Tela, over in Honduras, and joking about how our families in Ecuador and Argentina wouldn't recognize us on the phone because our time here had blended our native Spanish into a hodgepodge of Mexican, Nicaraguan, Honduran, and Salvadoran Spanish, I thanked him for the breakfast and pulled my battle board from my ALICE pack and began reviewing the short sheet on our principle. Looking at the topographical map, I checked our position in relation to the San Vicente volcano that made an excellent bearing.

We waved over our local FMLN-defector who had become a major anti-communist operator and asked him to check the short, cheat sheet dossier to see if he could add anything more from his time in Zelaya's group. The three of us checked the map for where the local FMLN bases had been moved to. Like with the Kit Carson Scouts in Vietnam, captured Vietcong who had defected and been turned into fighters against their own, we had our program working well in Central America, with captured Gs who turned out be much better fighters at getting their own former comrades. I wouldn't completely trust them because if they could be turned once, they could easily be turned around again.

They defected for a variety of reasons. One of the most influential national events that helped the cause was when President Duarte opened up landownership to the campesinos. When he offered this small gesture, he took so much out of the communist propaganda, that it forced the Gs to increase brutal conscriptions, and that in itself was a losing campaign. Another reason captured guerrillas were turned was for money. They got better pay than they got from the communists, and when we used them to train regular forces in their guerrilla tactics, we were that much more effective in being ahead of the enemy's maneuvers.

When I asked one of the counter-intel interrogators back in San Salvador why he thought guerrillas who had been turned were such fierce fighters, so fierce that a couple times I felt compelled to rein them in, else suffer an atrocity as the result of the actions of one who was under my command, she said that it could be a variety of reasons, but the most striking was that it was a way for them to take out those who might point them out later as traitors. As one who was more interested in capturing and bringing back live prisoners for the wealth information they could provide, I had to keep my eye on those who were cleaning up loose ends.

Most of my time in central El Salvador, I navigated during the day by referring to the variety of inactive volcanoes. We were on our way to our second waypoint and all looked good. We were only 5 klicks from the village and the little glen we had found to rest was a good place to wait and then get ready to move in toward our target in the last hour.

Our next waypoint would give us a full view of the village. I checked the photo of the American who had had been in the USAF in Vietnam during the mid-1960s and was now using his knowledge in FMLN operations against the government. One of them were car bombs that created such a visceral reaction from me whenever thought about them—I'd learned to hate indiscriminate use of explosives in urban areas. There are two kinds of responses to IEDs left to maim and kill indiscriminately: rage and fear. Of the former, I was of the type who was spurred on to hunt down and eliminate those who left landmines in our way.

Below the map was a photo of this man in his thirties, taken in Honduras. A list of possible contacts, and persons of interest, in the village we were headed towards, too. My fellow PMO and I went through the satellite photo we had rehearsed our strategy the previous four days. We had decided that we'd have two of our defectors who were from the area be the first into the village. All going well, we'd have one of those held responsible for the murders of US Embassy's Marines nearly three years earlier.

Zelaya was in a way, like me, born of an Anglo-Americano father, and a mother from Latin America. The difference to most fighting for the communists in El Salvador was that he had entered the US military and gone to Vietnam. He returned to the US from that war with a good knowledge of how to conduct operations. It still mind boggles me that people think things will be better under a regime that is based on more control of the citizens than even a military dictatorship. From all the places I've personally experienced that were under totalitarian control, the only difference was that communist dictatorships had better PR departments, initially.

This was a tricky situation. The US government knew that Gerardo Zelaya was involved with the assassination of the Marines at Zona Rosa, but he was also an American citizen. Terrorists of American origin was not something that started with born-again Islamists trying to prove themselves in Jihad. We in the United States have been confronted by them for decades, if not the last two centuries. Some of them didn't fare too well, such as Joe Sanderson and others who had been killed fighting for the communists in Latin America.

These were Americans who came down to follow some romanticized dream of Ambrose Pierce fighting alongside Pancho Villa, or who came down from the Communist Party USA (CPUSA) and other groups in Berkeley that were Anti-American and pro-communist—not much different from what's happening nowadays, except these new "*Internationalistas*" wear three-piece suits and have done much better than their earlier versions who still wear over-priced Birkenstocks and tie-dye. Many were recruited or simply enabled by such organizations as CPUSA and Committee in Solidarity with the People of El Salvador (CISPES). Internationalistas, or as they were also called, "*Sandalistas*" because of their preferred hippy footwear came in droves to help their compadres. Some brought medical supplies and aid, others helped carry the arms and ammunition provided by the Cubans and Nicaraguans, American armaments left in Indochina in 1975. It was good business for Hanoi, selling them to the Castro brothers and Ortega, paid for by the Soviet Union.

Figure 72. The author, excited to still be alive, after helping liberate a school house from the FMLN, who had turned it into a training center for building and deploying IEDs.

Unlike most of the Sandalistas who came down to Central America to join the FMLN in their fight to take over the country, Zelaya, was a citizen of both the US and El Salvador. During the Vietnam War, he learned English while a recruit in the USAF. An artist in the Mission District of San Francisco, he did business between artists and galleries in the El Salvador and San Francisco. According to an interview, he said that his artist friends were starting to disappear. He went down to find out what happened and ended up bringing his ability to strategy in in the USAF to aid the FMLN. He even became an operation chief for the FMLN.

An uneasy feeling suddenly overtook us as Guillermo, my fellow *teniente* (both of us were given the rank of lieutenant with which to work with and within the Salvadoran military), went over our plan and worked on our light lunch. It's hard to explain, unless you've really paid attention to that uneasy creepy feeling that works its way up your spine, or overwhelms you with a heavy sense of dread. I'd felt it many times before in war. Everyone has this extrasensory ability. Some have visions. Some hear sounds, of words. Others feel it in their gut. Women are more willing to call it psychic ability. Men more often call it a gut reaction. It's often felt when meeting someone you should be on guard with.

The first time I really paid attention to this feeling in war, I was with a team of Salvadoran Navy SEALs during *Operacion de Golfo III*, (Third Gulf Operation), a naval land and amphibious campaign through Usulutan Province in 1986. I was assigned to the Salvadoran Navy SEALs who were working in conjunction with the BIM (*Battalion Infanteria Marina*, the Salvadoran Marines). Originally, we were supposed to be at the head of the spear, moving ahead of the Marines as they moved forward, but ended up sitting on a Salvadoran Navy cutter waiting to be landed on the beach and move inland to cut off the any elements of the FMLN trying to escape the advancing Marines.

With seas too rough to make an amphibious landing in Zodiac, we were brought to port and were suddenly launched into an airborne operation supporting the Marine sweep, which was already moving in on Deuce-and-a-Halfs. An arrangement was made with the FAES that afternoon we were underway to the Puerto El Triunfo. For the next nine days, we participated in the operation.

On a Wednesday, I had been almost zipped up the back with three rounds from the machine gunner behind me, who thought it was a good idea to stick his thumb inside the trigger guard while adjusting the weight of the M-60 slung his across his chest.

At the first sound of fire, my feet were kicked out and I fell to the ground, my M-16 aimed toward where I thought the Gs were going to come running out of the bush at us. When I noticed everyone else was slowly getting up and their lieutenant was walking back annoyed, I took a deep breath and came to one knee to see the gunner looking at his weapon as though it had magically gone off on its own. A chill went up my back as I realized I had almost become a statistic of stupidity.

Figure 73. BIM moving along a cornfield, shot by the author from the Huey, as they leapfrogged over.

213

After a quick talking down by the Salvadoran officer, the gunner and the rest of us continued on our way down through some brush and intersected a road. We took a break, and I sat back against my pack. Replenishing my salt by sucking on the rings and lines of it that formed on my tunic after my sweat evaporated, I gazed tiredly at Rubio, our sniper. He had shucked his gear and began doing push-ups in the middle of the dirt road.

Almost immediately, I heard a voice. "He's going to get it."

It was so startling that I was compelled to look around and see who had said it. It was shocking in that it wasn't in Spanish, but in English. No one in this team spoke English. So bizarre, I had to look around to see who had said it. No one.

It was simply a thought. I racked it up to just being totally beat. Combat fatigue had set in days ago.

Figure 74. Hidden and taking a break in the tall grass, author's eyes wide from combat fatigue.

That was a Wednesday. Thursday we were coming into the town of *Las Arañas*, and I had come across a sign left by the guerrillas that I felt compelled to tell our sniper, Rubio, to read it and I took his photo. The sign said, in Spanish, "Soldiers—The mines are for the officers. Desert. FMLN. BRAZ."

A few hours and we walked through the village and were on the southside of it and had contact with a five-man squad of Gs who were just walking down the road. One of them was wounded as they tried to escape. The lieutenant called in a Huey Gunship and we continued our way down the road, stopping for a moment to acknowledge what hell must have dropped down on the guerrillas, who had tried to get away, but had clearly been found by the gunship. The commandos closest to me raised their eyebrows in a form of empathy and shock for those Gs being rained on by lead and copper. All I could say was, "Fuuuuuck..."

It sucked to be them.

Figure 75. Rubio reading a warning left by the FMLN.

After a day of recon south of Las Arañas, we were moving back up into the town that I had learned to hate: it was bursting with Gs. You'd walk past their smiling faces and then they'd pull a weapon out from under a cart, or a mound of corn and shoot you in the back. This was "Indian Country" for the Salvadoran military. The area around the town was also peppered with land mines and a variety of improvised explosive devices (IEDs). You took your life in your own hands just taking a quaint country stroll. The guerrilla-friendly campesinos knew where they all were, of course.

Twelve of our team had had walked down that trail before I saw Rubio, who was right in front of me, take what looked like a high and leaping step. A muffled boom hit me at the same time. I looked behind me and the corporal was to one knee just as quickly as me, our M-16s at the ready. We didn't know what it was, and thought it was an RPG about to bring on a whole ambush. There was only a moment of silence as I glanced at the corporal behind me, who shrugged his shoulders.

First it was a moan, and then it was, *"Ayudame...Ayudame. Enfermero!"*

Immediately, I ran for his position and began pulling items from my medical bag. It was my job on this operation, to be an extra corpsman for this team. Normally they had one, but if I was to be along, I had to serve some purpose, other than just auditing their performance in the field. Teams this small needed everyone to be a contributor, else they were undergunned. Their regular corpsman was on Rubio's leg administering a tourniquet, while I injected morphine into Rubio's arm. It took effect quickly.

Thankfully it was only a small mine. It took his foot off, instead of the bullets or a pieces of shrapnel as I'd seen in the previous two years I'd experienced combat. The blast had cauterized the stump when it took his foot, leaving only the skin of his heel, the size and shape of a gummy worm. A medevac was called, and I saw the RTO standing over to the side.

I called him and over and he refused, saying he wasn't going to walk across a potential minefield to aid in putting his teammate on a makeshift stretcher of Rubio's rain poncho. I was going to get up and beat the shit out of him for his cowardice, but the team's sergeant appeared, and we had enough men to carry Rubio out to a field of tall grass to wait for the choppers under a tree.

Just as annoyed as me at the radiotelephone operator, the lieutenant came up and yelled at the RTO to come over to us under the tree. The antenna on his PRC-77 made him look like a scared little bug as it vibrated, signaling his trepidation as he walked out of the brush to us.

An hour later, the UH-1D came down and we loaded Rubio onto the chopper with a team mate to hold his IV of Ringer's solution. After loading his scoped M-14 and pack, the chopper left us to continue our mission. Not until I had the chromes developed and reviewed the sequence did I recall that *voice.*

That same voice was calling out to me in San Vicente, and it made me very uneasy. It caused me to load up and after conferring with Guillermo, who was also now feeling the same, we got our teams back on the move.

Barely a half-mile from where we got back on the path, the brush in front of us erupted in small arms fire. Immediately our teams went to action. This is what training is all about. It's to act in a coordinated and accurate manner, without having to completely bring the conscious mind into play in order to accomplish it. It's almost surreal how it happens, as if your conscious mind is a third person player, observing the action, instead of participating.

Figure 76. Rubio's bad day.

Figure 77. Coming home on a Huey, tired after a long op...

217

One of the personal realizations of spending 11 months in prison in Vietnam, and after having come to the conclusions of what happened to American servicemen, who ended up as POWs, and then held as MIAs for later negotiations for war reparations to be paid to Hanoi, was I swore I'd never, and I mean, NEVER, be taken prisoner again. Having seen corpses in the field, of supposed American combatants who had been captured, and mutilated by the FMLN, was another bit of incentive, I was more than compelled to this belief. The FMLN was all about making statements by killing and mutilating those Americans captured while aiding the Salvadoran government.

At first, just like in Vietnam, Americans weren't being heavily targeted, but by the mid-1980s, killing Americans was a prime objective of the FMLN. When I was in San Miguel during the base overrun, there was an FMLN team whose sole objective was to get to the US Army Special Forces 7th Group advisers. Perhaps I would have been gotten away unscathed had I been with them that night. They made it to an escape tunnel that had been built for just such an event. Less than a year later, at the Salvadoran Army 4th Brigade Base at El Paraiso, thirty miles north of San Salvador, Staff Sergeant Greg Fronius wasn't as fortunate as his brothers at San Miguel. SSG Fronius went down fighting with his M-16 in hand.

When I heard, I thought it was the best thing he could have done considering the situation. Being skinned, and having your penis stuffed in your mouth while you were still alive was a much worse option. I knew this all or nothing attitude had pulled me and my combat buddies out of some really tight spots over the previous two years.

In the moment that the first shots came in, we immediately went to that training that had been drilled into us day after day, some of it totally contrary to what logic and genetic impulse would dictate, such as running into danger instead of into it. Everyone one of us charged straight at the firing positions, providing covering fire as we went on full-auto. To go anywhere else could have meant falling into a variety of boobytraps set for such a tactic, or another flank that hadn't yet opened up on us.

By charging directly into the firing positioners, our patrol line forming the point of our spear driving into them, we skirted the unknown and were confronted with the known ambushers. Two of them jumped up immediately and tried to run when we started to their firing line, being dumped with rounds to the back. It's amazing how quickly people can move when driven by fear or anger. It's for this reason the tactics of close combat are taught to even those wanting to just carry a pistol for self-defense. The twenty-one-foot rule is taught, which is a general estimate. Some people can close distances much faster. And the rule is not just for the time it takes to close that distance, but also your reaction time to such a threat.

In amongst our ambushers, we immediately went to machetes and knives. We trained with those machetes, hacking targets with strokes and stabbing, and sheathed, against blows from opponents. We were as deft with them as the Gs, some of who had become proficient with them long before they were issued guns by the FMLN. Our machetes appeared as we closed on them, as we couldn't use our firearms because our teams that fanned out and engulfed them in a line—for fear of shooting our own, either an accidental direct shot, or a through an enemy into a friendly fighting for his or her own life in the melee.

With our rapid closing of ranks with the Gs, they were left to react by going for their own knives and machetes. Already at a loss because they were reacting instead of acting, they did so only after realizing that firearms, especially long FN-FALs and M16A1s were impractical in such close quarters—they'd shot one of their own in an attempt to get a bead on us in the brawl.

Fractured and bleeding, what was an FMLN ambush team was now crashing through the brush to get away. Two groups of two of our men went off to search for their stragglers. The rest of us went about securing the area and checking to see who was still alive on the ground. I wiped the blood off my machete and stuck it back in its sheath, strapped running down the middle of my pack between the shoulder straps where it was fast and easy to get to by reaching over behind my neck.

Others carried it like a bowie knife on their combat belt, I preferred it on my pack so that it would be in play from the moment it was drawn, starting with a slicing chop down, from my right down to my left, which would then swing up in a loop that would create a cutting infinity symbol, or a figure-8 on its side. When President Trump mentions the MS-13 cutting heads off with machete, he's talking old school—They learned how to do it from their uncles, grandfathers and fathers who fought on both sides of the war, a cutting and hacking tradition of war fighting in this area going back further than the Mayans and the Spanish conquistadores.

While I took stills of the battlefield and of the faces of the captured and dead for our files, and those of analysts in San Salvador and back at Langley, Guillermo and I conferred on whether we had been compromised all the way back before we flew out of Ilopango Airbase, or that this was just bad luck. We wouldn't know until much later that an agent of the FMLN had told them that we were coming for Zelaya. We'd learned that TOP SECRET didn't mean much at the State Department—some US State Department employees revealed a poor understanding of prudence with regards to sensitive information, instead sharing it as a tool of rapport and persuasion, even with certain individuals of questionable loyalties. Ambassador Corr was a pretty straight shooting former Marine who understood the various discretions, so I never had any guff with him.

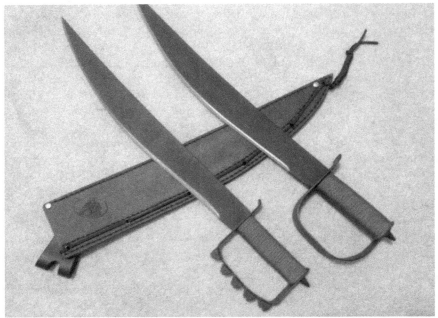

Figure 78. Prototypes I was working on to be manufactured and sold by a knife company with whom Mykel Hawke had a contract. It was based on the customized machete I carried in my pack during the Central America War, and was to be marketed as "Cork's Cutlass."

A call went out for a gunship and a couple choppers to pull our wounded, prisoners, and a few able-bodied commandos out of there, along with a Deuce-and-a-Half to take the bodies of the FMLN and the rest of the team to guard them. The FMLN's dead had a habit of disappearing off the battlefield, in the FMLN's drive to keep their casualty numbers down— even Raoul Castro didn't like throwing money at efforts and numbers being so heavily whittled by anti-communist forces.

Back in the mid-1990s, CBS's 60 MINUTES did a piece on gaining recognition for military veterans of the war in Central America, and Gerardo Zelaya came up, with his real name, too, Romeo Gilberto Osorio. In an old tradition the United States has with former enemies, going all the way back to WWI, he was living peacefully in the Mission District of San Francisco, back to being to be an artist, last seen in 2009 in an article about him and his history, and still unanswered questions about how involved he was in the murder of four Guatemalans, three Salvadorans and four US Marines enjoying a dinner and good times with friends the evening of June 19, 1985.

Figure 79. The author waiting for his ride, refueling before returning to Ilopango Airbase after an operation.

Rage was an emotion that had clearly gotten the best of Jeremy Whalen. He was beside himself with envy that I was team leader and he wasn't. It didn't matter that he really brought nothing to the table, other than he had pushed and pushed to say he was a team player, especially on a team, unbeknownst to me, that was willing to do anything, and I mean, anything to further its agenda of getting another successful multi-season reality show.

Cappy was not looking good. He had been pounding back the rum since the night before. Earlier this morning he had told me how he was going to clock our set doctor. He blamed Dr. Petermann, and the local producer, Julio Noguera, for how we had been basically locked up at the mansion.

The problem with 'reality TV' is that it has nothing to do with reality and everything to do with drama. Discovery Communications' whole strategy of opening offices in Los Angeles and hiring female CEOs and vice presidents of programming was to build on the ability of drama to reach a female audience they found so lacking in numbers. They didn't go to Hollywood for nothing. After watching all the video footage. After finding out all the facts. It's hard for many to believe that what happened next was all accidental: nothing happens in Hollywood without a script.

By the time we'd begun filming the scene of following our two Guarani guides to their camp, that would lead to the scene of the treasure hunting team talking with the tribe of the Guarani, I was amazed that Keith was still able to stand up straight with all the rum he had coursing through his veins. Never underestimate the abilities of an old salt; old sailors don't survive to old age by coasting.

It's amazing, too, that Carr didn't think it unsafe to have had Keith working on set that day, considering you could smell the booze on him a mile away. All I knew was that Keith had reached the end of his rope with how Discovery Communications had us quartered at the Bemberg Mansion like birds in gilded cage. To think I never even used that gorgeous swimming pool, what with the amazing view of the Parana River from that infinity pool. We're talking big money, the Argentine equivalent of the Coors family, Guinness, types of wealth here, the kind that enabled the patriarch to spend most of the year at their home in Paris and spend a couple weeks at the hacienda. The mansion and that wonderful infinity pool wasn't even a mile from where were filming, just on the other side of the Hotel Bemberg.

Production all came crashing down once the yelling started. It was like someone yelling, screaming, to us from the other side of a canyon. It started with Carr asking us where Cappy had gone, as we were still in our roles, and the situation hadn't yet made itself clear that it was soon to spiral wildly out of control. Directing a reality TV show is like that, a sleight of hand. In a fakeumentary, such as THE BLAIR WITCH PROJECT and TREASURE QUEST: SNAKE ISLAND, the actors are paid to deliver that shock, fear, excite, joy, sadness, all the emotions needed to appeal to the law of emotional contagion. Humans are hardwired to see an emotion and their own reactions come about through a very genetic need to mimic, a need to human to be in synchrony. This is what actors are paid to do well on a traditional TV or film drama. Only in the last few decades have psychologists like Elaine Hatfield put names to these reactions. Hollywood's mega-wealth was built on this innate understanding of human psychology over the decades.

The problem with being an actor on "reality" TV is that it's very hard for a non-psychopath to pull up emotions while playing yourself under your own name on camera, doing things and acting in ways you would never do, especially when they go counter to your life experience and training. As one real gold miner told me when we talked about the validity of shows like GOLD RUSH and BERING SEA GOLD, "Do you think you'd ever get anything done, get gold from the ground if you were preoccupied dealing with all that fake drama? You'd be bust in one mining season!"

According to my friend, Vern Adkison, he's gotten more gold now that he's not on BERING SEA GOLD: When you have to reshoot scene after seen over the same area, go figure. Just a few months ago, he asked me if I'd like to prospect the Yukon as he planned to float his new dredging platform down to Nome. When he told me he wanted me to shoot some footage for Discovery in the hopes of getting something going like Dakota Fred Hurt had with GOLD RUSH WHITE WATER, I said—HELL NO!

I'd never find any gold. I'd be preoccupied videoing. And having learned how much gold Hurt and his team really got on that show, I'm just reminded of how real miners, successful miners, never, and I mean, NEVER, appear on TV. The types of personalities who appear are either trying to rewrite their family history, like the Kilchers, Haydens, and the Whalens, and or they're trying to sell something, like Keith, me with our books, or people with services and products—more on that later.

Figure 80. BERING SEA GOLD's Vernon Adkison and the author heading out from breakfast after conferring about our favorite subject—gold!

All a professional actor needs to do is bring up that emotional value that will illicit the mimicking through emotional contagion from the audience, especially the female audience—"Don't cry, Cork. You'll find the treasure!" Since Discovery would lose its profit margin (that CEO David Zaslav is so proud to tout in the media news), by hiring professionally-trained actors, and they still need to get that same type of emotion out of the subjects of its cameras, the showrunners play with the environment, instead of just asking for that emotion. Clancey though, who was the trained actor/director, and went more by the book. He asked for that emotion more than Carr, using the acting methods formulated by Lee Strasberg. David Carr relied more on just putting us in situations and seeing how we reacted. Like in Brazil, it was all a surprise until the morning when we got our day's call sheets, which had our shooting schedules of where we were going to be, what we were going to be doing and how to dress.

Keith was pretty good at hiding how much he had been drinking. The terminology is *functioning alcoholic*. Still, I'm surprised Carr wasn't aware of how emotionally charged Keith was when he sent him into the jungle to the play hide and seek for us to find him on camera. Keith was pointing at Dr. Gustavo Peterman our location medic and punching his fist. Keith for some reason was holding him responsible for us being quartered at the Bemberg. He resented the local fixer Julio Noguera's arrangements that had been made to garner special deals for his friends who had real estate in the area—our magic bus drivers were quartered at a cabin that belonged to Dr. Peterman's family. One of those drivers was also not happy at how the deals were happening as the Argentine fixer tried to get the biggest bang out of a Discovery production in the area.

That driver came to me once to show photo evidence of how Noguera was committing fraud, aside from getting all his buddy's with lodging into the Discovery Communications cash stream. We liked to have *parrilladas* (Argentine grill) for our lunch on set, Leo Ayala, who was not only our magic bus driver, previously on HUNTING HITLER with Tim Kennedy, was also a great grill master, or *parrillero*. That guy could cook with fresh coals and a haunch of meat like no other gaucho.

Thing was that Noguera was telling the butcher to stick price tags on the meat that were almost ten times as much as it cost him to buy the chorizo, morcilla, and beef cuts. He was making bank, and our bus driver was furious that the he was being undercut on his salary—this is why you always take care of your team first, treat them right, else they come back at you when you least expect, and rightfully so! The bus driver delighted in showing me the photos he taken on his cellphone that he was going to turn into the local police.

Figure 81. l.-r. Emilio White, our Argentine naturalist; Dr. Gustavo Petermann, set medic; Brett Tutor, our fake security/survival expert of TQ:SI and TLC's TRADING SPACES; Jimmy McCormick, local fixer; Keith Plaskett, Rolando Ramirez, one of our magic bus drivers; the author with a maté; and Leo Ayala, grand parillero and magic bus driver of TQ:SI and History Channel's HUNTING HITLER. Everyone getting ready for an Argentine parrilla.

All this had just fueled Keith in his anger at everyone on set who wouldn't listen to him. Added to that was his fear that Mehgan and Jeremy were going to be successful in their bid to get the show as their grandstanding production. Drinking was the only place he knew where to go.

It was shocking to see him in the hole, as he lay there on his side, like a fetus curled up in a womb. But, to see him going into an abreaction wasn't: I'd seen it many times as a counselor and recognized it immediately. Others saw something was wrong, but were dumbfounded, even our doctor. Keith had been in Vietnam as a combat engineer, which entailed clearing mines and IEDs—the real hurt locker that Bryan Grieg-Fry always liked to refer to in his self-aggrandizing in Brazil—which was when Keith was first introduced to the use of metal detectors. The psychological effects on combat engineers were as extreme as those hitting tunnel rats who survived their own trials.

While Mehgan, and the rest were blindly screaming for medical assistance from Gustavo, I was doing what I was supposed to do—go to the one in need and provide assistance from my years of counseling in PTS had given, and the years before in Central American when I aided those who had been wounded. When Dr. Petermann came up to Keith, I gave him two pieces of information: Keith was drinking since the night before, and he was having a PTS-related abreaction. Petermann at first didn't recognize what I was talking about with regards to the PTS, but he definitely saw the need for Keith getting hydrated. Keith just needed reassurance and grounding to get him back from his memories and using deep breathing to do it. We talked him through. Once he was calmed enough, Dr. Petermann provided those much-needed fluids to combat the dehydration caused by the alcohol, and I went off to deal with my own memories that had come up while talking Keith through his.

In therapy, it's like walking into the dark jungle, finding the one needing the counseling, and then walking them back out of that dark, traumatic place of memories. As a counselor, you know you're there because you're feeling your own emotions from your own experiences, as you pull the effective emotions from the client. There's no avoiding feeling those emotions if you're doing it correctly: getting into rapport. It's just tiring, and you need your own time away to process your own stuff. My time away was about twenty yards from where all this was happening.

Blading, on the other hand, is what happens when someone is getting ready to attack you. When Jeremy Whalen made that walk from twenty yards away, there would later be no question as to whether it was pre-mediated assault and battery. At the time all I could think about as he came up to me, as if from nowhere (my mind was in a totally different place and time), was, "Is he really doing what I think he's doing?!"

Normally, when an aggressor blades their body to present a smaller target and hide the dominate side that's either pulling a weapon, or coiling a fist for a strike, these are pretty good indictors that something bad is about to happen. Clearly Jeremy had done this before. It takes practice to sucker punch with your weak side. Had I paid attention and not still been caught up in my own thoughts after Keith's abreaction, Jeremy's pumping fists and the proximity with which he closed on me, I would have been more focused on that, than his repeated statement, "No one tells me what to do!"

What drew my attention, though, were his eyes. There was something really weird about his eyes. They were large and black, just like a great white shark's. In a great book on self-preservation in combat, or dangerous areas for that matter, titled LEFT OF BANG, the authors caution toward keeping an eye out for anomalies. By doing so, you can keep ahead of the threat, or remain outside of a bad place: *right of bang*. Jeremy's heavily dilated eyes, clearly due to him being on something, likely the cocaine brought along with the artifacts smuggled from Peru by his brother Jaime, was an anomaly. The other anomaly was how out of character he was from his normally controlled and calculating state he was in with the way he was bouncing around through various forms of irritability.

Jeremy's fist was fast. One second, I was responding to what he said, and the next I was reeling and unable to see out of my left eye because of the blood gushing out of it. That was one calculated punch, initiated all the way back when he started walking toward me. For him to have specifically targeted my eye, instead of punching in me in the stomach said a lot: impact to the torso can hurt, but a blow to the head can kill.

Rage took over just like it did during ambushes twenty-five years earlier, but not as surgically. Blinded and not wanting to get hit again in the eye, the rage of being assaulted and receiving battery for no reason, other than only what I could surmise to be Jeremy self-inflated ego, overtook me and I charged into him, trying to defend myself—he was clearly still a threat. As we down on the ground, I heard this voice saying, "Don't go for the knife! Don't go for the knife!"

Just as suddenly as I had Jeremy on the ground, I was being yanked by my neck and onto my back, and put into a sleeper hold. "Are you done?"

"Yeah, I'm done." I said, disgusted.

Brett Tutor released his hold on my neck and I got up and Dr. Petermann came up to me. Just the fact that Tutor had grabbed me by my neck to pull me 180 degrees from a prone position onto my back immediately told me that Tutor didn't know what he was doing. There are so many other less dangerous ways to restrain someone, that have nothing to do with a maneuver that can either kill of crippled, especially when incorrectly done.

Tutor could have crushed my larynx, which would have required a tracheotomy. As it was, he put my neck out of whack, so that to this day, I've had to take pain killers, and muscle relaxants and still have a grinding and an inability to release a tightness in my neck, just below my cranium, though repeatedly having to see a chiropractor. Pretty amateur for a "security expert."

Everyone I've talked with in law enforcement has agreed a neck hold or sleeper hold is a poor option. Personally, I would have used a wrist, finger or thumb hold to get someone under control without threatening the person's life, or causing such injury. It all brought more questions as to exactly what was Brett Tutor's real background—what exactly did he learn in that SWAT class he said, even on his website, he took?

"Come with me and I'll help you," Gustavo said, when he got to me.

Glancing over my shoulder with my good eye, I could see Jeremy trading punches with Keith. I shook head and said, "What a cluster fuck."

Ariel, and Scottie were caught between shock and keeping the lens on us. Carr, and Dorman were trying to get back into the role of director and showrunner. As Dr. Petermann would later observe, in a very Germanic-Latino observation, owing to his family roots and place of birth, "It was highly charged with emotion." Pretty much a restrained description of what was playing out.

Jeremy had clearly lost his cool. While my requests to get the hell out of the way and stop preventing me from helping his friend were cutting into his ego, the stimulants he was high on took him of his comfort zone. His lashing out like a child in tantrum was indicative of someone who had known abuse as a child. Only now, while Gustavo working on my eye, was it all seemingly become apparent him what he had done, though his actions were actually calculated to get me off the set, especially after what I would later learn, and that he was on cocaine. He just didn't realize that by his immediate self-gratification of getting me off the set, he had gone against his ultimate objective. As said in an April 13, 2015 article on sociopaths (easily describing psychopaths) in PSYCHOLOGY TODAY, by Carrie Barron M.D., titled *When a Sociopath Is Hell Bent on Destroying You*:

"Those afflicted can be calculating, cunning, charming, organized and disarming. Because guilt, shame and remorse are absent yet entitlement, egocentricity and greed reign, the suffering they cause others is meaningless to them. Self-gratification is really all that matters, the guiding principle of daily life."

Figure 82. Author's eye immediately after Dr. Petermann wiped away most of the blood, resulting from Jeremy Whalen's assault and battery.

While I sat by the doctor's medical bag and he washed away the blood from my ripped open eyelid, Jeremy said from down the way, "Will you take my apology?"

"Cork, will you take Jeremy's apology?" Carr said, from further down the road, over toward where all this started with the staged hide-n-seek.

"I'm sorry," Jeremy said.

"You're unprofessional," I said. "We're done."

As I kept my good eye on Jeremy, I noticed something interesting in his mannerisms. He was totally void of emotions, as if he were out of his body looking at everything happening, as if from a third-person point of view. It was bizarre. It wasn't because he was in shock, like the rest there on set. I've seen something similar in survivors of a major battle, or car crash, who walked aimlessly around.

No. Jeremy was different. His mind was processing, not in static numbness, like when people are in shock. He was clearly calculating his next move. You could hear it in him not just coming forth and saying, I'm sorry, but instead asking me would I take his apology. It was as if he wouldn't offer it, if it didn't have the effect he wanted. He wasn't offering an apology; he was negotiating a deal.

It's kind of creepy looking back at it now, how unemotional he was in his calculations. Arnold Schwarzenegger's Terminator had more expression on his face than Jeremy did in that moment—but that's the numbing part of cocaine, too. It made it that much easier to say, to hell with his apology. It wasn't heartfelt, or had any meaning in any way, and really just one more indicator of a psychopath working his angles.

"How does it look? Do you have a mirror?"

Gustavo nodded and drew a small hand mirror from his bag. Looking at my eye, I immediately thought there was no way they were going to keep shooting with me on the show. That's when I started really thinking perhaps Keith Plaskett was right. Jeremy and Mehgan were trying to get us out of there and attempt some weird and twisted coup to put them as the leads. If that was the case, Jeremy was using Mehgan, because she had the fame, and he had nothing other than what he could weasel.

Thinking about how I was going to get the hell of there and get a plane ticket home, because if MAK Pictures and Discovery Channel had let things go this far, they surely couldn't be trusted to get me safely home. If a production company like Discovery Communications was willing to have its whole crew and cast of TQ:SI working for two months out of three on tourist's visas, what other illegal activities would they be willing to participate in? People disappear in Latin America all the time.

Carr, Dorman and the rest of the production crew were conferring with each other, dumbfounded as to what to do next. They'd let Jeremy get out of hand and did nothing until it was too late, which really started to make me wonder about all this drama that was happening on reality TV with fights. There was already the fistfight in Oregon that led to Dave Turin leaving GOLD RUSH. There was the fist fight between Vern Adkison and Scott Meisterheim on BERING SEA GOLD shot at a reunion in Southern California. According to Steve Riedel, also of BERING SEA GOLD, producers on the show were always egging on Meisterheim to create a dramatic scene by trying get him to pick a fight with Reidel. There was so much history at Discovery to make me believe that this wasn't all a set up for drama.

If Discovery had used up my personal history and really couldn't do a character assassination because that personal history is what made the show, they had to do something drastic to explain my leaving the show. As Mark Kadin told me when he said Discovery would pay me $6,000 an episode instead of the $3,000 they were paying the rest of the cast, it was because, "We have no show unless you're on the show." Discovery had to do something radical to explain my departure. What better way than to make it look as if I was losing my mind—just like Discovery Communications character assassinated Cody Lundin with matches in the pool scene—and had a fight between Jeremy to explain my disappearance from the show, even though first season was basically written around my background? They could then say that the reason I wasn't later in Bolivia for the fall 2017 production of Season 3, which was wrapped as TQ2B, was that I was done, just like Dave Turin.

Media character assassination for profit is nothing new. Look at what happened to Jesse "The body" Ventura, former Governor of Minnesota, and UDT 12 during Vietnam. The publishers got former-US Navy SEAL Chris Kyle to lie about battering Ventura in a bar for badmouthing Navy SEALs, saying that SEALs should die. How ludicrous is that? If a person were to have said that, why in the world would he be at a UDT/SEAL celebratory bar party the night before class graduation? Ventura was there to welcome in the new graduating class. Ventura was there out of respect to the graduating class and tradition—why in the world would anyone with those actions, use words so contrary to what Chris Kyle said compelled him to punch Ventura at that bar?! The media, of course, jumped on it, but they didn't do their due diligence with regards to research, and ended up wrongly crucifying Ventura. Or frankly, they didn't care, and knew the controversy would, and did, sell books!

If you're trained in recognizing facial expressions, you'll find that original interview of Chris Kyle in which he first mentions the supposed assault and battery against Ventura fascinating; it's a very interesting study in a person lying. Check the YouTube video of THE OPIE AND ANTHONY SHOW, which aired from 1995 to 2014, when Kyle said about

Ventura, "He went down." He puts his finger up to his mouth. That's a major tell, but there are several others. He was clearly deceitful—but where was the press in digging deeper into this story, that instead just jumped on the book publicity train?

Real military heroes hate to be called heroes. Perhaps it's time to remember military veterans are still human. We humans all have our vices, and when money comes calling some are willing to do anything. A former-Special Forces/Global Response Staff (GRS) buddy of mine and I were in a supermarket when a passerby came by and after seeing his veteran pickup plates, said, "Thank you for your service!"

"Did you serve?" my buddy responded.

"No, I didn't…I saw your sticker. I just wanted say, thank you."

We thanked him back and after he left, my buddy, said about that often repeat phrase, "It's the least he could."

I nodded.

He looked at me, straight in the eye, and then said, "No, man, I mean: IT'S THE LEAST HE COULD DO."

I smiled and said, "I know…"

It's one thing to pay respect to those who have served this country, either as military personnel, or those who willing went into harm's way to defend their country—Surprisingly, with all the patriotic rhetoric it's normally only a few (only about eight-percent actual responded to the call of duty during the most patriotic war, World War II; can you imagine how fewer went to Vietnam and the GWOT?! Of that percentage, only twenty-five percent of the military go into combat: the other seventy-five percent are support—but everyone has the potential of being killed or maimed, what with all the accidents.), and the demands are great. Going to war doesn't define whether a person is good or bad—it shouldn't be the get out of jail free card it has become, just because the rest of society feels guilty about not answering that important call. If society feels so damned guilty about it, why not bring back the draft we had in this country from 1939 until 1971? I'm for it: it'll at least teach the lesson of mortality to children and turn them into adults, and at least teach them how to say, yes, sir, and no, ma'am!

There are basically two famous Navy SEALs that draw media attention these days: CMDR Dick Marcinko, author of ROGUE WARRIOR, and James G. Janos, AKA Jesse Ventura. When you're publishing a niche book, which AMERICAN SNIPER was, and you need publicity, what better way than to suck some off someone already famous with the added spice of controversy? In an interview, Ventura mentioned that presales were only 2,000 copies, but after the character assassination by Kyle, sales went to 102,000. That's a big leap in sales. Mainstream media that didn't do their job threw lawyers at Ventura…and still Ventura won the case.

As I sat there having blood wiped from my face, I didn't know which I was more pissed off at, the fact that Jeremy sucker punched me; that I let him get close enough to do so in the first place (anyone with training knows that distance equals time to react to a threat); or that Discovery Communications scripted his assault and battery against me. It was sure looking more like it was staged than just happening on its own.

Caught in a whir with what to do, I watched Jeremy as he walked around lost in thought, talking with himself. Keith was off on his own. So too Brett and Mehgan. Everyone was pretty much lost in their own worlds, except for Mehgan who went into conversation with Carr and Dorman. Later, after all had settled down, and I had left the set, the doctor told me that Mehgan, crying a torrent of tears, pleaded with them, "I've got everything riding on this! I've put too much into this—It can't fall to pieces!"

A 250cc dirt bike caught my eye. The hotel desk attendant had ridden it down from the hotel. I asked him if I could borrow it to get out of there and to the hotel. He asked me in Spanish if I could drive one.

"*Claro que sí!*" I said. I've been driving motorized two-wheel vehicles since I was eleven years old. The Argentine fixers, and the rest of the hotel employees who were watching the production, told him to let me take it. Turning the key, I kick-started and fished-tailed the wheel for my own little get out of Dodge drama.

B-lining it for the Bemberg mansion instead of the hotel, I parked the dirt bike. The grounds keeper and his wife were shocked to not only see me rush up on a motorbike but show a large patch over my eye. They must have already heard, as they didn't greet me with questions about how my day had gone, as they normally did.

They were such a nice couple, trying not to pay too much attention to my eye as I kicked out the kick-stand and dismounted, which made me think that I must have looked really bad. Hinting that I probably wouldn't be coming back, I thanked them for their gracious hospitality, said I was going to take a shower and clean up and head over to the hotel. A quick shower, a clean pair of jeans and black T-shirt, and after having to replace my bandage, I headed downstairs and jumped on the bike and said, good-bye.

I made it back to the Hotel and then walked into the lobby that MAK Line Producer Cathy Grant, and Tambo Film of Peru's local production coordinator Paulina Cacho-Sousa, and fixer David Rivas, had commandeered into their own production company office. Rivas had left back to Peru more than a month earlier, after Carr lit into him one night that we were shooting a boat scene on the river: If you have to ask your co-showrunner and crew whether you had been a bit too harsh, you've pretty much answered your own question.

The wide-eyed and concerned looks on Cathy and Paulinas' faces said it all. They quickly asked me if I wanted lunch. I said sure and went outside on the hotel's veranda to think more on what to do. A nicely braised chunk of pork and mashed potatoes arrived and then the rest of the crew started appearing, all except for Jeremy, who likely was in the showrunner's office that had been fashioned out of the bar and wine cellar at the base of the hotel, talking with MAK in LA.

While I tried to take my mind off the pain overwhelming my eye and head, and waited for lunch to be served, Keith Plaskett who was still three sheets to the wind, was inside, and banging on the glass wall, yelling, "You fucker, you damned quitter—you pussy! You're gonna ruin it for all of us!"

Making a fist and pointing at me, he pounded the glass. I looked back at Paulina and Cathy and shook my head. Cathy was angry now. "Let me care take of this."

She got up to talk with Keith, and I tried focusing on my meal and the beautiful view out of the veranda of the Puerto Bemberg Inn. Apparently, he was ushered over to a van that took him over to the Bemberg mansion. While I finished my meal, I looked up at Cathy, and David Carr, through my good eye, and said, "I'm going to get out of here and go stay at the Amerian in Iguazu until I get my bearings."

"We'd like to get your belongings out of the Bemberg and bring them over here. We've got a freed-up room. We'll put you up in the hotel here with us, so we can get you away from them over there."

"I'm still not staying here this weekend. I'm going over to Iguazu...and as to whether I'll comeback on production that will have to depend on whether Jeremy's still here."

John Adams appeared and conferred with Carr away from the table while I finished up my lunch.

Adams and Carr came up and said, "Let's go with you over to the Bemberg and we'll have John go with you to your room and help you. Cathy and I will talk with Cappy while you get in and get out with your stuff. Is that okay?"

"Sure."

When we got to the Bemberg mansion, Cappy was in the foyer where he normally liked to commiserate with a bottle of rum at night.

Order of the day was to make our way toward the kitchen, then back over to the staircase and up to the second floor and my room. John Adams and I were in and out like Flynn. My gear was already packed from just before taking my shower earlier. All we had to do was grab it and get it down to the magic bus. Adams and I waited for only a short time, while Cathy and Carr exited the mansion over and joined us in the van.

Back to the hotel and I said, adios.

Figure 83. Cappy's favorite Bemberg Mansion foyer—beautiful.

A phone call was waiting for me at the hotel. It was MAK Pictures' executive producer and owner Mark Kadin's business partner, Will Ehbrecht. After pleasantries, I told Ehbrecht I had no interest in staying on a production with a psychopath. He said they needed to finish shooting.

More than disgusted with how Jeremy had successfully manipulated Ehbrecht and Kadin with his trinkets of research from Ecuador and Peru— I didn't know about the artifact and drug smuggling, yet—I let my anger overtake my self-control.

Ehbrecht responded furiously and so out of character, "I feel insulted you'd say something like that. We never colluded with Jeremy—"

I hung up. It hit me then how much Jeremy had been working them behind the scenes. By showing up for the second season, I had set myself up for an ambush. Remember LEFT OF BANG's advice to pay attention to "anomalies?"

Ehbrecht's response was totally out of character from the friendly demeanor that he normally used to put people at ease. He sounded not only angry but stressed. I had hit a solid nerve, when I told him I felt they had been working behind my back with Jeremy on the show, and to character assassinate me. While he tried to call me back, I ignored it. I was also furious as the feelings hit me for having been played by MAK Pictures and

Discovery Communications.

Then the what now thoughts came flooding in. *How the hell am I going to get out of here?! If they can bribe the local officials not check our passports, which would shown that our work visas had expired at the end of our first thirty days, what else can they do? I could try to buy a plane ticket but they could also have the police snag me at the airport.* No wonder Discovery likes to shoot productions in Latin America, the bribery of officials is a lot easier for them to do there than back in the States, or Canada. I had yet to hear what happened to Teti in Bolivia when he went off the deep end.

I also hadn't learned about Jeremy and James Whalen smuggling the artifacts for Discovery Communications. If I had, I would have been taking a bus to Paraguay, entering as a tourist, and catching a flight out of there back to the States, immediately. <u>Any corporation that is willing to break international laws concerning national treasures and artifacts will do anything</u>. I took the night to sleep on it.

Taking another round of painkillers, I was hit by those words I thought were actually coming out of my mouth when I defended myself against Jeremy's attack: "Don't pull the knife! Don't pull the knife!"

I realized then that they weren't coming out of my mouth. They were running around in my head, as I defended myself by charging and putting Whalen on the ground. I wasn't telling him not to pull a knife. I was telling MYSELF not to pull the large Super Bowie that SOG Knives had sent me to carry on the show, and always had on my belt during production.

This was the knife that I didn't just carry on the set of TQ:SI. I normally carry it when I'm in the field back home in Alaska. It's the only hunting knife I consider long enough to do any damage on a bear that large. It was a larger copy of an original my father picked up at the PX in Saigon when we were living there from Tet 1968 to 1972. I wore it as my last line of defense in varying degrees of separation: rifle, to pistol or machete, to knife, to hands—I would have been rusty, but it's just like riding a bike.

When I realized I had kept my cool during the whole defense of my life during Jeremy's attack, I was hit by two realizations. Even though two decades had passed since I was trained, and used, such tactics, I had charged him as if I had been in an ambush. Also, I was able to keep a sense of awareness in a situation where everyone was clearly turning off because of the intensity of emotions that had overtaken them, either exciting them to rash and ill-advised actions, such as Brett Tutor, using a sleeper hold that anyone in law enforcement will tell you is a horrible way to break up a fight (when my para-military team and I were taught how to use it in Central America by US Navy SEALs from ST3, we were cautioned it was mainly to be used for taking out sentries silently, and with the knowledge we could kill with it—jump to June 4, 2017 Bamako, Mali, and a US Army green beret being killed by two members of ST6 with a choke hold). I had felt good that I hadn't lost my cool and retained a sense of professionalism when those around were just falling over themselves. If I hadn't, had I succumbed to the same lack in discipline of Jeremy Whalen, I could have just as easily, just as rashly, gone fully back to that other training that got me and my teams out of ambushes in Central America using edged blades the way we did, old school...

When I woke in the morning, I was livid. My eye had a hematoma puffing out my eyelid. It was bad enough that I couldn't see well out of that injured eye. Looking in the mirror didn't do me any good in keeping calm. I was looking forward to flying planes when I got home to Alaska and having bad eyesight is a major negative!

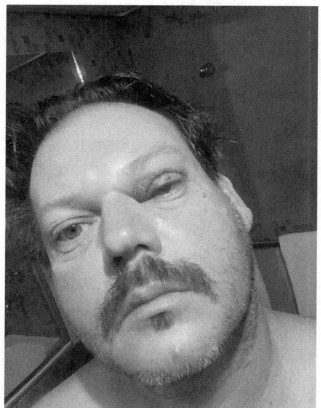

Figure 84. The morning after—my eyesight was definitely not as good as it had been.

Cooling down enough and calming myself, I checked my messages. First was Ehbrecht trying to get me to call him back. The second was from Mark Kadin. Emails were exchanged. I was learning that documentation with

Discovery Communications is very important. Verbal promises mean nothing with Discovery Communications: CEO David Zaslav was educated as a lawyer, and he employees fifty of lawyers on a full floor in Silver Springs, just to deal with the repercussion of their lies, deceit and outright illegal activities, such as fraud, defamation, and international artifact smuggling.

From: Cork Graham
To: "Cork Graham"
Subject: FW: Jeremy's expensive Daddy issue...
Date: Tuesday, April 17, 2018 1:44:16 PM

From: Mark Kadin ▮
Sent: Thursday, May 5, 2016 3:01 PM
To: Cork Graham ◄▮
Subject: Re: Jeremy's expensive Daddy issue...

Ok, I understand. Let's please talk first thing in the AM and please be ready to film tomorrow if we can come to an agreement on how to move forward.

On Thu, May 5, 2016 at 3:59 PM, Cork Graham ◄▮ wrote:

> I'm on painkillers the doctor gave that aren't working on the pain, but will prevent me from having a lucid conversation. That's why I'm trying to just rest for a conversation early tomorrow.
>
> Sent from my iPhone
>
> On May 5, 2016, at 7:29 PM, Mark Kadin ◄▮ wrote:
>
>> I absolutely respect how upset you are with this situation, as am I. I am more than willing to have discussions with you about how to move forward including additional compensation, however, every single day that we can't film with you costs the production an exorbitant amount of money, and every day that goes by will make the situation even more untenable for all of us and I will be less willing to be flexible. --
>>
>> Last season, you had an issue with Bryan, and as you can see, he is not part of the cast anymore.
>>
>> I can and WILL fix this situation, but I need your help. I suggest we discuss today if you can.
>>
>> On Thu, May 5, 2016 at 3:13 PM, Cork Graham ◄▮ wrote:
>>
>>> Tomorrow, Mark. I'm still pissed off that something as stupid as this happened. I'm also still in great pain.
>>>
>>> Thanks,
>>> Cork
>>>
>>> Sent from my iPhone
>>>
>>> On May 5, 2016, at 6:59 PM, Mark Kadin ◄▮

Figure 85. Imagine my later surprise to see Jeremy Whalen was the only one from the original cast to be on the Season 3; in Bolivia he's called the "tech specialist.": By then, I knew he had Discovery Communications by the balls—Jeremy Whalen and his brother go down for smuggling artifacts, and Discovery Communications down with them.

Kadin asked me what it would take for me to come back to production. I told him Jeremy had to go in order for me to even contemplate returning. He was clearly unstable. Who knew when he was going to go off the handle, or whatever else he could do. We had edged weapons on the set. Kadin said it was impossible to get rid of Jeremy. Not yet learning that Jeremy Whalen had MAK and Discovery by the balls with his artifact smuggling, I said, write him out due to an injury, hinting toward what they were already planning to do with me, like Jeremy's attempt to put himself in my place, but punching me in the face.

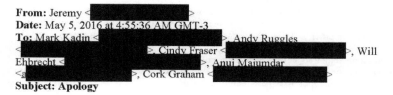

From: Jeremy ◄ ▬▬▬▬▬▬▬ ►
Date: May 5, 2016 at 4:55:36 AM GMT-3
To: Mark Kadin ◄ ▬▬▬ ►, Andy Ruggles
◄ ▬▬▬ ► Cindy Fraser ◄ ▬▬▬▬▬▬ ►, Will
Ehbrecht ◄ ▬▬▬ ►, Anuj Majumdar
◄ ▬▬▬ ►, Cork Graham ◄ ▬▬▬ ►
Subject: Apology

Hi Guys,
    Sorry I missed your skype call yesterday. I'd like to apologize for my part in the
altercation with Cork.
    I asked him not to pop off on me as he did a few minutes prior. His reaction
was to pop off on me again and unfortunately we both lost it.
    I feel deeply ashamed of myself. I should have been bigger than that and
walked. There's too much of a bigger picture here to mess things up with
pettiness. All of us are impacted by each others actions directly and indirectly and
I take that very seriously.
    Also, I apologize for the position that I've put you in. You all work so hard to
put out a great show and it's not fair to anyone to let anything risk that investment.
    Hopefully Cork will take the high road and accept my apology so we can
smooth things out and move forward.

    J

Sent from my iPhone

Figure 86. The blood wasn't even dry yet, and he sent out this email to try and clear up his coked-up screw up. Remember that Jeremy walked almost 20 yards to confront me...Jeremy's whole psychotic life receives meaning only through this show. In the States, he would have been walked off the set and sent home—fired, along with a date being set for his appearing in court on assault and battery charges.

His email infuriated me.

From: Cork Graham [mailto█████████████████]
Sent: Thursday, May 5, 2016 3:04 AM
To: Mark Kadin <█████████████>; Will Ehbrecht <███████████>;
aruggles█████████ cfraser ███████████ David Carr <█████████>;
Tom Dorman <T██████████>; Cork Graham <██████████>
Subject: Fwd: Apology

Mark, Will, et al:

The punk doesn't know when to quit: the arrogance is stifling...this is not an apology.

This is another attempt by an extremely manipulative one, who thinks himself better and smarter than everyone else...this is just the same asshole who spent an angry summer in his teens walking up a stream in WA, chopping spawning salmon in half with a new machete his father bought him, in order to deal with his poor little me family issues at the time.

Jeremy needs some major anger management counseling. I'm not willing to waste my time with someone with such a psychological makeup--his attempt to control this situation with an email, trying to make me look like the villain. Laughable.

Watch video of the event: I was a drug and alcohol with 7 years experience specializing in PTSD, providing aid to his friend Keith Plaskett, who was clearly dealing with the symptoms, while under the influence of alcohol.

Jeremy was no longer acting, for some reason in a fear and jealously mode, that I might come between the relationship between he and his friend, and was dealing with this reality and was preventing me from doing what I know what to do. You will even hear the dialogue of him trying to belittle my background and experience--Dave Carr and Tom Dorman heard this while recording the event.

Jeremy has constantly tried to belittle my background, both in front of others, and behind my back. There are two kinds of expats: one that runs to other countries in order to do something great and wonderful for the world, and one that is overseas in order to run away from themselves by hiding in another country. I recognize both from my childhood growing up as the son of an American expat--Jeremy is the latter.

It was also mentioned to me by one of the locals yesterday, that Jeremy has the energy of the local druggies. Has anyone done a piss test on him? After all, Jeremy was the one who brought a gift of drugs to Bryan on Ilha Bela the first day we were there, and prided himself on telling the cast how he was his high school's most successful drug dealer, who almost got caught, but due to his slyness, foiled the high school narc and principal.

I'm done turning the other cheek for this arrogant idiot in order to complete production--like Plaskett likes to say: "Cut this guy away like a bad parachute!"

Cheers,
Cork

Figure 87. And I didn't even know, yet the level of family issues that Whalen was dealing with through his psychotic behavior—interview any psychopath in prison and you'll get the most eloquent "poor little me" stories.

Twenty-thousand was my offer to come back to set and finish the two weeks of shooting—to be deposited immediately into my account: that amount, I felt would trump whatever Discovery Communication, through its local representative, MAK Pictures, had bribed the local law and government, and get myself out there if it all went south further than it already had, and I had to bribe my own way to safety. It's not that much, considering a proper payment for an actor on TV is paid $25,000 per episode. Kadin came back with $7,000. Funny how he came back with that offer through Andy Ruggles, as if he wasn't wanting to be associated with anything related to TQ:SI, even though it was their first real hit since a show called CAJUN JUSTICE: only now do I realize Ruggles was doing the talking, because Kadin was in conversation with Joseph Boyle and Discovery to see how much more money they could get to pay me off. Anuj Majumdar, the show's scriptwriter, hiding under a co-executive producer title, confirmed that Joseph Boyle was at all important meetings regarding the show—Alaska is a single-party recording consent state, by the way, unlike California, so good luck for Discovery getting out this: good thing I don't reside in California anymore.

Figure 88. Normally, when you put up a photo of yourself on LinkedIn, it's best to put up a photo that will create a feeling of rapport, and not the idea that the page owner is having a fragmentation of personal identity.

Discovery is so aware of how they're breaking a variety of laws, that they're constantly playing a balancing act between bathing in the accolades of a new hit series and at the same time keeping their mugs out of the mainstream, like Joseph Boyle, who is associated with the creation of some of Discovery Communications' most fraudulent and questionable shows: DEADLIEST CATCH; NAKED AND AFRAID; TREASURE QUEST: SNAKE ISLAND, COOPER'S TREASURE. For someone who works in Hollywood and is in the limelight, Boyle does a pretty good job of hiding in the shadows—check out his Facebook and LinkedIn pages. He'd do a covert operator proud.

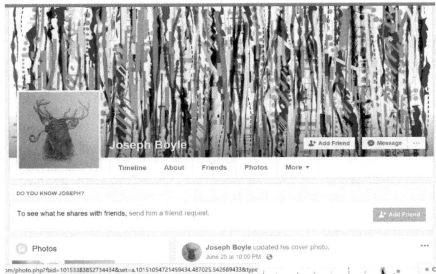

Figure 89. Remember, this is the name of the producer that's plastered on every credit for TQ:SI. He's the one we never saw in Los Angeles, Brazil, or in Argentina. Have you ever had an inkblot test? What does this choice of art tell you, instead of what a friendly, smiling human face would tell you...deception and hiding out?

It was decided that for me to return to set, they had to pay me $10,000 for the next two weeks of appearance. That was it. They bought $10,000 worth of acting from me. It would turn out not to be worth it in how it enabled them to complete the character assassination, for which they were pulling out of me through my acting, more content for them to fabricate story through images blurred for such a purpose.

David Carr and Dr. Petermann were sent to Iguazu to check out my eye. They were more there to see how long it would gum up production than to see how I was personally doing. The doc treated me the way you would a boxer, and suggested heat pads to replace the cold compresses that I had been using for the last two days—I was ordering a bucket of eye twice a day. The heat got the blood flowing and I took a ride back early that next Monday morning with Omar Armoa and Leo Ayala, our drivers who lived in Iguazu and had acted on HUNTING HITLER as fake locals of the town in the scene with Gerrard Williams and Tim Kennedy.

My greatest fear were the new migraines that I hadn't had since the crippling headaches that lasted for fifteen years after my TBI in San Miguel. Unlike those migraines that were like a railroad spike running through the center of my head, from temple to temple, these started right above my left eye, right where Jeremy suckered punched me, and reached to the center of my brain, and stopping there. As I write this book, I still have them—I hope they don't last for fifteen years or more, like the migraines I received in the war.

We had to shoot three more important scenes for Discovery to have their script completed. There was what they liked to call the hero shot. In writing it's called a climax which can also be the denouement. In this book, the denouement will be in the epilogue. In Season 1 the climax was the hero shot in the cave with the fake treasure chest in the hero cave noted in the shoot schedule for March 25, 2015. In Season 2, it was Mehgan coming out of the pool below the waterfall with the look of surprise on her face as she held up the fake gold mask of the Incan sun god Inti.

On Ilhabela, the hero shot was produced in the "hero cave." The denouement was my tearful scene and then boat scene where they had me look at constellations to realize it was Eridanus and that we were going to go inland. And here we were, having followed that script to Argentina. Now, we had to have climax. Jeremy donned his neoprene freedive suit and placed the mask of Inti, that Sebastien Baille cut from tin and painted with gold paint, along with the real Incan fetishes his brother had purchased through Jeremy' old drug and artifact contacts in the Peruvian blackmarket and smuggled to Argentina.

When Jeremy came out of the water, Carr winced and rolled his eyes, as he said to Dorman, "Fuckin' Jeremy." Jeremy had sat right down on his mesh goodie bag. The mask inside was crushed. When we did the money shot with Mehgan coming out of the water with the look of astonishment on her face, we had to be careful to place our fingers and hands over where Jeremy had broken off the gilding, revealing the blue primer that had been painted on the tin to hold the gold paint.

Treasure Quest: Snake Island

December 14, 2016 · ⊗

"This is one of the most significant finds of Incan treasure in the last 500 years."

Figure 90. Discovery Communications defrauding its audience, advertisers, education, and archeology community, again—fake, gilded tin mask is the most significant find in 500 years—if so why haven't we seen these most amazing finds in museums around the world?

The first few days after returning to set after Jeremy's assault and battery, I was assigned a makeup artist for the very first time since appearing on the show. It was to continue the façade that nothing had happened, and we were continuing to run the show as one happy treasure hunting team. Truth be damned.

Just about every take, she was running up to check my eye with some very irritating make up. The itching did its best to compete with the migraines and pain in my eye, the pain from the extra punches Jeremy had landed in my stomach before he went down were slowly disappearing. By the end of the second day of shooting since returning to the set, I was ready to tell her she wasn't needed. The ice compresses had done their job. So, by the time we were shooting the fake brocket jaguar kill scene, I was free of unpleasant effects of makeup on my eye.

Figure 91. Real grave-robbed Incan Tumi, held by real drug and artifact smuggler, who had his brother, James Whalen/Kendall Mckibben, be the mule for the cocaine and graverobbed artifacts to the set in Argentina.

The fake jaguar kill would be one of the most hilarious scenes, not only because the brocket deer was a roadkill that had been found by the local Argentine fixer, but because of how it was written into the story. It was to show how dangerous it was to hunt treasure in Argentina—at least the snakes on Snake Island were real.

It was so contrived I had to really bite my lip not to just break out laughing. Anyone who recognizes what a scalpel wound looks like in contrast to the real puncturing and tearing of predatory cat's claws and teeth on one of its favorite prey, would have easily recognized the fakery in that scene. Evidently, nobody did when it was broadcast...

While Sebastien and Julia were responsible for the creation of every, non-stolen and smuggled national treasure, prop used in scenes, Dr Gustavo Petermann was the artist on this piece. He went to work crafting pseudo-claw marks with his scalpel and a spray bottle of theater blood.

Our last shoot aside from the OTFs that would to be shot later this day, were down a bamboo lined path to a waterfall, pool and crystal cave. It was an amazing cave of quartz, and amethyst. The Puerto Bemberg area, just down the road from Puerto Libertad, was mined for years. All kinds of crystals unique to the area are in the ground. Where they reach the surface in caves and washes, they can catch the light in a most magical way.

Had I been on my own, or enjoying a hike and spelunking with real friends, I would have truly enjoyed the experiences of checking out all these crystals in the wall of the cave that Dorman had Jeremy, Keith and me acting as if we were investigating this small cave in the ground for possible artifacts. It would have also been nicer if I'd had some actual sleep. Those last two weeks, I was running on two-thirds empty, staying up late as I had during the war, my PTS coming back in spades due to the duress of being around someone who was a verifiable psychopath, one who abused cocaine and was unpredictable as a result. The scene in the crystal cave appears in the show, but what you don't see is my final crash after having come to full, and clear understanding that this fake show and industry was going to just keep going on as long as no one said, "ENOUGH!"

Figure 92. Poor little roadkill brocket deer, used as a prop for the fake jaguar scene.

As an absurd side note, when my lawyer contacted MAK Pictures/Discovery about their involvement in the assault and battery case against Jeremy Whalen and Brett Tutor, they had the audacity to say they didn't know I had post-traumatic stress. This is ridiculous, considering they hired me because of my memoir, and even used a real incident with Richard Knight finding Grand Pirate Island in 1983 by looking for an island the Thai Gulf with topography similar to those in Captain Kidd's map, in order to create a totally contrived TQ:SI scene that was broadcast of me putting the flipped over and spun upside down map to fit Snake Island. The subtitle of THE BAMBOO CHEST is AN ADVENTURE IN HEALING THE TRAUMA OF WAR, for a reason.

That moment when I said, enough, was when the very guy who had only two weeks early gotten into a hissy fit because, no one tells him what to do, Jeremy Whalen, became annoyed because I wasn't following his direction. Suddenly, Jeremy was now the director and telling Keith and me what to do. I smiled at Keith and went very Buddhist monk. I just shut up and let Jeremy become even more annoyed that I wasn't doing what he was directing me to do—He had become just like Mehgan, in the staged car chase scene, when she took the walkie-talkie from me and was in two roles that made it even more fake and stupid-looking. First, we had camera operators directing actors, who were supposed to be on a reality show how to act, and now we had actors directing actors.

Paresthesia is the scientific term given to the sensation of pins and needles, numbness, or other tingling feelings that can be experienced in different parts of the body, particularly in the limbs and their extremities (arms, hands, legs, feet). A couple days after we restarted production, Jeremy told the showrunners that he couldn't perform that day. Dorman boarded the bus after having run up to Jeremy's room in the Bemberg Mansion. He told David Carr that Jeremy wasn't able to get out of the bathtub that morning. I blurted, "Somebody needs to give that guy a drug test."

It was clear that Jeremy Whalen was having withdrawals from his use of cocaine—who knows how long he'd been using since his brother's arrival and quick departure almost three months earlier. Keith said later that Jeremy had told him that the numbness and inability to move his legs frightened him because he thought it was something like the paresthesia his mother had experienced when she had lost her mind. Paresthesia can come on as the result of various psychological events, such as anxiety.

"No, Keith," I said. "He's been high for a while, and I'm sure he had his brother bring cocaine with him when he visited from Peru." Drug dealers are often dealers in a variety of illegal offerings, like artifacts, sex slaves, children, etc. They use the same routes around the world, and the smuggling routes from Peru to Argentina are used by all variety of such scumbags.

For the last three months, I had to act in scenes that any newsman, or documentarian would be livid to take part in, in any form. While reviewing Sue Aikens own dilemma with the fakery of reality TV that had even infected a network I previously thought incapable of being drawn to the dark side: National Geographic—if NatGeo can take this highway to hell, who's safe? The public awareness of what was really happening on set was made clear when Aikens broke her shoulder in a so apparently contrived scene of her speeding like a demon down a slippery ice river and then hitting a bank and tumbling.

What came out in the lawsuit, which was easily searched on the Internet, was that the British producer on set drank all her booze and then ordered her to stage an idiotic speeding down an ice river (basically setting up herself for a crash) and then make it look as though that's what any Alaskan would do on a snowmachine. Easy for a network to pull this off, since most viewers don't live in Alaska, and don't' know better. Those who do, saw it for what it was—idiocy and stupidity and totally staged for the camera.

Figure 93. Tom Dorman checking with soundman Brett Ulery, while our little roadkill brocket deer waits his cue...

It was revealed later in the lawsuit, that the producers even told her to say on camera that it was her idea and decision. Aikens' enlightening comments appeared in a January 5, 2018 article of *Earn the Necklace*:

"In February 2017, she sued producers of the television show for breach of contract, interference with Aikens' business, and intentionally causing her emotional distress. Most of these issues stem from what Aikens says was "an unsafe working environment." Due to her contract, she reportedly felt that she couldn't say no to producers' requests. One such request had Aikens working outside without a face mask or helmet so that viewers could see more of her face, and connect better with the audience. She alleges that she got frostbite and was unable to work at the camp for several days."

Boy, could I relate. The producers do make it seem as if you can't say, no. This was why, though I completely understand the FAA's resting the responsibility on the pilot in command for the helicopter crash that killed CSM Michael Donatelli, camera operator Darren Rydstrom, and the pilot David Gibbs, I totally hold Discovery Communications responsible for what happened on the set of Joseph Teti's debacle, LONE OPERATOR— and especially in later using their PR and legal department to protect a psychopath, who should have never been given a production gig in the first place. It's amazing what producers on location for a reality show can do, seemingly well-read in all of Dr. Robert Cialdini's six principles of persuasion: reciprocity, commitment and consistency, social proof, liking, authority, scarcity—authority, and commitment and consistency can work wonders in keeping people on board, when they should have jumped ship long ago.

A month before the contrived TQ:SI scene in the crystal cave with Jeremy and Keith, was the fake car chase in which Mehgan drove the vehicle as if we were being harassed by another vehicle in the night. I just didn't know how much further in this clusterfuck it was going to go. Keith had made a comment about David Carr's directing. "He just lets them do whatever. He's really got to lead his thing."

When Mehgan turned all crazy, like a Medusa, snakes coming out of her head, because I wasn't acting as excited and dramatic and fake as she was in the scene, she yanked the walkie-talkie from me and started doing the dialogue herself, in true Hollywood form. She was furious that I was talking the way I would if we were really in danger—as slowly as I could to keep and share calm. They wanted Hollywood fake over the real deal, but they just needed my credentials to bring credibility to a fakeumentary. It was all leading up to this when Zaslav went to Hollywood for "true-life" documentary.

Hollywood scenes where you hear people screaming and yelling is just that: Hollywood. When that level of overt emotional intensity appears in truly dangerous events, it's because all hell has broken loose and you're pretty much lost. The only times I've seen it get to that point in real-life was when I've seen someone totally in the throes of alcohol and drug abuse, or the base overrun at San Miguel, where soldiers were shooting soldiers in the fray, and a couple ambushes that were instead just emotions focused and directed like hot burning lasers.

Figure 94. Brett Ulery on sound, Scottie McKibben on camera, and co-executive producer, Tom Dorman, during the very last seconds of filming of TQ:SI Argentina. Dorman is asking me what if questions OTFs that will be folded in by post-production to create the fakery. There's enough sleight of hand during shooting, but the real magic happens in post-production.

In her acting, what Mehgan depicted was the character of someone who had lost control and was treading water. Sadly, this is the emotional intensity that appeals to the mind stimulated by voyeuristic drama. What makes it that much more attractive to a reality show main audience is that it's all the emotional reward, without all the real dangers and threat of danger that an audience imagines the subject on a reality show is going through. Snakes, jaguars, drownings, killing falls, these are the threats that a reality TV audience can emotionally experience through the physically safe, vicarious thrill of the TV monitor.

Heaven forbid the audience actually get on a plane and head out to Alaska's gold fields, or after old Incan treasure in the jungles of South America. When they do, like the poor sixty-year-old woman who had sold her house, pulled all her savings to find gold in Nome, because she watched the Discovery Channel fakeumentary called BERING SEA GOLD, it becomes a tragedy.

A week after the assault and battery by Jeremy Whalen and Brett Tutor, Cathy Grant came up to me while no one was around. We were in the restaurant lounge of the Bemberg Hotel, where I was now lodged for safety sake. Even Keith was in the hotel now, too, to keep him away from Mehgan, Brett and Mehgan, and to hopefully make sure he wasn't by himself with a bottle of rum.

Keith had drunk so much one day, less than a week after the big event, he just came out and said he was totally drunk and he wasn't going to work that day, yelling to everyone in the bus, "To hell with you guys—I'm done!"

Jeremy said to Carr that Keith had been up through the night, drinking, mumbling and spouting threats, and that when they came down in the morning there was a knife stuck in a post in the dining room.

You know when you get this feeling that the person talking to you is lying through their teeth, but they have this wide-eyed, stare as if they're trying to the truth, but aren't? That's the look Jeremy gave everyone in the bus. As I looked at him, I suddenly felt the creeps. If he's willing set up his friend like this, to get his supposed best buddy, and surrogate father, fired, what else is he willing to do?

Keith was also quartered at the Hotel Bemberg from then until our last day. Brett Tutor had the whole house to play his guitar in, and Mehgan and Jeremy could fornicate and plot to their heart's content. I was happy to leave them to it. Keith, on the other hand, was stewing and blaming Mehgan for the backstabbing manner in which his supposed friend of eight years had treated him—it would be a long time before Keith would finally realize, it was a meeting of minds, and if anything, it was Jeremy working his own angles: he'd played the devil to make the deal with Discovery Communications and seduced the freedive champion he'd lusted after since long before meeting on the chem test in Los Angeles.

"I saw the video," Cathy said, as she looked around to make sure we were alone.

"What do you mean...You did?"

"I'm really sorry about what happened to you."

"What did you see?"

"I just wanted to warn you—I saw how Mehgan jumped on Jeremy after Brett pulled you off him. She straddled him and put her hand on his chest, and said, 'are you okay?'"

I kept my mouth shut and waited for her to say more...

"You could tell there was something there...The way she put her hand right on his heart—there's something going on between those two."

"What are you saying?"

"You need to watch your back."

Cathy's words sat with me for the rest of the day, a like a heavy boulder on my chest—like I needed more stress. By the time of that shoot in the crystal cave, barely a week later, I was on automatic pilot and already counting the days. I would be on edge the rest of my time there. If there was a greater impetus for a return of PTS, on the level comparable to that which hit me when I came back from Central America, I don't what would. Every night I was jamming the back of a chair against the door knob and slept with my Super Bowie and machete under my bed for immediate reach should Jeremy delve further into his apparent, predatory, psychotic tendencies.

Figure 95. A piece of tin covered with gold paint worth $250,000?! If that's not fraudulent advertising by Discovery Channel, I don't know what is—yet, again: where is the treasure? If it was real, it should be on display in a variety of museums around the world...The press, Interpol, ICE, and the FBI, need to finally do their job and ask Discovery Communications where they hid it: They've all been notified more than a year ago, and yet still silence!

EPILOGUE
THE RECKONING

Discovery should stay out of Bolivia. It should stay out of South America and Los Angeles, too. Frankly, for society and the mental health of the world, it should just stay in Silver Springs, Maryland. Most definitely, it should just stay of Bolivia, because Bolivia is one bad luck place for Discovery Communications.

Back in the 1990s, my colleague, Dr. James A. Swan, a TV and film and actor and most importantly, an environmental psychologist, wrote a couple excellent books on the native traditions related to the power of place, THE POWER OF PLACE and SACRED PLACES. In these books, he wrote about the importance of place, and how ancient cultures had a much better understanding of this, how some places are good, and some are very, very bad.

In May 2015, Joseph Teti and Matt Graham were in Bolivia to shoot an episode of DUAL SURVIVAL for Discovery. It quickly all went south from there. Who's to say why Teti did what he did. Personally, I think all the lies he had built around his life, and the hollow coveting of other's successes, such as Mykel Hawke's, and the ill deeds committed in order to steal it, had overcome him and in true psychopathic form, he went ballistic and sought solace in the harm of another living being—pretty much like Jeremy Whalen when he walked up a river in Washington State and chopped spawning salmon in half with a machete in order to deal with his anger at his father. What Teti did was kill three dogs with a knife in the Bolivian town of Coroico. When he told cast and crew about what he had done, they didn't know how to respond.

He clearly noticed that they found it pretty sick and twisted, and he said, he had done it to save a cat that been attacked by the dogs. Evidently, they didn't believe him. When the producer challenged Teti, he went into a rage and threatened to kill everyone. Teti left the Viejo Molina Hotel and then returned with the cat he said was being attacked by the dogs. When the crew checked the cat, they saw that the wounds had been made with a knife, and not the claws or teeth of a dog.

Teti went about the crew and cast threatening to kill them if they didn't appear on video and state they wouldn't tell anyone about his dog killing spree. With a situation that had completely gotten out of hand, and truly fearing for the safety of the crew, the local production company, Tambo Film (yes, the same company out of Peru that was our local production company in Argentina, represented by Paulina Cacho-Sousa and David Rivas) got the crew moved to another hotel. Tambo Film then moved the crew out of the country, and Claudio Aliaga, of Xentrax Group, a local security firm was hired to take Joseph Teti to the airport and deport him.

Initially, Discovery Communications tried not to broadcast that episode, but they were locked into a contract with an advertiser to put out a certain number of episodes with their ads. The first airing didn't even have final rolling credits, which is unheard of in the business. On Discovery's part, this was to keep Mykel Hawke's legal team from knowing who was on production, crew on whom they could conduct depositions. It was known something horrible had happened, but no one was talking, for fear of losing their jobs at Discovery.

This is the insidious quality of Hollywood and now especially Discovery. All that big to do about Harvey Weinstein? He was just the sacrificial lamb for all that has happened and continues to happen in Tinseltown. It's easy to attack a producer and Hollywood mogul, when they've seen better days and been defanged by the time everyone in Hollywood comes at them like rabid dogs with a "#metoo" on their Twitter feed. It's the psychopaths, predators, and Hollywood moguls who are still working and thriving in Hollywood that I'm interested in seeing in prison. The problem is that silence is often, not always, but often enough, rewarded handsomely.

Everyone in that town is either trying to get to the top, or at the top trying not to be toppled. If you air the laundry of a production or producer in Hollywood, you'll never get another job as a camera operator, soundman, or anything related to TV or film. Not until enough of the audience disappears in revolt against what has developed into a quagmire of delusion, undermining our society to the point that evil is accepted as just part of the business, and will no longer be tolerated.

Take for example Mark Kadin, owner of MAK Pictures, and his business partner and executive producer, Will Ehbrecht. Kadin graduated from Northwestern University's Medill Journalism School, known as one of the best. Ehbrecht came from a film background and even traveled to Africa produce a documentary on the children in Uganda. You'd think that people with this background would have the integrity to turn away from what they had been doing for almost twenty years: submitting fiction as non-fiction—where does a person's scruples go when they start working in the Hollywood reality TV genre? It makes all reality TV fiction, and the 2015 dramatic television show UNREAL, non-fiction.

Hollywood is a drug for those who let them be used by it, and probably a lot more attractive to those who get a little bit of success and can afford that new Audi or BMW, especially when true documentarians are notoriously always trying to make ends meet financially. Heaven forbid reality show producers deliver what they market, or worse for them, when it gets out what they really do, and how they sell it to the audience through fraudulent advertising.

How much differently would Mykel Hawke's lawsuit against Discovery Channel have turned out had the judge in that case had the depositions of those who were in Bolivia to observe Joseph Teti's killing and mutilating of cats and dogs? Discovery Communications should open its own legal partnership as another stream of cash flow, as it's been very successful at keeping Discovery Communications out of court: Discovery's fifth floor legal fleet is kept busy and earns their keep.

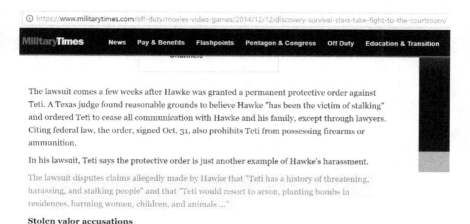

Figure 96. Capt. Mykel Hawke US Army (RET) definitely read the tea leaves correctly: six months before Joseph Teti went on his dog-killing rampage.

Covet is a powerful word. There's a reason it's in the Ten Commandments of the Old and New Testament. It drives all the ills of the world and has become very prominent as standard operating procedures at Discovery Communications. In so doing, it has left another powerful word,

INTEGRITY, a casualty on the battlefield of good against evil. From the very top with Eileen O'Neil, David Zaslav, Richard Ross, and now with the continued game shell game at Discovery, you'll see the same with Nancy Daniels following in form, coveting the audience numbers of A&E in the shrinking market of satellite TV.

As I said, I shot for CNN as a freelancer in the 1980s, when satellite TV was a great boon to the information age—to come back from a battlefield and see on TV the recorded events from that same battlefield only a few hours later. The man who I hold responsible for this in a good way, was Ted Turner. Let me tell you, I don't feel I'm stretching to say, if Ted Turner was dead, he'd be turning over in his grave now to see how satellite broadcast has been bastardized by such media as churned out by the present, Hollywood-driven reality TV industry. At least Turner did his best to deliver solid reporting when he was in charge at CNN. Now that can't be said of Discovery, A&E or even CNN.

This coveting that starts all the way up there with CEO Zaslav making more than $42 Million in the last year, while his next subordinate makes $8 Million is where it starts, but it trickles all the way down. Jeremy Whalen had been coveting my position on the show from the first day of meeting on the chemistry test in Los Angeles. If he had done a better job of keeping his rage under control, he might have gotten away with his crimes, as I'd likely not have learned about all that he had been up to with his brother.

By coveting he was displaying a truly sick and perverted form of *skincrawling*. He was already doing this with Keith Plaskett, who had become a pseudo-surrogate father to him, a relationship he jealously guarded and heavily controlled in order to achieve his aims, such as how he used it to get on the show in the first place. This wasn't hard for Jeremy Whalen, who had at least learned to speak some conversational Spanish, to pull over on someone like Keith Plaskett, who moved to South America more than ten years ago, but couldn't communicate with locals, except through interpreters and broken Spanish curse words, and sign language.

To covet is synonymous with greed. To covet to have something that isn't yours, and not something that you've worked hard for and paid the price. Fame and a different family and personal history was something that Jeremy heavily coveted. In so doing, he was very much like Joseph Teti coveting Mykel Hawke's successes, both in the military and in the world of TV.

This sick and twisted skincrawling, that reminded me of the psychopath character of Buffalo Bill in THE SILENCE OF THE LAMBS, was so bad that Teti was trying to get his webmaster to copy Mykel Hawke's official website. As if that wasn't enough, he was going after the same manufacturers that were sponsoring and using Hawke as a spokesman, like Smokey Mountain Knife Works and the watchmaker MTM.

My own Joseph Teti, as I started calling him, after I realized what criminal activities Whalen and his brother had been up to, was trying to get the manufacturers I had brought onto the show, such as Minelab and the manufacturer of the Hot Foot Rug metal detector to send him free gear. He even got Minelab to pay him as a treasure hunting specialist, to speak at an event—he's not a treasure hunting specialist; he's a boat yard manager hiding out in Salinas, Ecuador. As a testament to Discovery Communications propensity to protect the criminals in their employ, the only one from the first two seasons to appear on Season 3 in Bolivia is Jeremy Whalen.

It's one thing for someone without any integrity, and major psychopathic tendencies to go after you, but when two or more get together, it's like Kenneth Bianchi, who was spurred to outdo his cousin, Angelo Buono, two psychopaths charged for the Hillside Strangler murders of the late 1970s. They wouldn't have stopped had they not been arrested. Bianchi is serving a life sentence in Walla Walla, Washington.

Who knows what could happen if Jeremy Whalen and James Whalen feel even more emboldened than they already were, by successfully smuggling drugs and graverobbed Incan artifacts from Peru to Argentina and cyberstalking and harassing me from 2016 to 2018—their attacks didn't stop until the first lawsuit filed against Discovery Channel and Brett Tutor in Austin, TX in January 19, 2018. Mykel Hawke was spot on by predicting that a psychopath doesn't stop of their own volition. They instead take things to a higher and higher levels until they're finally apprehended.

Betrayal is another powerful word, too, one of the most deplorable acts one person can do to another. In the special operations community, there's such strong reliance on brotherhood, combat buddies, and esprit de corps. That's why it's no surprise that a breach of such trust in the special operations community is so frowned upon. Such betrayal is unconscionable. To do it for reasons as cheap as to hopefully get another shot at being on TV, is just mind-blowing.

The other actor on LONE OPERATOR was not just Joseph Teti, but also former CAG member Dale Comstock. Donatelli and Comstock were both CAG (Delta Force). This esprit de corps is supposed to course deeply within the veins of those in the special operations community. I see it still in the PJs, the real PJs, not the Brett Tutor PJ-wannabe types. Of late, in the SEALs and the Green Berets, when they suddenly come out of the shadows and become the John Wayne Green Berets of TV, something really bizarre happens. It's no longer the brotherhood, it's the who was in SpecOps, now on TV, and how can I network myself into that person's web of influence?

Figure 97. Dale Comstock said in an affidavit aiding Joseph Teti, that in 2015 when he made his statement, he didn't know Mykel Hawke, but in 2011 they both starred on Discovery Channel's ONE MAN ARMY. Affidavit in appendix.

6. Although I do not know Mykel Hawkeye ("Mr. Hawkeye") personally, he has called me three times on the telephone to talk about his relationship with Mr. Teti.

Figure 98. Clearly a lie by Dale Comstock on his affidavit for Joseph Teti. Full document from four years after Comstock's handshakes with Hawke on TV, in the appendix.

Once Joseph Teti learned that Mykel Hawke was doing well on TV, he contacted him with the request to be his bodyguard and provide security. An old team mate from his days in his SF Group in the National Guard, Hawke, of course brought him into his circle. Hawke didn't know that the day before the military enacted stop-loss in response to 9/11, Teti bailed on his unit and went military contractor, taking a position with the CIA. It has always been a bit of contention between active-duty military and contractors, and how though both are serving their country in harm's way, and often private secure can be the tip of the spear in the worse places, active military aren't receiving anywhere near the pay contractors receive. The unknown part of that departure was that Teti left the military just before potentially receiving a dishonorable discharged. Until corrected by fellow SF Group members, Hawke thought Teti was a straight shooter.

Sadly, once Hawke learned the truth, Teti was already proving otherwise—worst, Hawke had already brought him into his circle. Being around him all the time, gave Teti the opportunity to learn about the TV business. What it also did was give him the opportunity to get was enough information about Teti and his family to be a viable threat. A judge found this to be true, and gave Mykel and his wife Ruth, a restraining order for the protection of the family against Teti.

When I learned how Teti worked his way into Mykel's graces, all I could think about was how Jeremy Whalen had tried to do the same thing, in true psychopathic predator fashion. As I've said, there are nice people and there are good people; and good people are not always nice.

Psychopaths are nice people all the time, until they drop the veil and reveal how truly evil they are. They're charismatic (Ted Bundy had charisma in spades—so many couldn't believe the monster lurking inside until it was too late), playful (John Wayne Gacy was a clown that everyone loved), and this is the clincher, people who come from a good place in their souls, of which I think most people do, just can't believe that there are truly people like real predators, so friendly, charming ,and yet, can have no thought, no remorse in getting something over you, or even strangling you to death—they'll actually get a rush out of doing it from the sense of power and control it offers their sick minds.

Hawke couldn't believe it at first with Teti. I didn't want to believe it at first with the Whalen brothers. Think about it, when you have a predator in your midst, and you can't immediately remove yourself from their proximity, as you would from a rabid hyena, you don't want to believe you've put yourself in such a situation by having found yourself in a restrictive environment, such as the workplace, and you also don't want to admit that you have been had.

Frankly, when I learned that Jeremy Whalen was in Bolivia acting on what was going to be Season 3 of TQ:SI, I thought everyone at Discovery Channel was either stupid or insane. I'd been keeping tabs on my fellow crew and cast to see where they were appearing. When I started to see photos of the crew in Bolivia, I knew that it was on. Discovery Communications is neither stupid nor insane. Like a psychopath who gets away Scott free with increasing degrees of lawlessness, Discovery Communications is that arrogant. Hard to say whether they're that way originally, or because they have learned that the government won't doing anything, and that the media, who should be an overwatch with an interest to keep the audience's trust, instead ignored Discovery Communications' wrongdoings.

It was one thing for Discovery to say that they didn't know that MAK Pictures had any dealings with the stealing of national treasures through Jeremy Whalen, when MAK Pictures lawyer Aaron Weiss and Discovery Communications VP of Litigation Leah Montesano, finally had a talk with my lawyer about what had happened on set in Argentina in the spring of 2017.

Evidently, they thought we had disappeared like so many others that Discovery Communications had kept logged in paperwork by make request after request in court. The most ludicrous I've heard about was the request for the names of students Cody Lundin had instructed in his time as a survival instructor: all of them! The reasoning is that if they keep Lundin's lawyers running around chasing paper trails (ever see that movie about law school with John Houseman?) they'll keep Lundin paying legal fees. This is good strategy when it's a battle between Lundin's coffers and those of Discovery Communications: millions will always win out. Jesse Ventura had to deal with the same dilemma in his own defamation lawsuit, while the legal fees for the Chris Kyle estate were paid by publisher's insurance company.

Some may think that I'm wrong in saying that every officer in land forces should be required to complete a sniper course. The reason I went through sniper training at El Salvador's sniper school at CEMFA in 1986 was not to become a better shooter. As I've said many times, you can teach a chimp to shoot (it's one of the reasons I laugh so hard when I've watched the video passed around the Internet of a chimp in Africa who finally gets his hands on an AK47 and opens up on a bunch of guerrillas—think about it; if you're a Green Beret or SEAL who can take a hilltribe member in Laos, or a Salvadoran or Nicaraguan recruit in Central America, who likely didn't even graduate middle school, and turn them into a very efficient shooter and killer, how hard do you think it really is to shoot well with the right training?). The reason to go through a sniper school is to learn all that other stuff, like keeping cool, knowing when to call your shot, building photographic memory and most importantly, tactics, strategy, and patience.

Patience rewarded my legal team with Discovery Communications giving the go-ahead to MAK Pictures to shoot in Bolivia, and to advertise the actual broadcast for August 24, 2018. According to Tom Dorman's profile at staffmeup.com, he had gone up in title from supervising producer to co-executive producer on TQ:SI Bolivia, and was working on it from

August 2017 until January 2018. That means pre-production, the writing of the initial script, and sending production scouts down to set up with local fixers started in August:

Thomas Dorman
CO-EXECUTIVE PRODUCER
LOS ANGELES, CA
AVAILABLE

💬 MESSAGE

Summary

For years now, I've been pushing the bounds of reality storytelling. Ever the production vagabond, I thrive on bringing the world's more obscure tales to life.

Credits

Co-Executive Producer – Treasure Quest: Snake Island (Season 3)   7/17 – 1/18
DISCOVERY – REALITY/DOC (TV) – MAK PICTURES

Supervising Producer – Untitled Custer Project (Season 1)   9/16 – 1/17
HISTORY – REALITY/DOC (TV) – WARM SPRINGS PRODUCTIONS, LLC

Supervising Producer – Treasure Quest: Snake Island (Season 2)   5/16 – 8/16
DISCOVERY – REALITY/DOC (TV) – MAK PICTURES

Figure 99. "pushing the bounds of reality" is an understatement with regards to Discovery Communications, wouldn't you say?

Reality TV is truly an addictive drug for these folks. Remember when I asked Derrick Nevot and Scottie Mckibben what in the world they were doing in Argentina, after they swore they would never work on TREASURE QUEST again? Well, seems the memories were forgotten.

Frankly, I was amazed, remembering that conversation with Scottie Mckibben in New Orleans for lunch, and his comments about my assault and battery, *"I really liked Jeremy. But, after that, I think we really lost respect for him."*

David Carr
September 12, 2017 · 👥

Finding innovative ways to transport gear in Bolivia...

😊👍❤️ Derrick Nevot and 59 others   7 Comments

👍 Like   💬 Comment

Figure 100. Production of Season 3 began in Bolivia in Sept. 2017.

I smiled. This was par for course when getting the details of what happens after a psychopath is found out. Ted Bundy. John Wayne Gacy. All of these psychopaths, and many more were described as such "nice" men, and those interviewed couldn't believe that they had committed such heinous crimes. Jeremy was always a very charismatic type, always trying to do something "nice." That's the difference between "nice" and good. Good people are not always nice, but good people are not psychopaths.

Later when I chatted with Scottie on the phone to see how much he knew about the smuggling of the artifacts by Jeremy Whalen and his brother, he immediately said, "Sebastien was really angry about that. He was furious as to what they were doing."

It made me think better of Sebastien Baille, our artifact fabricating wizard. He had been raised as an expat, too. Instead of Southeast Asia, his childhood was in Egypt and the Middle East. His father was a geologist.

But, then, just like Scottie and David Carr and Tom Dorman, and even Keith Plaskett, they kept working on a project that was clearly illegal in all senses of the word.

Good thing I didn't know about the artifact smuggling until Keith Plaskett told me months after I got back home. I wouldn't have just been furious, like Sebastien. I would have gone out of that country within a day. Can you imagine what would have happened to everyone who was involved in the production had it been found out by the non-bribed officials of Argentina?

Figure 101. The look of hate on Derrick Nevot's face, and Scottie McKibben's says it all— I'd been in Bolivia during the 1980s when it was an even worse hell hole than now. This photo made laugh, just like I did when I saw them in Argentina.

They would have had all of us in jail before the night was over. The artifact smuggling, the having all employees working on tourist visas the last two of the three months of production, these were all indicators that Discovery Communications, through its representative MAK Pictures, bribed local officials. As I mentioned in my open to this book, everyone who works for Discovery Communications has a non-disclosure clause in their employment contract.

Normally, this is used to keep creative ideas from leaking out to a direct competitor, in this case A&E. What it's not supposed to be used for is to keep criminal activities on the hush. As can be seen, Discovery Communications had been running way off the reservation ever since they opened an office in Los Angeles and let that office initiate production under Eileen O'Neill.

In research and investigation, you look for commonalities, common threads. You look for what hasn't changed. Eileen O'Neill is no longer at Discovery, nor Richard Ross; but, CEO David Zaslav is, and the fraud continues. Not only that, Zaslav is slated to be CEO of Discovery Communications until 2023! Are we, as a society, being taught that crime does pay—that it pays BIG?

In remotely observing their production of the third season of TQ:SI, I'd play with my idea of how they wrote it. It was so transparent and more than a little entertaining to observe the new players in this completely scripted show masquerading as "true-life" documentary as CEO David Zaslav likes to call what his network churns out. Most importantly, it removed any questions of whether MAK Pictures was just a renegade production company running on its own or was one-hundred percent told what to do by Discovery Communications. Discovery in Bolivia to shoot season 3, meant that they had waited to see if there was going to be a major lawsuit coming, if so how much would it cost, and how much could they make in order to cover any fall out for a season 3 (which would give a lot more evidence for my case—and other cases, such as Cody Lundin's defamation case). Could they have a big enough profit to make the juice worth the squeeze?

By March 2017, I had signed with a lawyer to go after Discovery Communications, MAK Pictures and Brett Tutor, because his US address was in Austin, Texas. Jeremy Whalen was already well versed in jurisdictions, so hiding out in Ecuador. In the process of putting Discovery Communications on notice, they knew everything about drug use, the artifact smuggling, the assault and battery, but not only that, I also knew how the idea for TQ:SI came about in response to Eileen O'Neill's RFP to MAK Pictures.

As I said, I was trained a long time ago on when to call a shot. When it became clear that Discovery was vested in keeping the fraud going, because they clearly felt they could profit, it was time for my lawyer to drop the bomb on Brett Tutor. Initially, it was to hit Brett Tutor because we had also learned that he had been given a reward for keeping quiet about the assault and battery he committed in Argentina—the whole case for that matter—rewarded with being groomed to be Discovery Communication's new pretty boy on TLC's TRADING SPACES.

This is nothing new. Discovery did this with Matt Graham after the Teti dog-killing spree. Suddenly, Discovery was doing the same thing with Jeremy Whalen. In his creepy skincrawling desires, he had gotten the role on a third season. But, unlike me or Keith Plaskett, he had no credentials to bring credibility to the fakery. That's why Shawn Cowles was brought on as team leader to replace me, bringing the inferred reputation of the Mel Fisher estate with him.

Jeremy Whalen did try to play with posed images in order to create some type of personal credibility all the way back in 2016. The problem was that to try and do it, he had published a photo of himself with treasure and metal detector in Ecuador: treasure hunting has been illegal in Ecuador since 2008. Published on Instagram, it still sits there waiting for Ecuadorian police to stop by and ask him some questions, the least of which would be about a few silver coins.

This using other people's gear to build credibility with a photo was all very humorous to me, because when Jeremy and his brother James were trying to defame me on the internet, they actually said something as stupid as that I had borrowed my M16 and CAR15 from soldiers to get my photo taken with them. Remember what I said about people communicating in vocabulary and language in which they're versed, such as when Jeremy and James Whalen were working their anger out at their father and his arrest for sex offenses in 1982, in some twisted form of transference, by using sodomy and pedophilia-related terminology in their libelous edits on my Wikipedia page? Well, here's what Keith Plaskett had to say on Facebook Messenger about Jeremy's treasure hunter credibility photos:

Figure 102. The photo that puts Jeremy Whalen in jail for illegal artifact gathering in Ecuador in 2016, eight years after it was made illegal.

Figure 103. It wasn't February, it was October 15, 2016, and dated on Jeremy Whalen's Instagram post.

Though I'm waiting with great excitement to see the show, to see how much more evidence could be brought against Discovery that only takes a trained eye to see, let's not wait. I'll use my skills as a writer to tell you what the storyline will be. In journalism, it's supposed to be the "five Ws": who, what where, when, how. In Hollywood, because this has nothing to do with reporting and getting the facts right, the model sequence runs like this: what, where, who, when, how.

Remember when Eileen O'Neill made the order for an RFP, from MAK Pictures? She asked first for a treasure hunting story to compete with History Channel's CURSE OF OAK ISLAND, which was the *what*. Then, she asked for it to occur on Brazil's infamous Snake Island, aka Queimada Grande, which was the *where*. That's when casting was put in play and the *who* was found. A go ahead was given, but the *when* was delayed because O'Neill was replaced by Rich Ross. Though there is an overall main script, since it's being shot to imitate a true documentary, and scriptwriters in Los Angeles have no idea what it's like to deal with realities of location in Brazil, or South America for that matter, the *how*, was an ongoing process, as the scripts were written daily and sent over the Internet to the showrunners to implement that very day.

Using that very same model, and tracking through social media, I quickly learned and kept tabs on the *what* and *where* from September to November of 2017. This was going to be a show in which our intrepid adventurers were to climb the mountains and jungles of Bolivia, and find the *treasure* in a mine. After climbing up from the jungle, rappelling and ziplining, they come on this secret mine shaft. Of course, as we've learned in the supposedly secret rivers, Jesuit ruins in season 2, these sites are only secret to those living outside of Argentina. Bolivia is much tougher to travel around due to the horrible, and very dangerous roads, which of course makes it that much more attractive to MAK so that tourists can't verify facts as easily as could be done in Brazil.

It's the players that make season 3 so interesting and compelling. First, there's the only cast member from season 1 and 2, the criminal artifact and drug smuggler, and possible pedophile, Jeremy Whalen. Then there are three other individuals who seemingly think that being on a reality TV show will somehow market their service or products. These people are Jack W. Peters, Robert Leonard, and Shawn Cowles.

Jack W. Peters has a company called American Explosives Group, based out of Springfield, Oregon. Though I was trained in the use of explosives as part of my counter-insurgency training in Central America, it's not my forte. My Green Beret buddy, MAJ John Donovan (RET.) has been professionally dealing with the subject since 1964, when he joined the army. He was instructing in Central America the five years before I first arrived in 1985. A former police lieutenant, EOD instructor, and a many decades long owner of a blaster's license, he was the first one I went to and asked about Peters' explosives group website: americanexplosivesgroup.com. What hit us first was that there were all these titles but no mention of certifications or where the instructors collected their experience and training, to qualify a background teaching "breaching, demolition, EOD-IED, K-9 detection, military munitions."

John said, "Here, look at TEES. I've worked with Alan Brosnan." A quick search brought up a website at energeticentry.com.

"Oh, he's a Kiwi," I said.

"That's what I said, brother. He's SAS; New Zealand." John responded in that endearing gruff Illinois farm boy staccato that you listen to because it's from someone who has also seen all the bullshit thrown around over the years, and you just don't have the patience for it anymore.

I went back to americanexplosivesgroup.com and saw the difference. All I could say about the contrast between a professional and a wannabe was, "Wow..."

"So, what I'm getting from this, is that he was either approached by Discovery, or he responded to another casting call on one of the many film and TV casting websites from MAK Pictures, and he thought, *hey, if I get on a new treasure hunting show on Discovery Channel, I can publicize my business!*"

"He does look like a good marketer, brother."

"Wow..."

When I looked at Robert Leonard, and his company Terra Exploration Group, it was clear he was in the business of selling metal detectors. Fine and dandy, but it was that he was on CURSE OF OAKLAND, that I almost snorted my cup of morning coffee, again. Once more, Discovery Communications had counted coup against A&E. First, they got David Carr and what was Beantown Productions, but now Downtown Television, in season 2, and now season 3, along with Tom Dorman, sans Aaron Benarroch, John Adams and Cathy Grant. I think they'll realized that you can play with fire for only so long before you get turned into a crispy critter. Now they had not only the showrunners from History Channel's production that led to O'Neill asking for Discovery Channel's own treasure drama, but they were also starting to get the cast from CURSE OF OAK ISLAND over to TQ:SI. It was one more opportunity for Leonard to sell his products and services.

Figure 104. Jack W. Peters brings the explosions that should excite. As explosives expert Major John Donovan, US Army (RET) said, he's more of a marketer than an explosives man based on his website--he's trying to sell services by being on the show.

It's all about creating credibility for a fake show. Jeremy Whalen has none; that's why he did his best to slander me behind my back to everyone on the set, and to use his brother to libel me on the Internet. In season 1 and 2, they had Mehgan Heaney-Grier with her freediving championship, Keith Plaskett with his bonafide treasure hunting and archeological credentials, Dr. Bryan Grieg-Fry with a PhD. in herpetology, and me with my internationally reported capture in Vietnam in 1983 while photographing a treasure hunting expedition. As Whalen had no credentials to carry the show on his own, so they needed someone with credentials as solid as Plaskett's and mine.

A newly formed joint venture between a Clearwater shipwreck recovery company and a Los Angeles entertainment firm aims to take viewers on the hunt for underwater treasure.

Endurance Exploration Group Inc. (OTCQB: EXPL) teamed with Downtown Television Inc. to produce entertainment content related to deep-sea exploration, historical shipwreck search and artifact recovery.

Endurance and Downtown will each own 50 percent of the new limited liability corporation, named Megalodon Entertainment LLC, a press release said. Specific financial details were not disclosed.

Downtown is owned and operated by CEO David Carr, who has produced adventure, science and exploration shows such as "The Curse of Oak Island," "Treasure Quest," "Extinct or Alive," and "Ancient Aliens." His productions have been featured on networks such as History, Discovery, TLC, Animal Planet and Lifetime.

Endurance is in the business of researching and recovering historic shipwrecks and their cargoes. To date, it has not generated any revenue and has relied on

Figure 105. What does it say about integrity and society when a media company uses a fakeumentary as a resume for archeological research—when do the flags go up that media is no longer recording the events, but fabricating and falsifying history? When does the federal government FINALLY step in to stop the fraud?

That person came in the form of Shawn Cowles. His name kept rolling around in my mind. I followed the link to his website and nothing was ringing a bell. There was information about his adventure travel business on his official website, along with his description as a treasure hunter. There was little information other than he has been associated with the Mel Fisher organization. That part about Mel Fisher didn't really resonate until I searched under his name and looked at other references, such as LinkedIn. That's when it hit—all the way back in 2015!

After we all returned home from shooting in Brazil, MAK Pictures set up a video conference on Skype between Shawn Cowles and me. At that time he was not a treasure hunter. He had the title of investor relations manager for Mel Fisher's Treasure, the Fisher organization in Key West, Florida. It was to be another credibility spot in the first season, to go along with the scene where Mehgan and I were verifying the authenticity of the corroded silver coins that we called "cookies" on the show. That was the scene in the *Museu Náutico de Ilhabela* with the proprietor, a retired Brazil Navy diver and author of books on treasure and diving ship wrecks in the area, by the name of Jeannis Platon. The recorded Skype banter back and forth with Shawn Cowles was never aired. The scene with Platon in his maritime store was enough.

When I realized this Shawn Cowles was the same person I had talked to almost two years ago, it all came together. It was so damned bizarre. I wondered if Discovery had given Cowles the same spiel they did me, about going on a treasure hunt. They probably also lured him in with the last two seasons, and how close they must be to finding the whole motherlode. Not until he arrived in Bolivia, did he probably also come to the same conclusion I did, that he had been conned, and that the non-disclosure agreement in his contract, along with stern words from Kadin about how the veracity of the NDA was nothing to mess with.

Figure 106. Just like in Argentina, the Bolivia season 3 team using tents to have actors do OTF in, such as Brett Tutor did, when he talked about how dangerous everything supposedly was, though the tents were staked on the lawn of the hotel, all shot from the inside with a GoPro to make it look as if we were instead deep in the jungle—back in Puerto Bemberg, it was the lawn of the Bemberg Inn. Shawn Cowles must have had some bit of humor adding the gag labels.

So there they were in Bolivia. Jeremy Whalen must have felt on top of the world thinking he had pulled off the greatest coup by not yet being arrested by the police in Salinas, Ecuador where he manages a boat yard, or Peru, where his wife is from and left to Ecuador for questionable reasons, possibly to avoid charges of artifact smuggling, or sex offenses similar to his fathers', according to Keith Plaskett: Peruvians and Ecuadorian aren't the best of friends—before my cousin was killed in a skydiving accident in preparation for Ecuador's independence day celebration, he was a special forces captain who was highly decorated for his actions in battle during the Cenepa War of 1995.

Then, to give the stamp of authenticity, what better person to bring it than someone who worked on bonafide treasure hunting expedition on Mel Fisher's team? Recall that all bonafide artifacts we had on the show that were *finds*, on season 2, were brought by Jeremy Whalen, and Keith Plaskett. Everything else was fabricated by Sebastien and Julia. Keith was no longer available to provide that bulk of artifacts. Jeremy could bring more stolen artifacts from Peru, but that would really be running the razor just a few too many times. What if Shawn Cowles also brought some real gold and silver artifacts from the Atocha find?

It's easy. You can go to the Mel Fisher website and they have a store that has variety of bright shiny gold and silver artifacts for sale, not to mention the treasure on display and the treasure in the safes. I'm sure that Cowles has his own collection that he would have been asked to bring down to Bolivia to salt the site, as had been done in Argentina and Brazil with musketballs and silver "cookies" from Peru by Keith and Jeremy. Sebastien Baille had probably realized he would have been putting himself in major danger of imprisonment by creating more fake artifacts for another season of TQ:SI.

Imagine everyone's surprise when Discovery was probably in the middle of post-production editing, when they received notification of a lawsuit against their newly groomed Ty Pennington heart-throb replacement on TLC's TRADING SPACES, Brett Tutor, that listed Discovery Communications as a defendant. Had everything gone on schedule, TQ:SI Bolivia should have broadcast in the winter/spring season, but it had yet to be released. Now, with more attention brought to bear on all the items listed in the case that are now in the public domain, it's going to be very interesting as we near the initial broadcast of Season 3.

Betrayal is a very emotionally loaded word. It brings up my memories as photographer and why I stopped thinking of myself as a career journalist, and it became simply another legend or cover, to use after my recruitment by the CIA: I accepted recruitment initially as an asset after witnessing an atrocity committed by the FMLN in 1986. The FMLN had cut the hands off a campesino as an example to stop them from picking coffee, for which they would be taxed, and those tax dollars would go towards arms and ammunition against the FMLN. What I had found was that the free press was only free to those who felt the FMLN should win—I took the story to the Reuters and the AP bureaus when I returned to the Camino Real Hotel, where most of the agencies and networks had their offices.

"If it was the soldiers doing this, we'd take it. We're not interested in this," was the response. My coming out twenty-five years after the fact really pissed off former members of the CIA, because it confirmed that the CIA, like the KGB back then and the FSB, like all clandestine services, used the press and the cover of the press. The press hated me for the same, even though I was a golden boy at the time—how many journalists actually got to see behind the veil in communist Vietnam?

This was a time when you had to really watch your back. *Peace demonstrators* were coming to Latin America from Europe and were riddled with East German operatives from the KGB, who had latched onto peace groups from Berlin coming to Central America. One was on the steps of government buildings on the day I was flying out of Tegus on a C47 for one of the FDN/Contra bases at the Honduran/Nicaraguan border.

The Jesuits who we were chasing all over Brazil and Argentina? I knew them long before rattling off their ancient history in South America. Contemporary Jesuit priests were actively working with the FMLN, much like the ancient Jesuits were aiding the Guarani in South America. The difference was that some of them were agents of the Soviet Union and Cuba in Latin America.

Liberation Theology was in my face every day that I was in Latin America, and it wasn't always some peachy, jump on the peace bus and sing kumbaya my Lord type. It was arms being smuggled in from Nicaragua and Honduras, into and out of Mexico and Colombia. Many like to think that the priesthood is all about love and kindness, unless you were actually raised by Jesuits and endured their use of the switch. It's no coincidence that my Ecuadorian special forces cousin, with whom I worked with on a contract to interdict the flow of FARC guerrillas and drug smuggling into Ecuador back in the early 1990s, illegal incursions that turned Ecuador from the idyllic Switzerland of the 1960s and 1970s into one of the kidnapping capitols of the world (PROOF OF LIFE was filmed around my mother's birthplace of Quito for a reason), went to school to become priest. Then, suddenly, we learned he had joined the Ecuadorian Army.

As you might have guessed, someone like Tim Kennedy spouting off about having killed women and children to draw attention to himself as a PR move is pretty revolting to me. Because of administrative changes in the White House, from Reagan to Bush Sr., and resulting unfulfilled promises by the US government, I can't even show a DD214 to the VA for my combat-related injuries. More than that, for twenty-five years I kept the full extent of my experiences secret, like so many from that time, in the last battle of the Cold War that we won, for fear another glory whore in the Hague might try to come after us for having participated, nay survived, in the one of the dirtiest wars of the 20th Century.

Paramilitary, in and of itself, is defined as *outside* of the military; even if a paramilitary officer commands foreign military unit within the military to achieve specific objectives aligned with the defense of the US: one of the reasons you run paramilitary units is that it's one of the best ways for an agency to keep their actions off the books, by staying out of the US embassy, and the record keeping that occurs there. If you're outside of the military, even if wounded in action, you don't receive the same benefits as regular military in the US.

Betrayal goes much farther in the TV industry with Discovery. It started for me with TQ:SI, but for Discovery Communications it goes to its network, but also its Discovery Education recipients. If the Discovery Communications' "last true-life network" is fraud, and Discovery Education would become one of Discovery Communications' biggest moneymakers (Discovery Communications has now begun broadcasting TQ:SI on the Science Channel—as historical fact!), what lens are we expected to look through at what Discovery Communications' CEO David Zaslav for meaning here in the August 19, 2012, *New York Times* quote?

> *"'It's kind of perfect for us,'" said David M. Zaslav, chief executive of Discovery Communications, which owns networks like Discovery Channel, Animal Planet and TLC. 'Educational content is core to our DNA, and we're unencumbered — unlike traditional textbook publishers, we're not defending a dying business.'"*

Frankly, this is chilling when we're reminded of what a fan commented on the TQ:SI Facebook page: *"Who needs books when we can get our history from TV?"*

Many more questions come riding in when we look at the backgrounds of those working in the reality TV industry, who went to seemingly great journalism schools, like Mark Kadin with the degree in journalism from Northwestern, who have no morals with regards to fabricating the news. For us on TQ:SI to supposedly have found such a major find that corroborates a centuries old story of a Portuguese conquistador who had been one of the earliest European paramilitaries in the Americas, leading native peoples in a concerted effort toward a military objective, is BIG NEWS. And it is news: all those fake finds, broadcast as real and true, will be entered in the books for some poor archeologist to try and follow.

When I realized it was time to make sure it was news, I contacted my first employers in the news business, the Associated Press. I then also contacted Reuters, my later employer as a freelance photographer, starting in Southeast Asia in 1983. Reuters and even *Agence France Press*, third of the news services I shot photographs for from 1983 to 1990, seemed interested in the story I had to tell of a major network participating in the fraudulent fabrication of "true-life" documentaries, going so far as to purchase illegally got artifacts from Peru and having them smuggled to Argentina to appear on set on a scripted show.

No response from the bureau chiefs for AFP in Los Angeles, nor Reuters in San Francisco from my initial call. I found this amazing. One of the most important resolves of the reparations made to nations, and individuals, after WWII, such as those in the Jewish community, whose art was confiscated by the Nazis, while those people were being sent to the death camps, was the making illegal of the taking of national treasures. In Europe, it was Renoirs, Rembrandts and the like. In South America, after the UNIDROIT Convention on Stolen or Illegally Exported Cultural Objects of 1995, it would the stealing of Incan mummies, and their belongings buried with them.

I thought perhaps I had some coverage coming with Anthony McCartney of the AP Bureau in Los Angeles. After all, he was the entertainment reporter for AP in Southern California. He asked for sources. I told him I had them and was ready to send. He said he had to talk with the New York office. Then silence.

Nothing in from the various news agencies, even Fox News, and TMZ, I went to the various embassies in Washington D.C. that should be aghast at such flagrant breaking of laws by such a large media corporation as Discovery: Peru, Brazil, Ecuador, Argentina. Not a word from ambassadors Carlos Pareja, Sergio Silva Do Amaral, Francisco Carrión Mena, Martin Lousteau. Nothing. *Nada*—for nations complaining about "gringo corporations" coming down to take advantage of southern cousins, that doesn't say much about their own *por la patria*.

Just before I started working on this book, I checked in and now not even a word back. I approached from another angle that should have gotten the word out, that something is greatly amiss. At this point, I was only thinking what was amiss was only with Discovery Communications and A&E in their false advertising, and lack of show disclaimers. Heaven forbid what the present White House administration calls FAKE NEWS has seeped into something more than just contemporary record, and as important as the record of past history.

I called the AP bureau in Buenos Aires, Argentina and was told that the bureau chief Victor Caivano was in Chile at a photography competition. Fine. I'd send an email with the facts. I had a long list of local sources with whom everything could be easily verified. I left messages and Caivano even accepted a friend request on Facebook. The AP bureau should have been running with this for no other reason than it would be a story that would appeal to an audience wanting to hear another story of the Gringos raping and stealing in South America (funny how Jeremy Whalen was always spouting off about how Gringos, and Europeans had come to the Americas to take from the Native Peoples, and yet that was exactly what he had done for two decades in Peru: his last recorded attempt was offering to sell Incan artifacts to Keith Plaskett's brother, when he visited Keith a few months after close of Season 2 production in Argentina. Keith's said his brother, an archeologist by training and previous profession, was aghast.)—and how much more controversial than the very media corporation that sells itself as the bastion of transnationalism? And then, yet again, continued silence from the news media.

My disgust took me back to El Salvador, a bloody stump left by an guerrilla's machete, a farmer who might have, or not, lived after I had done my best to stop his bleeding and help get him on a medevac—and ignorance at the bureau office. When I told my friend, and former boss at Human Events, one of the oldest political newspapers in Washington D.C. what had happened over the last year with my attempts to break a story, he said, "Journalists don't want to work...They are the laziest people on earth."

In a life circle that took me from an idealistic, pumped up combat photographer, filled with admiration for those journalists I thought risked everything, some paying with their lives, some of whom have become my friends over the years, like Joseph Galloway, Zalin Grant, Nick Ut, Tim Page, Steve Northup, Robert Capa, Dana Stone, and Sean Flynn; through Central America; the CIA; the corporate world; back into media with Discovery Channel; and then to where I started with at AP, Reuters, and AFP, this time trying to report a story with such ramifications by Discovery Communications on world history, the betrayal seemed constant and pretty damned tiring.

How to stop this merry-go-round?

Well, I'd hope the CEOs at Reuters, AP and AFP, would get their ship in order after reading this book and realize that they'll make more money by getting their reporters back to what they used to do, which is simply to just do their damned job. Discovery on the other hand is going to be a major quagmire to wade through until the shareholders realize fully what has happened under CEO David Zaslav's get rich quick, Ponzi scheme.

Like anything in the world, this can be fixed. First, CEO David Zaslav must be fired and the US government should seek legal action against him, Eileen O'Neill, and Rich Ross personally for criminal actions—did the US just go after Germany and the rest of the Axis powers as a whole for their actions, which included the stealing of national treasures? Of course not, they targeted first the leaders for if not for their twisted leadership, the masses below them wouldn't have gone down that road on their own.

There's an old Vietnamese proverb that goes: "The house leaks from its roof on down." This was used to describe the mindboggling amount of corruption that had occurred in South Vietnam during the war, namely how all that corruption started with the generals and government leaders who benefitted the most from all the corruption happening in Vietnam, and then that corruption trickled down to those below them, all the way down to what we called White Mice, Saigon police who wouldn't waste time waiting for a bribe (they asked for it), and didn't hang around to fight crime when VC shot at them, either. Discovery Communications is media's version of South Vietnam's government during the late-1960s through to the fall of Saigon—Like in Vietnam it was all done for greed and self-interest from the top on down.

If that's not enough to make you shiver, think about this: Zaslav received the NATAS Trustees Award in 2007. Past recipients of the Trustees Award were CBS founder William Paley, CBS Newsman Walter Cronkite, and President John F. Kennedy. He also captained NBC when that network was earning it stripes as a left elite-slanted network—I don't really care about it being leftist-slanted, I care that news media that should just report the facts have become just opinion platforms that most not trained in deciphering it all, are being put upon: how many have the time, like me, only because of my business, to watch three different networks in order to find the real news? Frankly, I think all previous recipients of the award would be rolling around in their grave. Add to that he was an adjunct professor at Fordham University, who created and taught a graduate level course in the business of cable television: shocking and frankly terrifying!

As I said, I'd carried a video camera as a freelancer for Ted Turner in Latin America, a man whom I consider the patron and *patrón* of satellite TV, and hence cable. He kind of shot himself in the foot with a sarin gas story that I think was more on Peter Arnett—all that had to be done was check the DD214 of one of the most vocal sources for that piece on Operation Tailwind, to know that the source hadn't even gone to Vietnam.

I've always felt that Turner carried the creed of the journalist to heart, though and the day he left CNN's command was the day that it was going to turn into the shit show CNN is now. He represents what class there was in media, kind of like the Charlton Heston and Jimmy Stewart of Hollywood. How often does a CEO of a media respond to a FUBAR situation with such apologies, as these included in former Secretary of the Navy James Webb's July 15,1998 commentary in the Wall Street Journal?

"CNN founder Ted Turner issued a fervent apology to Vietnam veterans for his network's false report that the military had used sarin nerve gas in Vietnam. "Nothing has upset me more probably in my whole life," Mr. Turner said, adding that he "would take my shirt off and beat myself bloody in the back""

Do you think CEO David Zaslav would do something as honorable as at least offering an apology to those actors who were hired simply as a means to an end, that end being the bottom line he's proud of touting in his annual reports, in the process endangering the welfare of those employees?

How about apologizing to the international audience for defrauding and them in his drive to collect $42 Million a year for him personally? Holding your breath?

Figure 107. What a CNN transnational epitaph to Anthony Bourdain, more than a week after his suicide, and they still haven't corrected—It's COLOMBIA, not Columbia!

I didn't think so. Instead, all he has done is use a variety of Discovery Communications producers and other executives, not to mention a fleet of lawyers to bog down the legal process, in order to protect people who should be in prison, for a variety of charges, such as pedophilia, drug-running, stolen artifact smuggling, cyberstalking, harassment, assault and battery, and even manslaughter—I'm still amazed Joseph Teti isn't locked up in a small little hole in Leavenworth: this is a predator who definitely isn't walking around freely because of his own personal abilities in the courtroom.

Even with all that is known about Joseph Teti, and now Jeremy Whalen, who are walking freely, while Will Hayden, and Rich Wyatt are in prison is only because Zaslav used all those millions of dollars and the legal fleet, in the protection of Teti and Whalen. It's all business sense to Zaslav, the longer they keep Discovery Communications, Whalen and Teti out of court and out of prison, the more money Discovery Communications can continue to pull in from all those fakeumentary, reality TV shows that they don't even have to pay their actors royalties on.

But, it's the idolatry that galls and especially frightens as media leads the common mind of society. By continuing to broadcast images of criminals such as Joseph Teti and Jeremy Whalen, which Discovery Communications is presently doing, they bequeath unto them the aura of a TV personality, for which many, especially in foreign countries, it provides hero status to those two, who if they had never been on TV, the average person wouldn't have paid a mind to.

This goes much farther than a network protecting its commodities. Many have asked, why take on such a mega-corporation with millions of dollars at its beck and call, to do whatever they desire, legal, or illegal? With a total revenue of $1.86 Billion in 2017, which translates to a net of $1.1 Billion, they have large coffers from which to draw. Still, it goes much, much farther than financial wealth.

Figure 108. Loan executing Lém, a photo story so poorly interpreted through history. ©AP/Eddie Adams.

My first memories of life started in Saigon during the Vietnam War. One of the most impacting images of that war and time, and probably one of the reasons I started off as a photographer, was an image that AP staff photographer Eddie Adams captured. He was there with a camera team from NBC, so there were also moving pictures of this traumatic event that was so poorly interpreted. Even now the photo continues to be mired in ambiguity in such contemporary media productions as should have finally cleared up history with some accuracy, such as the Ken Burn's PBS release of THE VIETNAM WAR, but didn't: yet, again, there it was the infamous scene of Nguyễn Ngọc Loan, South Vietnam's chief of police, putting a .38 Special Smith & Wesson Bodyguard revolver up to Vietcong Nguyễn Văn Lém, and executing him, without full explanation.

(NY16-Feb.1)DEATH OF A MILITARY FAMILY IN SAIGON SUBURB--South Vietnamese soldiers stand near bodies of a South Vietnamese commander of a training camp and command center and members of his family after the camp was retaken from the Viet Cong in a northern Saigon suburb today. The commander, a colonel, was decapitated by the Viet Cong and his wife and six children were machinegunned. On ground near the corpses are toys and food. At right are sandbags behind which the children hid.(AP Wirephoto via radio from Saigon)(see AP wire story)(nr50852nw)1968

Figure 109. Loan's friend, who was decapitated, and the officer's family murdered earlier that day. ©AP/Wide World Photo.

People who ignorantly continue to defend the communist invasion of South Vietnam by North Vietnam, refer to this event as an example of why the US was on the wrong side of the war, and should have never gotten involved in Vietnam in the way we did, that it showed Americans had just become party murder. I do agree that how we participated in Vietnam once Lyndon B. Johnson took over was a major travesty. I also think that things would have turned out differently had the world gotten the full caption.

What most didn't know was that Lém wasn't just some hapless VC, or civilian, that had been captured and had come face first into a police chief with a lust for blood. What most didn't know was that this VC Captain Lém had been captured after having executed not only one of Loan's deputies, a friend, an officer who had refused to give the VC captain information, but also his friend's family. The complete lack of understanding and comprehension of the whole story, due to the inability of a single photograph to accurately record what had happened didn't become completely clear until 1978. That year, after having escaped with many Viet refugees, the INS came after Loan as a suspected war criminal, based solely on the inaccurate interpretation of the famous photos Eddie Adams had taken. Loan was only allowed to stay after President Jimmy Carter stepped in.

As Eddie Adams said in TIME Magazine, "Two people died in that photograph: the recipient of the bullet and Gen. Nguyen Ngoc Loan. The general killed the Viet Cong; I killed the general with my camera. Still photographs are the most powerful weapon in the world."

Media can be misinterpreted when a too thinly written caption is provided. Imagine what happens when the caption is completely false, like the caption that CEO David Zaslav has inserted into every production broadcast at Discovery Channel, and all others under the Discovery Communications umbrella: "True-life documentary."

But, everyone knows it's all fake, you might say. I got that from a lawyer I approached about doing a defamation case against Discovery Communications in California, much like what Cody Lundin has been at for a few years now. I stated what I'm stating in this whole book: **if everyone knew it was fake and scripted, Discovery Communications wouldn't be bringing in $1.1 Billion a year.** In their 2017 letter to the shareholders:

Dear Shareholders,

At Discovery, we know that truth is stronger than fiction.
We serve a global audience of passionate enthusiasts with real-life
stories that inspire, inform and entertain. From distant lands to the comfort
of home and the drama of the playing field, our heritage lies in helping people
explore their world through stories they love and the brands that matter.

As our industry rapidly evolves, we are accelerating our commitment to great content and the innovation to ensure that our viewers can enjoy our stories across every screen, service and format, whenever and wherever they choose. We also are delivering new ways for advertisers and distributors to reach highly targeted audiences at scale.

As a global leader in real-life entertainment, we differentiate ourselves in a crowded and competitive marketplace which is primarily focused on high-cost scripted productions. We create exceptional value for our shareholders by bringing high-quality content to viewers through trusted brands that resonate globally.

2017 was a historic year for Discovery. We took significant steps to position ourselves for success in a changing industry, while driving growth from our traditional linear business and accelerating our investments in areas like digital and mobile to reach viewers on every screen.

Figure 110. The best combat shot at AP, for Christmas 1985. When the bureau chief bought it, a fellow freelancer in the office at the Camino Real asked me, "What are they shooting at—campesinos?" Reality was that a sneaky ambush by the FMLN nearly took out the PRAL unit being commanded by Captain Gustavo Perdomo, and the two gunships that day came in to provide covering fire to turn that ambush around. The journalist's comment was a reminder of how media can be misinterpreted by the bias of the viewer. ©AP/Cork Graham

When I saw the first line of that letter, I again choked on my morning coffee with shock and laughter. Is it just me, or is the marketing department copywriter of this letter living in a different reality than the reality I've seen at Discovery Communications for the three years? Under Zaslav's direction Discovery Communications has travelled so far from reality when it comes to documentary, that to say he and his Hollywood offices are from Venus and the international audience is from Mars would be an understatement. For Zaslav to state that Discovery Communications is the last "true-life" documentary network out there is pure defrauding of the shareholders, the advertisers and especially the audience.

I joked that if Ted Turner were dead, he'd be rolling over in his grave now to see what has happened a technology platform he nurtured into a thriving media base. What is passing for news and documentary these days, though makes Turner's heavily criticized feature on Operation Tailwind titled VALLEY OF DEATH a true docudrama, in contrast to the flat-out fake Hollywood scripted programming masquerading as "true-life" documentary in the reality TV industry.

I'd like to say that it's just one horrible mistake, that CEO Dave Zaslav is just being played by his VPs of programming and channel presidents as they tremble in fear of being *culturally relocated*, or straight fired, but one thing you learn about people in power is how they appear in the media. The darker the shroud, the larger the veil, the more likely there is a mountain and not a molehill of information being hidden for less than scrupulous reasons.

Take Ted Turner. Multi-millionaire. He appears on TV even now, actively doing his part to keep our world from turning into the picked clean bones of a dead bison. When I've written to him, he's written back, faithfully, even with news contrary to which I wished. There's a lot about him on the Internet and even his family—this is a person who's trying to connect with the world. That's someone who's a straight shooter. Some might stay that that's "old school," which is really sad, because what does that mean about the "new school?" I saw this in how he ran CNN as a media service reaching an audience.

Do a search on the Internet on David Zaslav and you have someone who is clearly gauging every bit and piece that comes out, and most of it is shrouded in a cloud of misinformation. His family doesn't come into his PR campaigns, though he's reaching directly in the privacy your family's own home. While in the privacy of your home, he's telling you about treasure hunts that find treasure that no one's ever seen in a museum, which is in itself amazing—why have so few of the viewers asked when will the finds of TREASURE QUEST: SNAKE ISLAND be available for viewing at a museum? The importance of such a historical find cannot be underestimated. Yet, I'm still waiting to see the real treasure, and I was the team leader of season 1 and 2.

Figure 111. Discovery Communications CEO David Zaslav   ©AP/Rick Bowmer

Could the secretive activities of CEO Zaslav, who's supposed to be the face of Discovery Communications, be for safety reasons against his own employees, because of that other part of Discovery Communications programming that relies on creating drama: hiring wild cards, aka psychopaths, to build that drama? When you play with vipers, there's a real threat that you can get bit. I know if I had been actively hiring psychopaths like Teti and Whalen, I'd like to be far as possible away from them, i.e. preventing them from having enough information to stalk me.

It made me think also about the aloof Joseph Boyle. Checking his IMDB profile, he too is one of those Hollywood office hires, not one bit of documentarian in his resume. As a matter of fact, his resume starts with an acting part on a horror movie called RAVENOUS, loosely based on the Donner Party in the California Sierras. From there are a couple of production management of jobs on films, and then it's off the races with reality TV. This is a common theme with these reality TV shows, that the players aren't necessarily from journalism (if they are, they've totally ignored the principles of accuracy that those backgrounds were intended to instill, as was lost on Mark Kadin and Will Ehbrecht), but more often from film or a theater background.

What's surprising is that Boyle is so secretive about his identity. I never met him, yet, according to Anuj Majumdar, whose real title of scriptwriter is hidden in the credits with an "executive producer" credit (reality TV shows, which by description means "fly on the wall" reporting, are not supposed to have scriptwriters), Joseph Boyle's hands were all over the scripting and directing of TQ:SI.

Figure 112. The gray man, Joseph Boyle, Discovery Communications VP of Production and Development at Discovery Channel.

I get it. If I were working for Discovery Communications and I was hiring unstable actors, in the form of psychopaths, like Joseph Teti, Jeremy Whalen, Richard Wyatt, Dale Comstock, Grady Powell, Bill Hayden, I'd be worried that when these people don't achieve the fame and notoriety that they lied and cheated for, basically sold their souls for, they'd be coming after me. In the end, I take it as just another piece of evidence that Joseph Boyle never appearing on set, even though he was listed as Discovery Channel's executive producer on both seasons of TQ:SI, was because he knew it was fraud and he didn't want to be publicly associated with it in any form, other than where he had to, as in credits, for which them being completely missing(as they had been for that infamous initial broadcast of DUAL SURVIVAL in Bolivia), would only bring more questions. As you can see with what happened to Brig. Gen. Loan, and Eddie Adams said so eloquently, "Still photographs are the most powerful weapon in the world."

Figure 113. Richard Wyatt, AMERICAN GUNS; Will Hayden, SONS OF GUNS; Mark L. Rackley, EXTREME ENCOUNTERS. Rackley's Florida mug shot is from 2010, a repeat drug offender after Mehgan Heaney-Grier got him off with her testimony in Beaumont, TX. Like attracts like and Discovery Communications' fake "true-life" documentaries have been attracting quite a lineup.

As my longtime friend Joe Galloway, of WE WERE SOLDIERS fame, and who's reporting speaks for itself, commented when I told him last year about the mess I had gotten myself into at Discovery Communications, "Looks like a real shit show they've got going on over there at Discovery."

So, how to clear this mess up? If it's not clear to the board of directors that they need to overhaul their executive board, they should do some major soul searching into the longevity of trying to overcome that old proverb, *"You can lie to some of the people all the time, and you can lie to all of the people some of the time; but you can't lie to all the people all of the time."*

If you really want to call yourself a "true-life" documentary network, then BE a "true-life" documentary network. Don't parade around saying you are what you aren't. Definitely don't open a shareholder's letter with: "At Discovery, we know that truth is stronger than fiction."

Close the Los Angeles offices for production and move them back to Silver Springs, or now that the Maryland offices are moving to New York, make it New York. Use the services of Hollywood, like the camera and sound guys. Don't use the scriptwriters from Hollywood. Make agreements with actual scientists, researchers, archeologists, and other specialists of their fields, like presently working treasure hunters in totally self-funded expeditions. Have the content direct the show, instead of the scriptwriters who shouldn't even be on staff.

Don't set up scenes: teach your Hollywood crews how to shoot like journalists if they don't already. It's not that hard. Some of the best combat photographers in Vietnam and other wars were those who were initially trained in the fine art of model, glamour and film. Larry Burrows is one those I highly admired, along with Sean Flynn.

There's the artist and then there's the documentarian. The artist collects the images and soundbites that stir the emotions. The documentarian makes it "true-life." Since 2011, Discovery Communications has only been producing "art" out of its Hollywood offices. Have all you want from Hollywood in post-production. That's where the dramatic magic really gets tightened up. Put your cameramen in the field with real gold miners, and treasure hunters, instead of hired actors. When the fishermen on DEADLIEST CATCH are taking another hit of cocaine or crystal methamphetamine in order to stay up those long hours, catch that, too—be honest. Get the full, "true-life" in reality TV. I guarantee it'll be dramatic enough without having to have your field producers and show runners egging on cocaine-pumped cast to pick fights with others.

Time for integrity to return to Discovery Communications, and move away from what had begun back in August 8, 2011, when Discovery Communications representatives, Jim Ford, VP, Talent Business & Legal Affairs, and Anna Geddes, Executive Producer and Director of Production, had a lunch meeting with Mykel and Ruth Hawke at Landry's in New Orleans. It should have been a wonderful time: They had two hit shows, MAN, WOMAN, WILD , and ONE MAN ARMY under their belt. MAN, WOMAN, WILD was already going into its third season. As such, Mykel asked for a created by credit for his brainchildren: MAN, WOMAN, WILD and ONE MAN ARMY (later DUDE, YOU'RE SCREWED, NAKED AND AFRAID, among others he's never been credited for). He said, he didn't want the money, and that he'd put that in writing. Mykel just wanted to make more shows to teach more people. It was in his contract, and they should honor it.

They told him the key word was IF and if anyone got it, he would; but they didn't want to give it and never do. When asked why, they said, "if we give it to you, everyone will want it."

Mykel said, "But I created those; I earned them. If folks don't deserve it, then they don't get the credit, that simple."

Ford responded, "It would mean lots of money lost to them, so, no, was the final answer."

"You have lied to me and stolen from me and I will leave," Mykel answered.

Ford fired back, "You should shut the fuck up and be happy."

"I can't believe you'd say something like that, to a man like me. I will quit."

"You won't walk away from two hit shows."

Mykel looked at him, and said, "Watch me."

Mykel and Ruth left Discovery and went to Travel Channel, and Outdoor Channel, where he produced and hosted LOST SURVIVORS and ELITE TACTICAL UNIT. Soon after, Discovery fired Dave Canterbury for lying about his army schools, which they didn't vet in the first place. They then hired Joseph Teti, failing to vet his military records, yet again. Teti lied and sold them a bill of goods and he was rewarded with LONE OPERATOR and the slow role on DUAL SURVIVAL. Discovery thought they had the perfect replacement for Mykel Hawke: a former Green Beret and Marine, and CIA paramilitary contractor, and survival guy.

According to Hawke, "The entire first season of dual survival with Teti was a fake season where he did nothing because he didn't have the survival background like Hawke's, so they tried to make him look like a hero as they were planning to make LONE OPERATOR, his show, based on his lies, right after DS began airing and they did, they started filming three weeks after DS with Teti aired and on the first day of filming, three men died. They died for something that could have easily been prevented; if Teti had not lied they would not have been there. If Teti was what he claimed, he could have caught all the mistakes that occurred.

"That said, the FBI Tampa told me, Discovery could be criminally liable for negligent homicide, and since then, Teti has attacked me to silence me and Discovery has let him, and helped him. In 2013, when Teti started and I had left and had two new shows [one at Travel Channel], Discovery wanted to buy Travel Channel. So, when Teti, their new star, attacked me, they protected him and helped him attack me, and they asked Travel to bury me. I have the emails to prove it all so, yeah, do I think discovery is a criminal organization? Yes."

Canned TV is a great way to look at the programming coming out of Discovery Communications. They've got a model and they just look for the dancing monkeys to fit—that's why they don't want talent working on scripts of storytelling: that's what the executive producers are hired to do. Mykel Hawke fit the SpecOps model, or profile. I fit the treasure hunter model or profile. Then, when they lost Mykel, they got Joseph Teti. Done with Teti, and needing a body to fill that vacuum, they're now grooming Tim Kennedy, with his show HARD TO KILL. For treasure, they're grooming Shawn Cowles to fit the new treasure hunter model and profile on Season 3 of TQ:SI. Until Discovery Communications is finally called to the mast, nothing will happen: too much pleasure in contrast to the pain right now for them.

As James Taylors sings, "I've seen fire, and I've seen rain." I've seen what seems so easy to achieve, fall by the wayside. I've seen things so impossible and seemingly unattainable; and yet totally embraced, focused on, and achieved against such immense odds. These challenges have taught me that anything can be corrected and fixed. But, it takes devotion, and the honesty to see that something has gone horribly wrong, and it needs to be corrected.

Mykel Hawke and I have talked about what would we do to fix this, if Discovery Communications actually tried to make amends with the despicable manner in which they've handled themselves in dealing with him and me. There are so many anecdotes of people pitching ideas for shows to the networks, only to have them appear on a show produced by that network. This is age old, and why if you're pitching a show idea, it's best to do so through a lawyer.

Story ideas are tricky, though. One person comes up with an idea that is never seen by production at a network, but someone at the network comes up with a similar idea, and there's really nothing that the former can do, because they would have to prove the show idea the network ran with actually came about from stealing idea from the private individuals how tried to submit it. Having an agent submit it provides that documentation that will more likely stand up in court.

It's when networks steal ideas from writers, and they do, such as when they had me move the map around to make it look as if I had found Snake Island that way, that it becomes ridiculous. If you remember the scene, it was in the Ilhabela HQ club house where we did our prep for the trip to the Snake Island and Bryan talked about the dangers of the vipers. Discovery showrunners had me hold up a copy of the treasure map that was found in India and that Paul Thiry had used in his research. What they did was have me spin it around and then flip it over to sort of fit the profile of Snake Island. They took that idea from having read my Vietnam political prisoner/treasure hunt, where I described how Knight had found *Iles Des Pirates* and specifically Grand Pirate Island by reviewing old French nautical maps—When Knight did it, there was an exact match without any map flipping and spinning mumbo-jumbo, which Discovery's scriptwriter's tried to explain away with contrived dialogue about Jesuit chicanery and misdirection.

It's just TV, many like to say, but for those who've never taken that step into the unknown but are searching for that opportunity, it becomes the dream. It's like the retired lady from New Jersey who met a gold miner on a flight from Anchorage to Nome. She said that she'd never done anything adventurous in her life. She had lived that security dream paying the house off and building a solid retirement. She then saw Discovery Channel's BERING SEA GOLD, and the impact of feeling she'd never taken a real risk, never done anything adventurous, hit her like a strike of lightening.

Within a month, she'd sold her house and pulled her savings to be on the plane that led to this moment in which a long-time miner was having this shocking conversation with her. He felt so sorry for this poor woman, who made such a rash decision based on a reality TV show that she thought was as CEO Zaslav said, "true-life."

Hawke and I feel that if Discovery Communications—or A&E and all these other networks—continue to offer "reality" TV but staff their productions teams with Hollywood crews hoping for that that next big television drama, or feature film, it will continue to be a losing war: these crews are building portfolios for a completely different genre than documentary or reality. It's the old story of the leopard or the scorpion. How can you ask them to do something they don't know how to do, because they're not experienced or trained in reporting?

If you want to see what "true-life" documentary really is, you need to watch a documentary on PBS, where you have people like Sir David Attenborough spending months and sometimes years on a production, shooting schedules that Ty Clancey at least knew when we commiserated on how a proper TQ:SI in Brazil would have taken about five years to shoot—ironically, the original TREASURE QUEST, which did find real treasure, took about that long to produce. But that was the problem: it wasn't as cheap as shooting TQ:SI. That was the problem, Clancey mentioned, with a stereotypical Hollywood tone, as if to say, "And that's why we're doing it in three months by totally fabricating everything as if this were just another made for TV dramatic mini-series."

Like anything in life, it's easy to fix something that was so easy to get into: eight years is not a long time. If Discovery Communications really wanted to fix things, Mykel Hawke and I would be happy to be of service. They could bring us on as VPs of programming—we've been in the fields of TV and news for long enough to see what's wrong, what needs to be fixed, and how to fix, and to do it fast. But, they'll have to follow the trail of shame to where it starts, where the spider webs all feed to and that's CEO David Zaslav, who will probably weasel and talk his way out of the repercussion of what he's done, after the public, and especially the FCC and the board of directors, gets wind of the full scope of what he's been up to.

When a society is told a lie enough times—as when the world was told that Brigadier General Loan, a person was highly revered by his colleagues, had summarily pulled a South Vietnamese civilian from the streets of Saigon, and murdered him, instead of the truth, that he was legally executing a Vietcong assassin (the VC was not in uniform and was killing women and children and mutilating those he killed)—the society believes that lie, and it becomes factual history, and then the righteous are wrongfully accused. When a society is prepped by lies, and begins making decisions based on those lies as in accepting what has been coined as "fake news" of late, the society will implode. When you look at reality TV, and the amount of money these people are making, do you think it's worth it? I'm sure CEO Zaslav is thinking it is. Why else would he be so focused on the financial bottom line in a field that is supposed to be one of service (how many of you remember when it was NEWS "SERVICES" and TELEVISION "SERVICE" and being asked are you receiving "service" regarding your transmission reception?), not just profit, especially a profit not based on the ideal of journalism, but on the philosophies of P.T. Barnum? If there was ever a time to fix what has gone horribly wrong, it's now.

The warning Discovery issued to their NC office, where Teti lives. This was sent right after they pull the crew out of Bolivia as a result of the alleged domestic animal & crew threat incident

ACTIVE: May 11, 2015

DO NOT ADMIT

Name: **Joseph Teti, Joe Teti**

Description: W/M/50 yrs, 5'9, 190 lbs, dark hair, typically has a beard, home address in New London, North Carolina

Information: Joe Teti is a Discovery talent, starring in the reality show ***Dual Survivor***. The network is currently evaluating the series and has requested that Teti not be admitted to any Discovery office during this evaluation.

If seen: Do not grant access. Call Security and the office manager immediately.

Security will respond to the area and politely inform Mr. Teti he is not allowed in the building and must leave the premises. If Mr. Teti does not comply, discreetly contact security the police and advise them of the situation.

The Security Control Center technician will monitor the situation through the CCTV system. Notify Director of Security as soon as possible.

- [redacted]

Confidential: Security and Reception Teams Only

Figure 114. When your talent is prevented from entering your corporation's work place because of psychopathic activities, such as knifing three dogs in Bolivia, but you're still broadcasting the show in which he stars, solely for revenue, and ignoring the fact that his appearance in your show makes him a hero, there's something horribly wrong with the working of your corporation...

ABOUT THE AUTHOR

Cork Graham received international notoriety in 1983 as an 18-year-old photojournalist, and US Naval Reserve midshipman, captured and imprisoned by the Socialist Rep. of Vietnam for 11 months while photographing a clandestine treasure hunt and reports of American MIAs lost in Indochina in 1975. This story became the subject of his first international bestselling memoir, THE BAMBOO CHEST: An Adventure in Healing the Trauma of War. Soon after his release from Vietnam, he was in Central America continuing his career as a photojournalist. He is the second American to have completed the Salvadoran Navy Special Forces course. With combat experiences spanning ten years in Southeast Asia, and Latin America, both as a combatant and photo historian/photojournalist and later as a paramilitary officer, he has advised and instructed a variety of military and LE units in counter-terrorism, counter-insurgency, and counter-piracy. His latest media adventure was as an actor on Discovery Channel's, 2015 #1 non-spin-off hit series, TREASURE QUEST: SNAKE ISLAND of which this exposé is about.

APPENDIX

STATE OF NORTH CAROLINA

COUNTY OF MECKLENBURG

IN THE GENERAL COURT OF JUSTICE
SUPERIOR COURT DIVISION
14-CVS-21803

JOSEPH N. TETI,

    Plaintiff,

vs.

MYKEL HAWKEYE, MONIQUE HAINA,
SCOTT A. HUGHES, GEORGE
DAVENPORT, and SPECIAL FORCES
ASSOCIATION.

    Defendants.

**AFFIDAVIT OF DALE ALAN
COMSTOCK**

NOW COMES Dale Alan Comstock, being duly sworn and deposing as follows:

1. I am over the age of 18 and of sound mind to give this affidavit.

2. I am a citizen and resident of ˉSAY County, FLORIDA .

3. In August of 2001 I retired from the United States Army after twenty years of service, with an honorable discharge.

4. During my military service, I was assigned to units including the 3rd Special Forces Group (Green Beret), the 1st Special Forces Operational Detachment – Delta (the Delta Force), and the 82nd Airborne Division.

5. After retiring from active duty military service, I served as a military contractor with Joseph Teti ("Mr. Teti") in a combat zone.

6. Although I do not know Mykel Hawkeye ("Mr. Hawkeye") personally, he has called me three times on the telephone to talk about his relationship with Mr. Teti.

7. During one of these telephone conversations, on or about February 2013, Mr. Hawkeye told me "that he would do whatever it took to destroy the reputation of Joe Teti."

-1-

8. From the tone of Mr. Hawkeye's voice, I took this threat seriously.

9. On a Facebook thread, I declared that I did not agree that Mr. Teti had misrepresented his military career, which was met with an angry response by Mykel Hawke and Monique Haina.

10. Shortly afterward, I continued to see Internet posts critical of me from Mr. Hawkeye and a woman named Monique Haina ("Ms. Haina"). Currently Ms. Haina has posted a YouTube video declaring that I am worse than Discovery Channel for supporting Joe Teti (https://www.youtube.com/watch?v=YOaXkW3OtQM).

11. Both Mr. Hawkeye and Ms. Haina accused me of threatening and harming Mr. Hawkeye's family. Neither of these statements is true.

FURTHER THIS AFFIANT SAYETH NOT.

Dale Alan Comstock

County BAY

State FLURIDA

Sworn to and Subscribed before me
This the 3rd day of March, 2015

Notary Public

Printed Name of Notary: Patrick N Drury

My Commission Expires:

PATRICK N. DRURY
Commission # EE 071533
Expires March 7, 2015

CAUTION: NOT TO BE USED FOR IDENTIFICATION PURPOSES | THIS IS AN IMPORTANT RECORD SAFEGUARD IT | ANY ALTERATIONS IN SHADED AREAS RENDER FORM VOID

CERTIFICATE OF RELEASE OR DISCHARGE FROM ACTIVE DUTY

1. NAME (Last, First, Middle)	2. DEPARTMENT, COMPONENT AND BRANCH	
COMSTOCK, DALE ALAN	ARMY /RA	

4.a GRADE, RATE, OR RANK	4.b PAY GRADE	5. DATE OF BIRTH (YYYYMMDD)	6. RESERVE OBLIG. TERM. DATE
MSG	E8	19630521	Year 0000 Month 00 Day 00

7.a PLACE OF ENTRY INTO ACTIVE DUTY	7.b HOME OF RECORD AT TIME OF ENTRY (City and state, or complete address if known)
SACRAMENTO, CA	SACRAMENTO, CA 95828

8.a LAST DUTY ASSIGNMENT AND MAJOR COMMAND	8.b STATION WHERE SEPARATED
SF BN 03 SF GRP C CO SF	FORT BRAGG, NC 28310-5000

9. COMMAND TO WHICH TRANSFERRED
USAR CON GP (RET) AR-PERSCOM, 9700 PAGE BLVD, ST LOUIS, MO 63132

10. SGLI COVERAGE ☐ None Amount: $250,000.00

11. PRIMARY SPECIALTY (List number, title and years and months in specialty. List additional specialty numbers and titles involving periods of one or more years.)
18Z5P SF SENIOR SERGEANT--12 YRS-2 MOS//11B5P
I_NfANTRYMAN--20 YRS-0 MOS//NOTHING FOLLOWS

12. RECORD OF SERVICE
a. Date entered AD This Period
b. Separation Date This Period
c. Net Active Service This Period
d. Total Prior Active Service
e. Total Prior Inactive Service
f. Foreign Service
g. Sea Service
h. Effective Date of Pay Grade

13. DECORATIONS, MEDALS, BADGES, CITATIONS AND CAMPAIGN RIBBONS AWARDED OR AUTHORIZED (All periods of service)
BRONZE STAR MEDAL WITH COMBAT DISTINGUISHED DEVICE "V"//DEFENSE MERITORIOUS SERVICE MEDAL //MERITORIOUS SERVICE MEDAL (3RD AWARD)//JOINT SERVICE COMMENDATION MEDAL WITH COMBAT DISTINGUISHING DEVICE "V"//JOINT SERVICE COMMENDATION MEDAL (2ND AWARD)//ARMY COMMENDATION MEDAL (3RD AWARD)//JOINT SERVICE ACHIEVEMENT MEDAL//ARMY ACHIEVEMENT MEDAL//CONT IN BLOCK 18.

14. MILITARY EDUCATION (Course title, number of weeks and month and year completed)
RADIO.TELEPHONE OPERATOR COURSE, 2 WEEKS, 1983//DRIVERS TRAINING COURSE, 1 WEEK, 1983 //PRIMARY NONCOMMISSIONED OFFICER COURSE, 4 WEEKS, 1983//BASIC NONCOMMISSIONED OFFICER COURSE, 4 WEEKS, 1984//ADVANCED LAND NAVIGATOR COURSE, 1 WEEK, 1985//SPECIAL FORCES MILITARY FREE FALL COURSE, 4 WEEKS, 1987//SPECIAL FORCES QUALIFICATION COURSE, 18//CONT IN BLOCK 18.

15.a MEMBER CONTRIBUTED TO POST-VIETNAM ERA VETERANS' EDUCATIONAL ASSISTANCE PROGRAM	Yes / No X	15.b HIGH SCHOOL GRADUATE OR EQUIVALENT	Yes X / No	16. DAYS ACCRUED LEAVE PAID NONE

17. MEMBER WAS PROVIDED A COMPLETE DENTAL EXAM AND ALL APPROPRIATE DENTAL SERVICES AND TREATMENT WITHIN 90 DAYS PRIOR TO SEPARATION | Yes / No X

18. REMARKS
DATA HEREIN SUBJECT TO COMPUTER MATCHING WITHIN DOD OR WITH OTHER AGENCIES FOR VERIFICATION PURPOSES AND DETERMINING ELIGIBILITY OR COMPLIANCE FOR FEDERAL BENEFITS//IMMEDIATE REENLISTMENTS THIS PERIOD--19810707-19850627, 19850628-19890116, 19890117-19901212, 19901213-19950912//SUBJECT TO ACTIVE DUTY RECALL BY THE SECRETARY OF THE ARMY//EXTENSION OF SERVICE WAS AT THE REQUEST AND FOR THE CONVENIENCE OF THE GOVERNMENT//SERVICE IN SOUTHWEST ASIA 19900919-19991124//MEMBER HAS COMPLETED FIRST FULL TERM OF SERVICE//SERVICE IN SOMALIA 19991006-19991032//SERVICE MEMBER HAS BEEN PRESENTED A FLAG//CONT FROM BLOCK 13. //JOINT MERITORIOUS UNIT AWARD//VALOROUS UNIT AWARD (3RD AWARD)//ARMY GOOD CONDUCT MEDAL (6TH AWARD) //NATIONAL DEFENSE SERVICE MEDAL//ARMED FORCES EXPEDITIONARY MEDAL WITH ARROWHEAD DEVICE //ARMED FORCES EXPEDITIONARY MEDAL (3RD AWARD)//SOUTHWEST ASIA SERVICE MEDAL WITH 2 BRONZE SERVICE STAR (BSS)//NONCOMMISSIONED OFFICER'S PROFESSIONAL DEVELOPMENT RIBBON WITH NUMERAL 3 //ARMY SERVICE RIBBON//KUWAIT LIBERATION MEDAL//KUWAIT LIBERATION MEDAL (K)//COMBAT INFANTRYMAN BADGE//EXPERT INFANTRYMAN BADGE//MASTER//SEE ATTACHED CONTINUATION SHEET

19.a MAILING ADDRESS AFTER SEPARATION (Include Zip Code)	19.b NEAREST RELATIVE (Name and address - Include Zip Code)

20. MEMBER REQUESTS COPY 6 BE SENT TO NC DIR OF VET AFFAIRS	Yes X / No	22. OFFICIAL AUTHORIZED TO SIGN (Typed name, grade, title and signature)
21. SIGNATURE OF MEMBER BEING SEPARATED		CHERYL B. JOHNSON, CW3, CHIEF, TRANSITION CENT

SPECIAL ADDITIONAL INFORMATION (For use by authorized agencies only)

23. TYPE OF SEPARATION	24. CHARACTER OF SERVICE (Include upgrades)
RETIREMENT	HONORABLE

25. SEPARATION AUTHORITY	26. SEPARATION CODE	27. REENTRY CODE
AR 635-200, CHAP 12	RBD	4R

28. NARRATIVE REASON FOR SEPARATION
SUFFICIENT SERVICE FOR RETIREMENT

29. DATES OF TIME LOST DURING THIS PERIOD	30. MEMBER REQUESTS COPY 4
NONE	Initials

DD Form 214-AUTOMATED, NOV 88 | Previous editions are obsolete. | MEMBER - 4

Figure 115. After seeing Dale Comstock on ONE MAN ARMY on Discovery Channel, and then reading the flat out lie in his affidavit for Joseph Teti, it's hard to say, whether he had just been punched in the head too many times, or he's just plain dumb. Sadly, what he's done now, puts a pallor on what he achieved in the military. Side note: Comstock was with CAG, one step to CIA in secrecy, yet no redaction on CHARACTER OF SERVICE, or NARRATIVE REASON FOR SEPERATION—Why such secrecy on my co-star's separation from the USAF, after only completing Basic?

IN THE CIRCUIT COURT FOR
MONTGOMERY COUNTY, MARYLAND

FREDERICK "CORK" GRAHAM   :

     :

          Plaintiff,   :

v.   :

     :

DISCOVERY COMMUNICATIONS, INC.,
1 DISCOVERY PLACE   :
SILVER SPRING, MD 20910

     :

         SERVE:
         THE CORPORATION TRUST, INC.   :
         2405 YORK ROAD, SUITE 201
         LUTHERVILLE-TIMONIUM MD 21093   :

and   :

DISCOVERY COMMUNICATIONS, LLC,   :
1 DISCOVERY PLACE
SILVER SPRING, MD 20910   :

         SERVE: :
         THE CORPORATION TRUST, INC.
         2405 YORK ROAD, SUITE 201   :
         LUTHERVILLE-TIMONIUM MD 21093

     :

and   :

DISCOVERY TALENT SERVICES, LLC,
1 DISCOVERY PLACE   :
SILVER SPRING, MD 20910

     :

         SERVE:
         THE CORPORATION TRUST, INC.   :

1

RECEIVED

JUL 2 3 2018

Clerk of the Circuit Court
Montgomery County, Md.

Case No.

Figure 116. The author's 2018 lawsuit against Discovery Communications.

297

GRAHAM

2405 YORK ROAD, SUITE 201   :
LUTHERVILLE-TIMONIUM MD 21093

                                  :

Defendants.

                                  :

PLAINTIFF FREDERICK "CORK" GRAHAM'S ORIGINAL COMPAINT

COMES NOW Plaintiff, **FREDERICK "CORK" GRAHAM,** files this original petition and request for disclosure against Defendants, **DISCOVERY COMMUNICATIONS, INC., DISCOVERY COMMUNICATIONS, LLC, and DISCOVERY TALENT SERVICES, LLC,** and alleges as follows:

I. PARTIES

1.   Plaintiff, Frederick "Cork" Graham, an individual, is a resident of Alaska, and can be served through his attorneys of record, Guy Fisher, of Provost Umphrey Law Firm, LLP, at 490 Park St., Beaumont, TX 77701, and Matthew Watts, of Mooney, Green, Saindon, Murphy & Welch, P.C., at 1920 I. Street, NW, Suite 400, Washington, DC 20002.

2.   Defendant, Discovery Talent Services, LLC,[1] a business entity, is a Delaware registered company whose registered agent is the Corporation Trust Company who can be served at Corporation Trust Center, 1209 Orange St., Wilmington DE 19801, or wherever it may be found.

3.   Discovery Communications, INC.,[2] a business entity, is a Delaware registered company whose registered agent is the Corporation Trust Company, who can be served at Corporation Trust Center, 1209 Orange St., Wilmington DE 19801, or wherever it may be

---

[1] Herein sometimes referred to as the "Discovery Defendants."

[2] Herein sometimes referred to as the "Discovery Defendants."

2

found. Upon information and belief, Discovery Communications, INC. formally converted to Discovery Communications, LLC in 2007, but continues to operate and do business as Discovery Communications, INC.

4.   Discovery Communications, LLC.,[3] a business entity, is a Delaware registered company whose registered agent is the Corporation Trust Company, who can be served at Corporation Trust Center, 1209 Orange St., Wilmington DE 19801, or wherever it may be found. Upon information and belief, Discovery Communications, INC. formally converted to Discovery Communications, LLC in 2007, but continues to operate and do business as Discovery Communications, INC.

II. JURISDICTION

5.   The Court has subject-matter jurisdiction over the lawsuit because the amount in controversy exceeds this Court's minimum jurisdictional requirements, and because a contract clause designates the State of Maryland as the proper venue for disputes arising between Plaintiff Graham and the Discovery Defendants.

III. VENUE

6.   Venue is proper in Montgomery County, Maryland because Discovery Communications, INC.'s corporate headquarters in in Silver Springs, Maryland located at: One Discovery Pl, Silver Spring, MD 20910.

IV. FACTS

---

[3] Herein sometimes referred to as the "Discovery Defendants."

7.   On May 4, 2016, while filming in the jungles of Argentina for the Discovery Communications, Inc. television show *Treasure Quest: Snake Island*,[4] Plaintiff Cork Graham suffered an assault and battery from Jeremy Whalen, a "treasure Recovery Specialist," and Brett Tutor a "Security Expert."

8.   *Treasure Quest* is a semi-fictional, scripted show currently producing its third season. One or more of the Discovery Defendants hired and employed the actors/cast, producers, productions company, and security for *Treasure Quest*.

9.   Keith Plaskett, a *Treasure* Quest actor/cast member, suffered a mental breakdown of some sort during filming for a scene. Plaintiff Graham calmed Mr. Plaskett.

10.   Shortly after Plaintiff Graham treated Mr. Plaskett, and while still filming for the show, Jeremy Whalen did commit an assault and a battery by striking Plaintiff Graham in the eye with Mr. Whalen's closed fist.

11.   Jeremy Whalen continued to strike Plaintiff Graham. Brett Tutor then did commit a battery on Plaintiff Graham by choking Plaintiff Graham. All this did cause injury and damage to Plaintiff Graham. The entire incident had been recorded by the camera.

12.   The Discovery Defendants became aware of the situation or should have become aware of the situation. Plaintiff Graham requested additional funds to complete the filming and that his assailants would not be at the film location and Plaintiff Graham. These terms were discussed orally and then reiterated in an email. Plaintiff Graham prioritized that Brett Tutor and Jeremy Whalen must be removed from filming for Plaintiff Graham to return due to their joint attack on Plaintiff Graham. However upon returning, Brett Tutor and Jeremcy

---

[4] Herein sometimes referred to as "*Treasure Quest*."

4

Whalen were not terminated, nor were they removed from filming. Plaintiff Graham was forced to film with his assailants for an additional two weeks out in a remote jungle.

13.   One or more of the Discovery Defendants ratified these actions by not terminating Brett Tutor and Jeremy Whalen.

14.   Due to damages sustained by these events Plaintiff Graham cannot work.

15.   The Discovery Defendants are in charge of the hiring and firing of all the actors/cast members, producers, production company, and the security for *Treasure Quest*.

COUNT I - NEGLIGENCE

15.   Plaintiff Graham reasserts, repleads, and incorporates by reference the factual allegations contained in the preceding paragraphs and those that hereinafter follow.

16.   Plaintiff Graham sues Discovery Defendants for negligence.

17.   Defendant owed a legal duty to Plaintiff. The Discovery Defendants owed a duty to supervise their employees' activities as a Respondeat Superior.

18.   The Discovery Defendants breached their duty to Plaintiff by failing to supervise their employees' activities as a Respondeat Superior. The Discovery Defendants failed to have a representative from the network at the film site to monitor the day-to-day activities as a Respondeat Superior.

19.   As a producing and/or proximate result of Defendants' negligence, Plaintiff has suffered injuries and sustained harm, including, but not limited to, physical pain and suffering, medical expenses, physical impairment, disfigurement, lost wages, and loss of earnings.

20.   Defendants are liable to Plaintiff for damages in an amount to be proven at trial for all such physical pain and suffering, medical expenses, physical impairment, disfigurement,

5

lost wages, and loss of earnings caused by the Defendants' negligence, as well as an additional amount in exemplary damages because Defendants acted with malice.

COUNT II - NEGLIGENT HIRING

21. Plaintiff Graham reasserts, repleads, and incorporates by reference the factual allegations contained in the preceding paragraphs and those that hereinafter follow.

22. In the alternative to other counts, the Discovery Defendants negligently supervised and retained Defendants' employee.

23. Defendants had a legal duty to supervise and retain competent employees.

24. The Discovery Defendants breached the duty when Defendants negligently supervised and retained Brett Tutor and Jeremy Whalen. By negligently supervising Brett Tutor and Jeremy Whalen before, during, and after the attack on Plaintiff Graham, and then by negligently retaining Brett Tutor and Jeremy Whalen for the following two weeks after the attack, the Discovery Defendants breached their duty by not terminating the employment of Brett Tutor and Jeremy Whalen, and also by negligently allowing MAK Pictures, LLC to continue to film with Plaintiff Graham, Brett Tutor, and Jeremy Whalen in light of Plaintiff Graham's PTSD.

25. As a producing and/or proximate result of Defendants' negligent hiring, Plaintiff has suffered injuries and sustained harm, including, but not limited to, physical pain and suffering, medical expenses, physical impairment, disfigurement, lost wages, and loss of earnings.

26. Defendants are liable to Plaintiff for damages in an amount to be proven at trial for all such physical pain and suffering, medical expenses, physical impairment, disfigurement,

6

302

lost wages, and loss of earnings caused by the Defendants' negligent hiring, as well as an additional amount in exemplary damages because Defendants acted with malice.

COUNT III - VICARIOUS LIABILITY – RESPONDEAT SUPERIOR

27.   Plaintiff Graham reasserts, repleads, and incorporates by reference the factual allegations contained in the preceding paragraphs and those that hereinafter follow.

28.   The acts of Brett Tutor were performed while in the employment of the Discovery Defendants and were within the scope of that employment or within the authority delegated to the employee. Brett Tutor was hired and employed as a security expert by one or more of the Discovery. As the "security expert" for the show *Treasure Quest* Brett Tutor did commit an assault and battery upon Plaintiff Graham in the course of Brett Tutor's employment as a security personnel. Brett Tutor was not privileged to conduct such an action upon Plaintiff Graham, and therefore the Discovery Defendants are vicariously liable for the actions of Brett Tutor, including, but not limited to, the actions resulting in the injuries described in Counts I and II.

COUNT IV - VICARIOUS LIABILITY – RATIFICATION

29.   Plaintiff Graham reasserts, repleads, and incorporates by reference the factual allegations contained in the preceding paragraphs and those that hereinafter follow.

30.   At the time of assault and battery, Brett Tutor and Jeremy Whalen were acting on the Discovery Defendants' behalf. Brett Tutor and Jeremy Whalen were hired and employed by the Discovery Defendants. The assault and battery committed by Tutor and Whalen did occur while filming an episode for the Discovery Defendants. MAK Pictures, LLC is the production company hired and employed by the Discovery Defendants to produce and direct the show.

7

31.   After the events complained of, the Discovery Defendants were fully aware of Brett Tutor and Jeremy Whalen's acts and approved them by the Discovery Defendants' actions. The Discovery Defendants failed to terminate Jeremy Whalen and Brett Tutor after the two tortfeasors attacked Plaintiff Graham, and further, the Discovery Defendants did continue to have Plaintiff Graham work with his tortfeasors for two additional weeks with knowledge that Plaintiff Graham did suffer from PTSD the entire time.

32.   The Discovery Defendants approved Brett Tutor's and Jeremy Whalen's acts with the intent to validate them. The Discovery Defendants did use the film and video, taken during and after the attack on Plaintiff Graham, in the final edit of the episodes aired by the network, and thus the Discovery Defendants did profit on the actions of Brett Tutor, Jeremy Whalen, and MAK Pictures.

33.   Defendants' are therefore vicariously liable for Brett Tutor's and Jeremy Whalen's actions by ratification, including those actions resulting in the injuries described in Counts I and II.

PRAYER FOR RELIEF

WHEREFORE THE PREMISES CONSIDERED, Plaintiff Frederick "Cork" Graham moves and prays these Honorable Courts grant Plaintiff Graham the following Relief:

A.   That the Court enter an order awarding Plaintiff damages in an amount to be proven at trial for all physical pain and suffering, medical expenses, physical impairment, disfigurement, lost wages, and loss of earning suffered by Plaintiff as the result of Defendants conduct;

B.   That the Court enter an order awarding Plaintiff additional nominal, actual, compensatory, exemplary and punitive damages, as allowable by law;

8

C.   That Plaintiff Graham be awarded pre-judgment and post-judgment interest, as allowable by law;

D.   That Plaintiff Graham be awarded attorneys' fees and costs, as allowable by law;

E.   That the Court retain jurisdiction of this case pending compliance with its Orders; and

F.   That the Court grant such additional relief as the Court may deem appropriate.

RULE 1-313 CERTIFICATION

Pursuant to Maryland Rule 1-313, I hereby certify that I am admitted to practice in the state of Maryland.

Respectfully submitted,

Matthew D. Watts
Mooney, Green, Saindon, Murphy & Welch, P.C.
1920 L Street, NW, Suite 400
Washington, D.C. 20036
Tel: (202) 783-0010
Fax: (202) 783-6088
mwatts@mooneygreen.com
Counsel for the Plaintiff

Dated: July 23, 2018

9

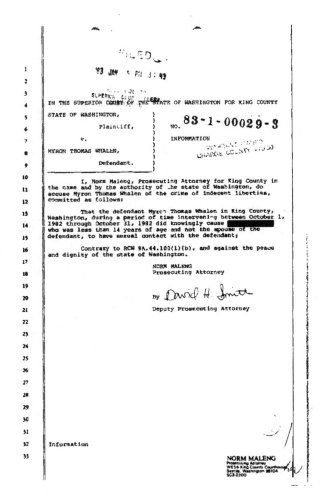

Figure 117. The apples sure don't fall far from the tree in the Whalen family: Jeremy and James/Jaime/Kendall's father's arrest for molesting their sister—Megan's Law doesn't apply, because he was arrested before 1994. Any child protective services would immediately conduct an interview with Jeremy Whalen after Keith Plaskett's testimony about Jeremy Whalen's sleeping arrangements with his daughter.

CAUSE NO. 83-1-00029-3

AFFIDAVIT FOR DETERMINATION OF PROBABLE CAUSE

STATE OF WASHINGTON)
                     : ss.
COUNTY OF K I N G)

DAVID H. SMITH, being first duly sworn on oath, deposes and says:

That he is a Deputy Prosecuting Attorney for King County and is familiar with the police report and investigation conducted in KCP case No. 82-217110;

That this case contains the following upon which this motion for the determination of probable cause is made;

The defendant, Myron Thomas Whalen, is the father of ■. The defendant has a date of birth of May 17, 1947. ■ was born ■ ■ lives with her parents at ■ Snoqualmie, King County, Washington.

In October, 1982, ■ went into her parents' bedroom to sleep during an evening thunderstorm. In the morning ■ awoke to find the defendant's hand on her breast, under her clothes. ■ got up and left the room.

On October 27, 1982, ■ got up early in the morning at the same time as the defendant. After ■ had dressed for school, the defendant called ■ and asked her to come into the family room. The defendant then had ■ sit on his lap. The defendant began breathing hard and rocking back and forth. The defendant then opened the zipper to his pants and exposed his erect penis. The defendant began touching his penis with his hand. When ■ attempted to stand up, the defendant pushed her down. The telephone rang and ■ got up and left the room.

■ then left for school. ■ told her mother of the defendant's actions when she returned from school on October 27, 1982. On October 28, 1982 ■ reported the defendant's actions to CPS worker Gerald Wood and KCP Officer Elaine Riches.

David H. Smith
DAVID H. SMITH

SUBSCRIBED and SWORN to before me this 3rd day of ~~December~~ January, 198~~2~~3:

Karen L. Granum
NOTARY PUBLIC in and for the state of Washington, residing at ___

Affidavit for Determination of Probable Cause

NORM MALENG
Prosecuting Attorney
W554 King County Courthouse
Seattle, Washington 98104
583-2200

GRAHAM

In the Superior Court of the State of Washington

For the County of King

THE STATE OF WASHINGTON,
        Plaintiff.

v.

MYRON THOMAS WHALEN
        Defendant.

FILED
KING COUNTY, WASHINGTON
MAR 31 1983
SUPERIOR COURT
W HELEN I BARILL
DEPUTY

No. 83-1-00029-3

Order Deferring Imposition

of Sentence

(PROBATION)

(vertical left margin) COMMITMENT ISSUED MAR 31 1983

The Prosecuting Attorney, the above-named defendant and counsel

Trip Hart   came into Court, the defendant having been charged by information with the crime(s) of INDECENT LIBERTIES

To this   information the defendant entered a plea of "Guilty" on the 27th day of January , 19 83 .

The Court having determined that no legal cause exists to show why judgment should not be pronounced, it is therefore ORDERED, ADJUDGED and DECREED that the said Defendant is guilty of the crime(s) of INDECENT LIBERTIES, Class "B" Felony, RCW 9A.44.100

The Defendant having made application to the Court for probation and the Court having found Defendant eligible under the law to be granted probation, and the Court being fully advised in the premises, it is therefore,

ORDERED that the imposition of sentence against the Defendant herein be, and the same is hereby deferred pursuant to RCW 9.95.200 for a period of (3) THREE years from this date upon the following terms and conditions, to-wit:

1) That the Defendant shall be under the charge of a Probation and Parole Officer employed by the Department of Corrections and follow implicitly the instructions of said Department, and the rules and regulations promulgated by said Department for the conduct of the Defendant during the term of his probation hereunder.

2) The Defendant shall not commit any law violations.

3) The Defendant shall pay all costs and the penalty assessment (RCW 7.68.035) of $50.00 within 90 days from release from date of this case custody.

4) The Defendant shall serve a term of 30 days in the King County Jail, (with) (without) credit to be given for time already served, to commence April 25, 1983 at 9 am. Work release is authorized.

(5) The defendant shall enter in, fully participate in, and successfully complete a counseling program with Dr. Kenneth McCleve.

(6) The defendant shall pay the costs of all counseling

DONE IN OPEN COURT this 31st day of MARCH , 1983 .

_____
JUDGE

Presented by:

David H. Smith
Deputy Prosecuting Attorney
Rev. 4/6/82

Copy rec'd
Trip Hart
Attorney for Defendant

308

THE STATE OF WASHINGTON   ADDITIONAL CONDITIONS

vs.   CAUSE NO. 83-1-00029-3

Myron Thomas Whalen

needed by ███████ related to this offense.

(2) The defendant shall have no contact with minor children except with the specific consent of his supervising probation officer and Dr. Von Cleve.

(B) The defendant shall not involve himself in a relationship with women with victim-aged children, unless specific written consent by his supervising probation officer and Dr. Von Cleve.

DONE IN OPEN COURT this 31st day of MARCH 19 _

_____
JUDGE

Presented by:

David H. Smith
Deputy Prosecuting Attorney

Tig Hart
Attorney for Defendant.

GRAHAM

IN THE SUPERIOR COURT OF THE STATE OF WASHINGTON FOR ___KING___ COUNTY

STATE OF WASHINGTON

Plaintiff

vs

WHALEN, Myron Thomas

Defendant

CAUSE NO. 83-1-00029-1

DEFENDANT'S PETITION FOR LEAVE TO WITHDRAW PLEA OF GUILTY AND ENTER PLEA OF NOT GUILTY AND ORDER FOR DISMISSAL OF CAUSE

COMES NOW the defendant ___WHALEN, Myron Thomas___ and respectfully petitions to this Court and represents as follows:

That he is the defendant in the above-entitled cause and on ___1-27-83___ entered a plea of guilty to the crime of ___Indecent Liberties___ that on ___3-31-83___ Petitioner was granted probation by the Honorable ___Herbert M. Stephens___ Judge of the above-entitled Court, under an order deferring imposition of sentence until ___3-31-86___ that the Petitioner has fulfilled the terms of his probation including the following specified conditions.
___See attached report.___

that the Petitioner was informed of and has obeyed the rules and regulations of the Office of Adult Probation and Parole; that the Petitioner has not been guilty of any offense against the law which he has failed to report to the parole officer; that the Petitioner's conduct during his period of probation has been to the best of his ability, satisfactory.

WHEREFORE, as provided by RCW 9.95.240, the Petitioner prays that he be permitted to withdraw or have set aside the plea or finding of "Guilty" to said charge and to enter a plea of "Not Guilty," and that upon entry of such plea of "Not Guilty" the said charges be dismissed and Petitioner discharged from all penalties and disabilities resulting from this cause.

Subscribed and sworn to this ___26th___ day of ___March___ 19_85_

Frances L. HUGHES, NOTARY
Notary Public in and for the State of ___Washington___

Residing at ___Renton___

ORDER OF DISMISSAL

Pursuant to the above petition, it is ordered that the defendant, ___Myron Thomas WHALEN___ be permitted to withdraw or have set aside the plea or finding of "Guilty" to the crime of ___Indecent Liberties___ an' enter a plea of "Not Guilty" it is further

ORDERED, ADJUDGED AND DECREED that the above-entitled cause be, and the same is, hereby dismissed and the defendant discharged from further attendance herein and is released from all penalties and disabilities resulting from the filing of said charge.

DONE IN OPEN COURT this ___2___ day of ___April___ 19_85_

Herbert M. Stephens

Approved for presentation

DPA 4/2/85

KRP:dh

310

BIBLIOGRAPHY

Van Horne, Patrick. *Left of Bang: How the Marine Corps' Combat Hunter Program Can Save Your Life*, Black Irish Entertainment LLC, 2014.

Navarro, Joe. *Dangerous Personalities: An FBI Profiler Shows You How to Identify and Protect Yourself from Harmful People*. Rodale Books, 2014.

Houston, Phillip. *Spy the Lie: Former CIA Officers Teach You How to Detect Deception*. St. Martin's Press, 2012.

Navarro, Joe. *How to Spot a Psychopath*. Amazon Digital Services LLC, 2011.

Navarro, Joe. *What Every BODY is Saying: An Ex-FBI Agent's Guide to Speed-Reading People*. HarperCollins Publishers, 2009.

Cline, Lawrence K. *Pseudo Operations and Counterinsurgency: Lessons from Other Countries*. Strategic Studies Institute, 2005.

Hazelton, Jacqueline L. *Insurgent Defectors in Counterinsurgencies*. Parameters 47, Autumn 2017.

Swan, James A. *Sacred Places: How the Living Earth Seeks Our Friendship*. Bear & Company, 1990.

Swan, James A. *The Power of Place: Sacred Ground in Natural & Human Environments*. Quest Books, 1995.

Hughes, Chase. *The Ellipsis Manual: analysis and engineering of human behavior*. Evergreen Press, 2017.

Cialdini, Robert B. *Influence: The Psychology of Persuasion, Revised Edition*. Harper Business, 2006.